S H A R K

STORIES OF LIFE AND DEATH FROM THE
WORLD'S MOST DANGEROUS WATERS

SHARK

STORIES OF LIFE AND DEATH FROM THE WORLD'S MOST DANGEROUS WATERS

EDITED BY NATHANIEL MAY
SERIES EDITOR CLINT WILLIS

Thunder's Mouth Press
New York

SHARK: STORIES OF LIFE AND DEATH FROM THE WORLD'S MOST DANGEROUS WATERS

Adrenaline® and the Adrenaline® logo are trademarks of
Avalon Publishing Group Incorporated, New York, NY.

An Adrenaline Book®

Published by
Thunder's Mouth Press
An Imprint of Avalon Publishing Group Incorporated
161 William Street, 16th floor
New York, NY 10038

Book design: Sue Canavan

frontispiece photo: Diver and Great White Shark, Australia © Cousteau
Society/The Image Bank

Library of Congress Cataloging-in-Publication Data

May, Nathaniel.
    Shark: stories of life and death from the world's most dangerous waters /
Nathaniel May.
        p. cm
    ISBN 1-56025-397-5 (trade paper)
        1. Shark attacks—Annecdotes. 2. Sharks—Annecdotes. I. Title.

QL638.93 .M39 2002
597.3'1566—dc21   2002018002

Printed in the United States of America
Distributed by Publishers Group West

For My Parents

c o n t e n t s

p h o t o g r a p h s

introduction

've seen one shark in the wild: a bluish-gray seven-foot mass flashing past me in five feet of water. I was busy looking for the best wave to ride, so it didn't occur to me to be afraid. I didn't know that my location—near Daytona Beach, Florida—has the highest incidence of shark attacks in the United States, or that researchers think yellow swimsuits (I was wearing one) are an especially appealing target for sharks. Had I known these things I probably would have thought twice about staying in the water. Still, I know that swimming there was neither dangerous nor foolish; the chances of suffering an unprovoked attack are extremely small.

When divers began spending time with sharks in the 1950s, many people thought there was great risk involved. Very little was known about sharks, and the anecdotal information people had gathered over the centuries seemed to prove that sharks were dangerous killers, predators who couldn't wait to get their teeth into human flesh.

Since then we've learned a lot about sharks. Shark scientists—and behaviorists in particular—now believe that sharks are pretty predictable. If you know what kind of shark you're swimming with, you can know what to expect in most cases, and you shouldn't expect to be attacked.

Nevertheless, horror stories about sharks abound, and we still love to hear them. A few shark attack stories are all journalists need to dub a season "The Summer of the Shark"—even in a year when shark attacks decline.

The writers whose work is featured in this book know (or think they know) sharks from a variety of perspectives. Some of them study or film sharks for a living. Some are recreational divers, who admire the shark for its form and its beauty. Others catch sharks for sport. All of them are moved to awe by their encounters with the creature. Peter Matthiessen describes his first underwater view of a great white:

> In the molten water of late afternoon it was a creature very different from the one seen from the surface. The hard rust of its hide had dissolved in pale transparent tones that shimmered in the ocean light on its satin skin. From the dorsal fin an evanescent bronze shaded down to luminous dark metallic gray along the lateral line, a color as delicate as that bronze tint on a mushroom which points up the whiteness of the flesh beneath. From snout to keel, the underside was a deathly white, all but the black undertips of the broad pectorals.

Even Zane Grey, who enjoyed hunting sharks, had this to say about a whale shark he encountered:

> The size was tremendous. From its dorsal fin to its head the length exceeded that of our boat, and it was wider than our beam. Lazily, with ponderous, slow weave of tail, it moved along, six or eight feet under the surface. Its dark blue color changed to a velvety brown, and the silver spots turned white. There was an exquisite purple along the edge of the broad pectoral fins. Altogether its colossal size, its singular beauty, its indifference to the boats, its suggestion of incredible power, made it the most wonderful fish I had ever seen.

Our sense of awe for these creatures is tinged with fear, as noted by sociobiologist Edward O. Wilson in an article about sharks:

> We're not just afraid of predators, we're transfixed by them, prone to weave stories and fables and chatter endlessly about them, because fascination creates preparedness, and preparedness, survival. In a deeply tribal sense, we love our monsters.

Do our monster stories perpetuate the myths about shark behavior? Do they encourage us to destroy the animals, acting from some misdirected survival instinct? I don't think so. We can love our monster stories *and* love the shark for what it is. Jacques-Yves Cousteau understood this when he and his son Philippe wrote *The Shark: Splendid Savage of the Sea,* one of the first books written entirely about sharks. The elder Cousteau wrote this about a diver's reaction to sharks:

> With or without special means of protection, alone or in groups, in warm waters as well as cold, it is now thirty-three years that I have been diving, and often in the company of sharks: all kinds of sharks, sharks of every disposition, sharks reputed to be harmless, and sharks known to be deadly. I and my diving companions fear them, laugh at them, admire them, but are forced to resign ourselves to sharing the waters with them.

I don't know what to make of sharks. I'd like to think that I'm not afraid, that I would be happy to swim with one, glad for the chance to observe and appreciate the subtle power of its body, the cold, absent stare of its eyes, the steady pulse of water through its gills. For now I'm content to read and reflect upon these stories, which remind me that there are things in the world I'll never understand.

—*Nathaniel May*

from Blue Meridian
by Peter Matthiessen

Peter Matthiessen (born 1927) brings to his work an interest in exploration and a respectful curiosity about the natural world. He accompanied Peter Gimbel's 1968 expedition to find great white sharks for a feature film. Here Matthiessen rejoins the group—which has yet to find a great white—in Australia, more than a year after the project began.

The whale-oil slick had drifted a mile or more up the blue gulf, and the crew settled down to wait. The cages, corroded by use in the Indian Ocean, were checked out in the water; both had air leaks in their flotation systems which were quickly fixed. Cameras were given final adjustments, tanks were filled with compressed air, and new powerheads were assembled. Each cage was fitted with two powerheads in case a shark tried to dismantle it: Ron Taylor, for one, has no doubt at all that a white shark could bite through the aluminum bars.

In midmorning a seal broke the surface of the cove, thrashing and playing off the bows; it was an eared seal, the South Australian sea lion. A crested tern, bright-white in the blue sun, appeared and vanished. From time to time, small sprays of bait fish showered the surface, but no shark came. There was only a great stillness, and sere islands in a metal sea. In the late afternoon, when underwater photography was no longer possible, cages and cameras were taken to the bottom on a test run; the water temperature was 60 degrees, and before long the divers were shaking with cold. Back on deck, Waterman called down to Gimbel that he should swim from the cage to the ladder instead of trying to haul himself aboard. "I'm not swimming here," Gimbel said shortly, clambering up the ship's side, tank and all.

At twilight a small party went ashore to explore the mallee scrub behind the beach, and with Jim Lipscomb I walked inland across the peninsula to gaze from the sea cliffs at what Australians call the Southern Ocean. Thirty miles to the south, out of the wind haze, rose the Neptune Islands, and beyond lay the Antarctic Ocean, which was, in my travels, the last of the Seven Seas. Brown swallows called fairy martins crossed from headland to headland, and below, big black-backed Pacific gulls came sweeping in across the broad wash of the reef. On this lonely coast, with the wind from the south out of Antarctica, it occurred to me that the air we breathed might be the last clean air on earth.

During the night I hoisted the lines to which the dead fish had been strung; they were untouched. The whale oil, which sometimes congeals when the air is cold, was still dripping silently into the sea, and I refilled the container. Overhead, the southern stars were round and bright in a ringing sky: Canis Major and Canis Minor, Castor and Pollux, the Southern Cross, Orion. Orion's belt is the leg of a mythical South American Indian, Nohi-Abassi, whose wife had him bitten to pieces by a shark for having persuaded another shark to devour his mother-in-law; the pieces were scattered all across the heavens. Shark legends occur around the world; the Jonah of the North Australian aborigines is Mutuk, who was swallowed entire, and some say that "the fishe" that swallowed the Biblical Jonah was the great white shark.

At daybreak the water was as still as lead—no sign of life, no bird. The skiff crossed Thorny Channel to the islands. In the distance, on the ocean points, the black rocks shone, and the still bodies of the sleeping sea mammals were brilliant, reflecting the dawn like things being given life. On the nearest islet the sunrise spun on the white heads of gulls and turned the amorphous forms of sleeping sea lions to gold. Golden animals lay on bronze carpets of algae, and glistened in the white surge of the shore. They reared high to see into the skiff, and one flashed like a porpoise through the shadows of the morning sea, curving away under the hull. Near a strange balanced rock, upright as a monolith at the water's edge, two young gulls haggled, yanking at the downy body of a bird still younger.

To bait any sharks drawn to the colony, we ran a whale-oil slick around the islets, then back across the channel to Memory Cove; later in the day the *Sea Raider* ran a slick out to Cape Catastrophe. In the silence, porpoises sliced softly through the waters of the cove, and gulls came to the fish scraps in the slick, but the white shark did not appear. After forty-eight hours the *Saori* returned to port, passing the cove under Cape Donington where Jim Veitch had caught his monster shark.

According to Veitch, who has studied them for forty years, the largest white sharks caught in South Australia have been found close inshore, and all were females; sharks taken at Dangerous Reef in the middle of Spencer Gulf are almost invariably males. This led Veitch to suppose that the females come inshore to drop their young, which might be eaten by the males in the open water, but this sensible theory had to be discarded, since none of the females contained embryos or young. Its reproductive cycle is one of many mysteries surrounding the white shark; few embryos or young white sharks have ever been recorded. The smallest white shark Jim Veitch has ever seen was five feet long, and he commented that he would rather catch an 800-pound female with eggs or unborn young than an 8000-pound world record for rod and reel.

Though larger specimens are regularly reported (Cousteau saw a white shark in the Azores that he estimated at twenty-five feet), Veitch has strong doubts about unmeasured whites over eighteen feet long. In fact, he has made a standing offer to *eat* that part of any specimen exceeding eighteen feet, starting at either end. A hooked shark alongside his boat at Streaky Bay, carefully estimated at just over seventeen feet before it got away, was the only one he has ever seen over sixteen, and his record fish was one of the few over fifteen. (A sixteen-footer was the largest of the 141 white sharks that have been netted since 1964 along the coast of Natal.) In Veitch's opinion, a fourteen-footer is a "good big shark." According to museum measurements of the bite wounds, the one that hit Rodney Fox "like a submarine" and bore him away through the water was a mere ten-footer.

Fox, a fair-haired jaunty man of thirty, has been involved in more white-shark attacks than any living person, and the pattern of his experiences is weird. In 1961, when he won the South Australian Skin-Diving and Spearfishing Championship—this is free diving, without aid of scuba tanks—his chief competitor was his friend Brian Rodger, who had been state champion the year before. Late one afternoon of March, during a "comp" at Aldinga Beach, south of Adelaide, the two were swimming close to each other when a shark seized Rodger by the leg. Rodger wrenched himself free, but the shark came in again, and this time he deflected it with a point-blank shot from his sling spear gun. Though the barb scarcely dented its tough hide, the shark veered off, and Rodger, bleeding badly—his wounds required some two hundred stitches—used the rubber sling from his spear gun as a tourniquet on his leg, then struggled on, unaided; he was finally picked up by a rowboat near the shore.

Fox was beneath the surface during the attack and was never aware of it; all he saw was the swift approach of a white shark that came in and circled him closely, so closely at times that he could have touched it with his spear gun. Even as he spun desperately in the water, he had to keep going to the surface to get air. Then he would dive for the bottom, thirty feet down, seeking protection, and creep a little way inshore. Relentlessly the big shark circled, and Fox is convinced that this was the one that Rodger had driven off, returning now along the trail of Rodger's blood; since both men wore black suits, it might have mistaken Fox for its original prey. This distraction, which Rodney thinks could not have been less than ten minutes, may well have spared his bleeding friend from further attack.

As the minutes passed and the shark persisted, Rodney had to fight a growing panic. He was still a half mile offshore, and was spending his last energies going to the bottom. Even when the shark was gone, he felt certain that it would return, and the day was growing late; he was most frightened of all that dark would fall while he was still alone in the open water. But the shark never reappeared, and he got ashore.

Fox became state champion that year and was runner-up the next; in 1963 it was expected that he would regain the South Australian title, and Ron Taylor, who was champion of New South Wales, thought that Rodney was the man to beat for the championship of all Australia. Once again the South Australian competition was held at Aldinga Beach, which is noted for its plentiful fish and is only thirty-four miles south of Adelaide, and this time Fox was swimming near Bruce Farley, whom he had taught to dive. That Sunday there were forty divers in the competition, which was based on the number of fish species taken as well as total weight; all contestants wore black wet-suits, and all dragged their fish behind them in a plastic float to minimize the amount of blood in the water.

By early afternoon, when he started his final swim, Fox appeared to be well ahead. On his last trip to the beach with a load of fish, he had noticed two large dusky morwongs near a triangular coral head, about three quarters of a mile offshore. Returning to this place, he parted company with Farley. "He went one way and I went the other," Bruce recalled, making a diving flip with his hand, "and the next thing I knew, the shark had him."

One of the big morwongs was out in the open in a patch of brown algae, and Fox was gliding in on it, intent, spear gun extended like an antenna, when he felt himself overtaken by a strange stillness in the water, a suspension of sound and motion, as if all the creatures of the reef had paused to watch him. "It was just a *feeling*," he says. "I didn't tense up or anything—I didn't have time to." For at that moment he was struck so hard on his left side that his face mask was knocked off and his spear gun sent spinning from his hand, and he found himself swirled swiftly through the water by something that enclosed him from the left shoulder to the waist. A great pressure made his insides feel as if they had been forced toward his right side—he seemed to be choking, and he could not move. Upside down in the creature's mouth, he was being rushed through the water, and only now did he make out the stroke of a great shark's powerful tail. He was groping wildly, trying to gouge its eyes, when inexplicably, of its own accord, the shark let go.

Out of breath, pushing frantically to shove himself away, Rodney jammed his arm straight into its mouth. For the first time he felt pain, a pain that became terrible as he yanked the flesh and veins and tendons out through the back-curved teeth. He fought his way to the surface and grabbed a great ragged breath, but the shark was right behind him. When his knees brushed its body, he clasped it with arms and legs to avoid the jaws, and the beast took him to the bottom, scraping him against the rocks. Once more he fled for the surface, and again the shark followed him up: his moment of utmost horror came when through his blurred vision he saw the great conical head rising toward him out of the pink cloud of his own blood. Hopelessly, he kicked at it, and the flipper skidded off its hide. At the last second the head veered toward his float, which contained a solitary small fish, and a moment later the float raced off across the surface; either the shark had seized the float or had gotten entangled in the line.

Once again he found himself being dragged through the water; already he was far below the surface. He tried to release the weight belt to which his float line was attached, but his arms did not work, nor his mutilated hands. And at this moment, when he knew finally that he was lost—"I had done all I could, and now I was finished"—and was on the point of drowning, the next event occurred in the series of miracles that were to save his life. Presumably the shark's razor teeth had frayed the heavy line that connected the fish float to his weight belt, for at this ultimate moment it parted. For the third time he reached the surface, and this time he screamed, "Shark!" There was no need of it; a boat which had brought a young diver from the beach was only a few yards away. "They thought that lad would be safe with Fox and Farley," Bruce Farley said. "They'd hardly dropped him in the water when they had to yank him out again, because there was Rodney, screaming, in a pool of blood. They hauled out Rodney, then came for me, and we headed for shore."

The bones had been bared on Rodney's right arm and hand—his hand alone required ninety-four stitches—and his rib cage, lungs and upper stomach lay exposed. "Bruce thought I was done for," Rodney said. "The rotten dog sat up in the bow with his back to me—wouldn't even look at me."

Farley grinned. "I just didn't like the looks of all them guts hangin' out," he said. In the boat there was nothing he could do for Rodney, and he tried to concentrate on how best to find help on the beach. "I knew everything had to go one-two-three if we were going to save him, and I didn't even know how bad he was. Oh, there was a little bit of intestine stickin' out, but we never opened his suit up to really see. We made that mistake on the beach with Brian Rodger, and his leg fell all apart." Fox himself feels that his suit, holding his body together until it could be reassembled, was one of the many things that saved his life.

The first person that Bruce met as he ran down the beach was a policeman who knew just where to telephone and what numbers to call. And someone had happened to bring a car down the rough cliff track to the beach—a very rare occurrence; this car was able to bump out onto the reef to pick up Rodney, and it carried him back up the cliff to the highway and eight miles down the road toward Adelaide before he was transferred to the ambulance sent to fetch him. Already the police were manning every intersection on the way, and because he was traveling just before the Sunday-afternoon rush he actually reached the hospital within an hour after he was picked up in the boat. His lung was punctured, he was rasping and choking, and that he did not drown in his own blood or bleed to death within that hour was miraculous. Nor were the miracles over: the surgeon on emergency duty that day had just returned from England, where he had taken special training in chest operations.

While Rodney was being prepared for the four-hour operation, he heard urgent voices. One said that someone should go for a priest, and Rodney realized that they thought he was unconscious and did not believe that he was going to make it. Desperate, he half sat up on the table, saying, "I'm a Protestant!" before they got to him and calmed him down. "He's a bloody mess," the doctor told Rodney's wife after the operation, "but he's going to be all right."

Two reasons for Fox's survival were his excellent condition and the fact that he never went into shock. "It's shock that kills most people in a shark attack," Ron Taylor says, and Valerie agrees. Experienced divers are more apt to survive an attack because they are less apt to go into shock; sharks are a reality that they must live with, and therefore they are psychologically prepared.

"I guess I just wasn't supposed to go," Rodney says cockily. After two weeks he was home in bed, though he had to pay daily visits to the hospital. Six months later he made himself dive again, and he has been diving ever since. In 1964 Ron Taylor's team in the Australian championships was beaten by the team of Brian Rodger, Bruce Farley and Rodney Fox.

The 1963 attack on Fox occurred only a few hundred feet from the place where Brian Rodger had been attacked; forty divers were in the water on both days, and on both, it was the reigning champion who was hit. In 1964 Bruce Farley was state champion. One competition day he was to drive down to Aldinga with Rodger and Fox, but somehow got left behind. By himself, Bruce drove five miles out of town, then turned around and went home. "I can't account for it," he says, "I just lost interest."

That same day at Aldinga, a year to the day after the attack on Fox, both Rodney and Brian separately, simultaneously and for no good reason started for shore. The competition had another hour to run, and both men habitually stuck it out to the very end, but today they each had an instinct to leave the water. Perhaps the two had heard that stillness which precedes the coming of the white death, because before they had reached shore someone came yelling down the beach. A young diver named Geoff Corner had been bitten just once, on the upper leg, but the great bite had severed an artery and he had died. Geoff Corner was the reigning junior champion.

Since that time, Bruce has never dived Aldinga Beach. "We're nice to Bruce," Rodney Fox says, teasing him. "We always decide we'll go and dive somewhere else, because he can't dive Aldinga with his heart and soul."

Bruce Farley is an honest man with a sad humorous bony face. "I haven't dived *anywhere* heart and soul," he says, "since Brian got hit in 1960."

Valerie thinks that the same animal was involved in the series of attacks off Aldinga Beach. In any case, the records indicate that the species is more common in Spencer Gulf than at Aldinga. Everyone is confident that white sharks will be encountered here, but whether they can be photographed is another matter. Many whites are extremely wary, and compressed air bubbles are said to put them off; the divers searching for abalone in these waters use compressed air piped from their boats, and in Australia there is no recorded case of a white-shark attack upon an "ab diver."

Like most ab divers, Ian McKechnie has never laid eyes on a white shark, though once one came and took a seal close by. According to Ian's mates, who were yelling to him from the boat, the seal had been swimming only twenty yards behind him. Rodney says that local fishermen in small boats fear the white death and its sinister habit of rearing its head out of the water; when a big one comes near, he says, they crouch below the gunwales to avoid being seen, then start up the motor and escape.

At dawn on January 21, the *Saori* put to sea again, bound this time for Dangerous Reef, an east-west litter of reefs and low rock islets where Rodney once saw seven whites together. With the sunrise, a strong northeast breeze increased to a battering wind, and there was no lee at the reef, which is marked by a solitary light. The ketch trudged west across the gulf to a lee behind Taylor Island, where a sheep bought from the local slaughterhouse had its throat slit and was strung over the side; the smoke of sheep blood in the water drifted down the shore. The wind shifted to the south, then backed around to the northeast again during the night, but no shark came.

By morning the wind was easterly, at 10 to 15 knots; it slacked off after sunrise, then picked up again at midday. The *Sea Raider* reconnoitered Dangerous Reef, and a party went ashore on its main islet while awaiting the *Saori*. The skiff entered a rock pool in the broad granite ledge used by the seal pups as a nursery, and the lion-colored cow seals, howling, hurtled past the skiff into the water, then reared up all around it, trying to frighten it away. Everywhere rushed new seal pups and small yearlings, fat and astonished, and scattered through the herds were harem bulls with a golden nape on their big neck muscles and dark brown coats which on the older bulls looked black. One cow rushed up out of the water as her pup was approached, barking aggressively and flopping with great agility from boulder to boulder; when faced, she stopped, swaying her head and neck in consternation. Up and down the rocks the young pups shrilled, adding their voices to a din of life that from a distance sounds like one mourning cry.

On the rocks, facing upwind, stood companies of Pacific gulls, a sooty oystercatcher, and small bands of sandpipers and turnstones, picking crustaceans in the rich algal mats that covered the granite platforms washed by tide. Offshore a sooty shearwater pointed its long wing at the water, stiff as a boomerang. In the high sea wind and cold austral light, the black-faced cormorant, stark black and white, came up in strings out of the south; other cormorants stood snow-breasted on the white-stained boulders. Their nest, of a lavender kelp and a brown rockweed stolen freely by the birds from unwary neighbors, held two or three eggs of a watery sea-green blue, though here and there a brown egg lay beside a blue one. The reptilian birds croaked dismally, hissing at the pirate gulls; as fast as a cormorant left its nest, the gulls fell upon its eggs with a horrid squalling. On the high ground under the light was the islet's only growth, a small succulent burned by guano and beaten flat by salt and wind.

At nightfall the wind was still out of the east, but the weather report predicted a shift to the southwest. Since any such shift might put the *Saori* on the reef, Captain Ben decreed that his ship would go in under Cape Donington for the night. By now everyone was so anxious to get to work that the decision was accepted with the greatest reluctance. "You can't go against the *captain* of the vessel," Ron Taylor exclaimed, dismayed by the mutinous mutterings; it was one of the rare times that Ron ever offered a strong opinion.

Before sailing, a four-gallon kerosene can full of chum and whale oil was anchored to the bottom to attract any passing sharks into the area. Next morning the can was gone. Possibly a big sea lion had taken it, parting the buoy line by force, but the sharp cut on the line—the rope strands had not unraveled as they do when parted under strain—suggested the sharp teeth of a shark.

As predicted, the wind had come around to the southwest, but there was a lee on the far side of the islet. The *Saori* anchored close to shore, scarcely more than a hundred yards from the sea-smoothed beaches, and for the next three days, alone in the lunar emptiness of Spencer Gulf, she was washed by a cool southwest wind, sea moaning and the parched stink of guano.

Day after day, sky and sea were the same oily gray, and the sea glimmered dimly like the old seal-polished stones. Rips and the low spine of rocks at the east end of the islet parted a high chop so treacherous that the surf seemed to fly in all directions, a true maelstrom. With the mourning of the sea mammals and the hurtling black birds, the air of this bare reef carried an infinite foreboding that boded well for the coming of the great white shark. And still it did not come.

On the foredeck, Jim taped Rodney's harrowing account and photographed his scars. The divers sewed hoods onto neoprene surfers' vests to be worn under our wet-suits as extra protection against cold, but otherwise there was little to do except watch for sharks in the empty slick that trailed away into the northward. That afternoon, for want of a better plan, Ron, Stan and Peter ran another check on cameras and cages, and I went with them; we took the cages to the bottom, thirty feet down. The cold sea was full of long pale shreds of a drifting algal bloom, and visibility was no better than thirty feet. The bottom itself was strange and dead, a coarse bed of myriad bits of crumbled coral-like gravel haired over with beds of a broad-bladed turtle grass that swayed in the surge and current. In open places in the grass the sand was broken by protruding pen shells, like small gravestones, and scattered everywhere were limy skeletons of scallops, cockles and clams. While the cameras were being checked, I reached out of the cage to collect specimens. Then I remembered how Henri Bource's leg had been removed, and peered into the restless blue-gray murk. Overhead, at the silvering surface, hung the black oval of the *Saori*, where a pair of rotting sheep, heads down, did a grim dance with the ship's rise and fall.

Each night when the sun sinks beyond the Eyre Peninsula, the air turns cold. The nights are clear, and since Ben Ranford's cabin is quarters for five people besides himself (its spare berth and adjoining floor are nominally shared by Gimbel, Cody, myself and the Taylors), Gimbel and I sleep ordinarily on deck. In my own niche well forward by the anchor windlass, out of the way of nighttime feet, I listen to the groan of the reef and the surf breaking on its weather shore and the wind of the universe spinning a full moon through blue-black skies. The Pacific gull adds its weird cry to the plaint of seals, and often the night voice sounds prehuman, a cry out of lost childhood or another world. Half asleep, I hear the calling of my name and listen fiercely, but there is nothing, only the black mainmast tossing, the black wind and whirling stars.

Saturday morning, January 24, and still no sign of shark. Gimbel is muttering about bad dreams. In one dream, he and Peter Lake had mutilated their legs with knives, then swum in the water to attract sharks. Their effort was in vain, and afterward they sat on the deck and compared their legs, which would have to be amputated. "We realized we'd made a mistake," Gimbel said, still worried by the dream; he looked up in surprise when everybody laughed, then laughed himself. In this time of stress, he is upset unduly by a cold sore at the corner of his mouth, which he chooses to see as an intimation of his own mortality.

The day is a good one, with light wind; the *Saori* will stay on here despite the absence of white sharks. But everyone is growing apprehensive. Even if sharks were numerous, it will be difficult to get good underwater film in the poor visibility of these cold turbid waters, especially if the whites avoid the air bubbles of the scuba tanks and cages. Dangerous Reef is a place notorious for the white shark ("The ab divers don't care for it," Bruce Farley says. "Took a quick look and decided they'd do better some place else."), yet no one has seen a fin. If only two years ago Rodney saw seven here at once, where are they now?

Rodney says that the sharks might be following the salmon schools that are moving through the gulf, and possibly their movements and feeding patterns have been affected by the past month of bad weather, which kept the water temperature well below the seasonal norm; though warmer than at Memory Cove, it is 4 degrees colder here than it was when Rodney came at this same time in 1968. In salt-water environments, a 4-degree gradient makes a big difference—it can keep oysters from spawning, for example—and it has been noted with captive specimens as well as in shark-attack statistics that a shark's interest in food rises markedly with an increase in temperature; in winter, captive sharks scarcely feed at all. The white shark is an exception to a general rule proposed by an Australian authority, V. M. Coppleson, that shark attacks around the world are rare in water colder than 72 degrees; nevertheless, its feeding may be inhibited by unseasonal cold water and unstable weather.

Or so we speculate. On the radio this morning, one of the tuna captains with a white-shark charter party out of Port Lincoln had some disturbing news: in his last three trips to Dangerous Reef he had raised only one shy white shark, and it would not come near the boat. "Not like it used to be," the radio voice said. "They're being slowly killed out, I reckon, like everything else in the world." This man blamed the gill-netters for the disappearance of the sharks, and certainly commercial netting is a factor. Like other large predators of land and sea, the white shark will not survive long without the protection that it is unlikely to receive from man, and possibly the Australians are correct in the opinion generally held here that the species is nearing extinction. I am happy that our expedition has no plan to kill one except in self-defense.

There are recent reports of white sharks farther north in the gulf and to the west of Cape Catastrophe, and there is a feeling aboard that the *Saori* should pursue these sightings. Pursuit might relieve the strain of waiting and improve morale, but chasing works no better with fish than it does with anything else: better to pick one likely place and chum the hell out of it, day and night. By the time the slow *Saori* got the cages to the scene of any sighting, the shark might be twenty miles away, and even if a shark was present, there is no guarantee that water clarity would be adequate, or that the shark would approach the cage. Possibly inshore sharks have a hunting circuit, moving from point to point as wolves do, but more likely they move at random, taking prey as chance presents, and congregating now and then at likely grounds like Dangerous Reef. Instinctively, I agree with Captain Arno, who is relieving Captain Ben over this weekend. Arno is a wonderful bent old salt with white broken bare feet that never sunburn; offered grog, he smites the table, crying out fiercely, "I *will!*" Says Arno, "Sharks have a head and a tail, and they keep swimming. Nobody knows where the shark goes. I reckon they don't know where they are themselves."

Although these days are painful for Gimbel, they are almost as hard on Rodney Fox, who must choose the fishing grounds and baiting techniques that will bring the missing sharks. Rodney performs his duties with efficiency and style, but his casual air of cocky indifference is deceptive. If anything, he takes too much of the burden upon himself, and tends to construe the discussion of alternatives as implied criticism. For those aboard with a long interest in the sea and sharks, such discussions are fun and ease the strain, but giving a hearing to amateur opinions is hard on Rodney's nerves in a nervous time. Rarely does he permit the strain to show, but sometimes, muttering "Too many cooks . . . !" he lies face down on the deck, feigning deep sleep, and one day he actually took refuge in the hold, refusing to come out to eat his lunch.

Nevertheless, Rodney says, he has never worked with a nicer group of people. I feel the same, and so does everyone else; even Lipscomb and I, who often disagree, manage to disagree in a friendly manner. After a year and a half, this film crew is truly a unit, and its strength is mutual affection and acceptance: each man knows precisely what can be expected of the man beside him and demands no more, because those who fail in one respect have made it up over and over in others. As relationships have grown, the people have become more self-sufficient; even the hearts game, a loud nightly event aboard *Terrier*, has given way to books and chess and backgammon.

There are other changes, in the crew's youngest members especially. A new confident Cody is so loose that he threatens to join the extroverts, while Lake has arrived at a new awareness in his dealings with others. One day on the deckhouse, watching for sharks, Peter said, "Remember when I wrote you that I didn't really care about this film? Well, that's all changed—I *do.*"

By now everyone cares about the film, quite apart from his own investment in it, if only because everyone cares about Peter Gimbel, who has his life's work on the line. A great part of the suspense of waiting for "Big Whitey," as the near-mythical ruler of these silent seas has become known, is the knowledge that his failure to appear could be fatal to the film. Therefore the ship is quiet. Against these stark horizons, even the throb of hard rock music has a thin tinny ring.

More than once I went ashore and prowled the tide pools. I have spent hours of my life crouched beside tide pools, watching the slow surge of simple organisms still close to the first pulse of life on earth. On Dangerous Reef are gaudy giant limpets, and companies of blue, black and banded periwinkles, and the green snail and a brown cone and a very beautiful cream volute with zigzag stripings; also rockfish and the great fire-colored rock crabs that grow enormous in the deeps, and a heart-colored sea anemone, and a garden of hydroids, barnacles and algae. In every tide pool the seal pups played, and others lay on the warm rocks in a sleep so sound that they could be petted without awakening. When at last one did come to, it would stare for seconds in bare disbelief, then bleat in dismay and flop away at speed over the rocks.

In the white surge along the shore, the seals rolled endlessly, turning and twisting, whisking clean out of the water in swift chases, or ranging along, the sleek sun-shined dark-eyed heads held high out of the sea. A small surge would lift them out onto the granite where, groaning, they dozed on the hot rocks in rows. The old bulls, though graceful in the water, were less playful; they stationed themselves on underwater ledges like old mighty sentinels and let the white foam wash around them. Onshore, competitors were driven off in heaving neck fights that were mostly shoving contests; the animals swayed their heavy heads and necks in the way of bears, to which, among land mammals, they are most closely related. Sea lions are agile on the land, and a golden-maned bull protecting a cow and a new pup drove me up onto high ground. One cow was raked drastically on her hind end and right hind flipper by the parallel black lines of an old shark bite, and it was notice-able that the young never left the shallows and that even the adults kept close to the reef edges when not off at sea.

At noon today the *Sea Raider* brought word that an eleven-foot white of thirteen hundred pounds had been hooked at Cape Donington, where the *Saori* had anchored two nights before. Psychologically this news was painful, but the water clarity at Cape Donington is awful and we could not have worked there. And at least it was proof that the species was not extinct.

In a letter to a friend this morning, Valerie wrote that no shark had been seen, but that she expected a twelve- or thirteen-footer to turn up at about 2:00. At 2:20, Peter Lake and Ian McKechnie saw a fin in the slick, some fifty yards behind the ship: the spell was broken. We dragged on diving suits and went on watch, but the fin had sunk from view in the still sea. A half hour passed, and more. Then, perhaps ten feet down off the port beam, a fleeting brown shadow brought the sea to life.

Suspended from a buoy, a salmon was floated out behind the boat to lure the shark closer. Once it had fed at the side of the boat, it would be less cautious; then, perhaps, the engine could be started and the cages swung over the side without scaring it away. But an hour passed before the shark was seen again. This time a glinting rusty back parted the surface, tail and dorsal high out of the water as the shark made its turn into the bait; there was the great wavering blade exactly as Al Giddings had described it, and the thrash of water as the shark took the salmon, two hours to the minute after the first sighting. Stan Waterman cried, "Holy sweet Jesus!," a very strong epithet for this mild-spoken man; he was amazed by the mass of shark that had been raised clear of the water. Even the Australians were excited, try as they would to appear calm. "Makes other sharks look like little frisky pups, doesn't it?" cried Valerie with pride. Then it was gone again. Along the reef, a hundred yards away, the sea lions were playing tag, their sleek heavy bodies squirting clean out of the water and parting the surface again without a splash, and a string of cormorant, oblivious, came beating in out of the northern blue.

Gimbel, annoyed that he had missed the shark, was running from the bow; he did not have long to wait. From the deckhouse roof, I could see the shadow rising toward the bait. "There he is," I said, and Rodney yanked at the shred of salmon, trying to bring the shark in closer to the ship. Lipscomb, beside me, was already shooting when the great fish breached, spun the sea awash and lunged after the skipping salmon tail; we stared into its white oncoming mouth. "My *God!*" Gimbel shouted, astounded by the sight of his first white shark. The conical snout and the terrible shearing teeth and the dark eye like a hole were all in sight, raised clear out of the water. Under the stern, with an audible *whush*, the shark took a last snap at the bait, then wheeled away; sounding, it sent the skiff spinning with a terrific whack of its great tail, an ominous boom that could have been heard a half mile away.

For a split second there was silence, and then Lipscomb gave a mighty whoop of joy. "I *got* it!" he yelled. "Goddamn it, I *got* it!" There was a bedlam of relief, then another silence. "Might knock that cage about a bit," Rodney said finally, hauling in the shred of fish; he was thinking of the baits that would be suspended in the cage to bring the shark close to the cameras. Gimbel, still staring at the faceless water, only nodded.

Just after 5:00 the shark reappeared. The late sun glistened on its dorsal as it cut back and forth across the surface, worrying a dead fish from the line. There was none of the sinuous effect of lesser sharks; the tail strokes were stiff and short like those of swordfish, giant tuna and other swift deep-sea swimmers. This creature was much bigger than the big oceanic sharks off Durban, but for a white shark it was not enormous. Estimates of its length varied from eleven feet six inches ("Ron always plays it safe and underestimates," said Valerie) to fourteen feet (Peter Gimbel: "I saw it alongside that skiff and I'm certain it was at *least* as long—I'm *certain* of it!"), but much more impressive than the length was the mass of it, and the speed and power. "It doesn't matter *what* size the bastards are," Rodney said. "A white shark over six feet long is bloody dangerous."

The day was late. In the westering sun, a hard light of late afternoon silvered the water rushing through the reef, and nearer, the blue facets of the sea sparkled in cascades of tiny stars. More out of frustration than good sense, the choice between trying to film the shark immediately and trying to lure it to the baits alongside, in the hope of keeping it nearby overnight, was resolved in favor of immediate action. The motor was started up and the cages swung over the side, and the cameramen disappeared beneath the surface. But the great shark had retreated, and did not return.

By dark the wind exceeded 25 knots, and went quickly to 30, 40, and finally, toward 1:00 in the morning, to 50 or better—a whole gale. On deck, I lay sleepless, rising every little while to check the position of the light on Dangerous Reef. The Reef is too low to make a windbreak, and even close under the lee, the *Saori* tossed and heaved under heavy strain. But Captain Ben, who knew exactly what his ship would do, slept soundly below. Toward 3:00 the wind moderated, backing around to the southeast, where it held till daybreak.

This morning the wind has died to a fair breeze. Waiting, we sit peacefully in the Sunday sun. The boat captains hand-line for Tommyrough, a delicious small silver relative of the Australian "salmon." Others tinker with equipment, play chess and backgammon, write letters and read. Peter Lake has put a rock tape on the sound machine, and on the roof of the pilothouse, overlooking the oil slick, I write these notes while listening to The Band. Onshore, for Jim Lipscomb's camera, Valerie in lavender is baby-talking with baby seals, and I hope that most if not all of this sequence will die on the cutting-room floor. Unless it points up the days of waiting, such material has no place in the climax of the film; it will soften the starkness of this remote reef as well as the suspense surrounding the imminence of the white shark. Stan and Valerie, with a background of lecture films and a taste for amateur the-atrics, share Jim's appetite for "human-interest stuff," which might yet reduce this film to the first million-dollar home movie.

Toward dark another shark appeared, a smaller one, much bolder. Relentlessly it circled the ship, not ten feet from the hull. On one pass it took the buoyed tuna at a single gulp.

Since it passed alongside, the size of this shark could be closely esti-mated: all hands agreed that it was between nine feet and ten. But if this was accurate, the shark yesterday had been larger than was thought. Rodney now said that it was over twelve, Valerie between thirteen and fourteen, and Gimbel thought that it might have been sixteen feet: "I thought so *yesterday*," he said, "but I felt foolish, with everyone else saying twelve." I thought thirteen feet seemed a conservative minimum. In any case, it had twice the mass of tonight's shark, which was plenty big enough. As it slid along the hull, the thick lateral keel on its caudal peduncle was clearly visible; the merest twitch of that strong tail kept it in motion. Underwater lights were lit to see it better, but this may have been a mistake; it vanished, and did not return the following day.

On January 26 the *Saori* returned to port for water and supplies. There it was learned that four boats, fishing all weekend, had landed between them the solitary shark that we had heard about on Saturday. The *Saori* could easily have hooked two, but what she was here for was going to be much more difficult. Meanwhile, a sighting of white sharks had been reported by divers working Fisheries Bay, west of Cape Cata-strophe on the ocean coast, where three whites and a number of bronze whalers had been seen schooling behind the surf; the bronze whaler, which may be the ubiquitous bull shark, *C. leucas*, is the chief suspect in most shark attacks on Australia's east coast.

On the chance that the shark school was still present, we drove out to the coast across the parched hills of the sheep country. Over high, wind-burnt fields a lovely paroquet, the galah, pearl-gray and rose, flew in weightless flocks out of the wheat; other paroquets, turquoise and black and gold, crossed from a scrub of gum trees and melaleuca to a grove of she-oak, the local name for a form of casuarina. Along the way were strange birds and trees in an odd landscape of wind-worn hills that descended again to the sea-misted shore. From the sea cliffs four or five whalers were in sight, like brown ripples in the pale-green windy water, but the white sharks had gone.

At daybreak on Wednesday the *Saori* sailed for the Gambier Islands, on the Antarctic horizon south of the mouth of Spencer Gulf. A big ocean swell rose out of the southwest, from the far reaches of the roaring forties, but there was a lee of sorts east of Wedge Island. The Gambiers are remote and no gill netting is done there, and white sharks had been seen often in the past; occasionally the sharks would seize a horse when the animals raised here in other days were swum out to the ships. Now the old farm was a sheep station, visited infrequently by man. With Ron, Valerie and Stan, I went ashore, exploring. Gaunt black machinery, stranded by disuse, looked out to sea from the dry golden hills, and the sheep, many of them dead, had brought a plague of flies; only at the island's crest, in the southwest wind, could one be free of them.

Wedge Island is a beautiful silent place, a great monument like a pyramid in the Southern Ocean. That night, white-faced storm petrels fluttered like moths at the masthead light. Some fell to the deck, and I put them in a box; once the deck lights were out, they flitted off toward the island. These hardy little birds come in off the windy wastes of sea just once a year to nest in burrows in the cliffs.

Overhead, shined by the wind, the austral sky was luminous. With the stem of his pipe, Ben Ranford pointed at the universe: "Canis Major," he pronounced with satisfaction. "The brightest star in all the heavens." In World War II Ben was captain of a destroyer in the Australian Navy, and is still the compleat seaman, clumping here and there about his ship in white coveralls and big black shoes without one wasted motion; he could have stripped the *Saori* from stem to stern and reassembled her in the dark. No man could do his job better than he, and yet Ben knew that this ship might be his last.

At dawn the day was already hot and still, the baits untouched, the ocean empty. Only a solitary eagle, white head shimmering in the rising sun, flapped and sailed over the sea, bound for the outermost islands.

Two weeks had passed, and there was no underwater footage, and running from place to place was not the answer. A decision was made to increase the volume of bait and chum and concentrate it at Dangerous Reef. The two sharks raised there were the only two that had been seen, the resident sea lions were an asset, and the Reef was only three hours from the abattoirs and fish companies at Port Lincoln. The ship sailed north again into Spencer Gulf, rounding the west end of the Reef and anchoring off its northern shore at noon; a southwest blow was expected that afternoon, backing around to the southeast by evening.

White shark number three came after dark on January 27, seizing the floating bait with a heavy thrash that brought a bellow of excitement from Gimbel, working on deck. No sooner had a light been rigged than the fish reappeared, making a slow turn at the perimeter of green night water. Then it rifled straight and fast for a carcass hanging at the ship's side, which it gobbled at and shook apart, oblivious of the lights and shouting men. Though not enormous, this aggressive brute was the one we wanted; by the look of it, it would not be deterred by cages or anything else. Then it was gone, and a cuttlefish rippled in the eerie light, and the sea thickened with a bloom of red crustaceans.

All baits were hauled in but a small flayed sheep, left out to stay the shark until the morning. At dawn, the unraveled bait line lay on deck. Taking the sheep, the shark had put such strain upon the line that, parting, it had snapped back clean out of the water. But there was no sign of the shark, and it never returned.

That morning the *Sea Raider* came out from Port Lincoln with big drums full of butchered horse; the quarters hung from the stern of the *Saori*, which was reeking like a charnel house. Buckets of horse blood, whale oil and a foul chum of ground tuna guts made a broad slick that spread northeast toward Spilsby Island. The cages, cameras lashed to their floors, were already overboard, floating astern. The sky was somber, with high mackerel clouds and a bank of ocean grays creeping up out of the south, and a hard wind; petrels dipped and fluttered in the wake. The ship was silent.

Vodka in hand, Gimbel came and went, glaring astounded at the empty slick that spread majestically to the horizon. About 5:30 I forsook my post on the deckhouse roof and went below. Peter was lying in a berth, face tight. I said, "I'm taking a shower even though there's still light enough to shoot; there'll be a shark here before I'm finished." He laughed politely. I had just returned to the cabin, still half dry, wrapped in a towel, when a voice yelled "Shark!" down the companionway.

By the time we reached the deck, bound for the wet-suits, the sun had parted the clouds; with luck, there would be underwater light for at least an hour. Already a second shark had joined the first, and both were big. I went into the sea with Peter, and Stan and Ron soon joined us in the other cage. Almost immediately a great pale shape took form in the blue mist.

The bolder of the sharks, perhaps twelve feet long, was a heavy male, identifiable by paired claspers at the vent; a second male, slightly smaller, stayed in the background. The first shark had vivid scars about the head and an oval scar under the dorsal, and in the molten water of late afternoon it was a creature very different from the one seen from the surface. The hard rust of its hide had dissolved in pale transparent tones that shimmered in the ocean light on its satin skin. From the dorsal fin an evanescent bronze shaded down to luminous dark metallic gray along the lateral line, a color as delicate as that bronze tint on a mushroom which points up the whiteness of the flesh beneath. From snout to keel, the underside was a deathly white, all but the black undertips of the broad pectorals.

The shark passed slowly, first the slack jaw with the triangular splayed teeth, then the dark eye, impenetrable and empty as the eye of God, next the gill slits like knife slashes in paper, then the pale slab of the flank, aflow with silver ripplings of light, and finally the thick short twitch of its hard tail. Its aspect was less savage than implacable, a silent thing of merciless serenity.

Only when the light had dimmed did the smaller shark drift in from the blue shadows, but never did it come to the hanging baits. The larger shark barged past the cages and banged against the hull to swipe and gulp at the chunks of meat; on the way out, it repeatedly bit the propeller of the outboard, swallowing the whole shaft and shaking the motor. Then it would swing and glide straight in again, its broad pectorals, like a manta's wings, held in an upward curve. Gills rippling, it would swerve enough to miss the cage, and once the smiling head had passed I could reach out and take hold of the rubber pectoral, or trail my fingers down the length of cold dead flank, as if stroking a corpse: the skin felt as smooth as the skin of a swordfish or tuna. Then the pale apparition sank under the copper-red hull of the *Saori* and vanished in the gloom, only to reappear from another angle, relentless, moving always at the same deceptive speed, mouth gasping as in thirst. This time it came straight to the cage and seized one of the flotation cylinders of the cage roof; there came a nasty screeching sound, like the grating of fingernails on slate, before the shark turned off, shaking its head.

The sharks off Durban had probed the cages and scraped past, but never once, in hundreds of encounters, did one attack them open-mouthed. The white sharks were to attack the cages over and over. This first one arched its back, gills wrinkling, coming on mouth wide; fortunately it came at cruising speed and struck the least vulnerable part of the cage. The silver tanks, awash at the surface, may have resembled crippled fish, for they were hit far more often than anything else. When their teeth struck metal, the sharks usually turned away, but often the bite was hard enough to break the teeth out. Sometimes as it approached the cage, one would flare its mouth wide, then close it again, in what looked very much like the threat display of higher animals.

To escape the rough chop at the surface, the cage descended to fifteen feet, where Gimbel opened the roof hatch and climbed partway out to film; he was driven back each time. At one point, falling back in haste, Peter got his tank hung up on the hatch, and was still partly exposed when the shark passed overhead, a black shade in the golden ether made by the sinking sun. From below, the brute's girth was dramatically apparent; it blotted out the light.

The shark paid the cages such close attention that Gimbel burned up a ten-minute magazine in fifteen minutes. When he went to the surface to reload, Valerie Taylor and Peter Lake took over the cage. "Listen!" Gimbel yelled at them, still excited. "Now watch it! They're nothing like those Durban sharks, so don't take chances!" Then Stan came out of the second cage, and by the time he was reloaded, Ron was ready to come out; this gave me a chance to go down a second time.

For a while the atmosphere was quiet as both sharks kept their distance from the ship; they came and went like spirits in the mist. But emergencies are usually sudden, and now there came a series of near emergencies. First the bigger shark, mouth open, ran afoul of one of the lines; the length of rope slipped past the teeth and hung in the corners of its mouth, trailing back like reins. So many lines were crisscrossed in the water—skiff lines, bait lines, hydrophone cable and tethers to keep the cages near the bait—that at first one could not tell what was going to happen, and I felt a clutch of fear. Swimming away, the shark was shaking its head in irritation, and then I saw that the line was the tether of the other cage, where Gimbel had been joined by Peter Lake. The line was very nearly taut when the shark shook free. Lake was using a camera with a 180-degree "fish-eye" lens, and was getting remarkable shots, but the close call rattled him considerably.

At the surface, he yelled all the obscenities. "To hell with *that* shit," he concluded. "I'm going below to hide under my berth!" But Lake's trials were not over. A few days later, when the *Saori* returned to Dangerous Reef for continuity shots and supporting footage, a shark, tangled in a bait line, bent the whole cage with its slow thrashing; it actually *stretched* five of the bars, shaking the whole cage like a dice cup before Lake could get his leg knife out and cut it free. At the surface, he had difficulty joking: "When I saw those bars starting to go I felt like I had jumped at twelve thousand feet with my parachute eaten by rats."

Often the larger shark would appear from below, its ragged smile rising straight up past the cage; already its head was scarred with streaks of red lead from the *Saori*'s hull. On one of these ascents it seized a piece of meat hung from the taffrail just as the current swung the cage in toward the ship, so that the whole expanse of its ghostly belly, racked by spasms of huge gulping, was perpendicular against the bars. I scratched the belly with a kind of morbid sympathy, but at that instant we were jarred by a thrash of the tail; the cage had pinned the shark upright against the rudder of the *Saori*. While Waterman filmed at point-blank range, it lashed the water white. "I wasn't really worried about you guys," Gimbel said later. "I just knew it would knock hell out of you." The cage was swiftly heaved aside, and the shark glided for the bottom with that ineffable silent calm, moving no more rapidly than before. Except for size, it is often difficult to estimate shark age, and watching it go, it was easy to believe that this beast might swim for centuries.

I turned to congratulate Waterman on the greatest footage of a feeding white shark ever taken, but bald eyes rolled in woe behind his mask, and he made a throat-slitting gesture with his finger and smote his rubber brow, then shook his fist at his camera, which had jammed. Gimbel got the sequence from the other cage, thirty feet away, and Lipscomb caught one angle of it from the surface, but Stan was inconsolable.

Gimbel was still trying to film from the roof hatch, and now he ducked down neatly at a shark's approach, only to find himself staring straight into its face. The main cage door had opened outward, and the shark was so near that he could not reach out to close it. Badly frightened, he feinted with his camera at the shark, which cruised on past, oblivious.

Between bites the sharks patrolled the cages, the *Saori* and the skiff, biting indiscriminately; there was no sense of viciousness or savagery in what they did, but something worse, an implacable need. They bit the skiff and they bit the cages, and one pushed past the meat to bite the propeller of the *Saori*; it was as if they smelled the food but could not distinguish it by sight, and therefore attacked everything in the vicinity. Often they mouthed the cage metal with such violence that teeth went spinning from their jaws. One such tooth found on the bottom had its serrated edge scraped smooth. It seemed to me that here was the explanation for the reports of white-shark attacks on boats; they do not attack boats, they attack *anything*.

When I left the water, there was a slight delay in getting the skiff alongside, and Rodney warned me not to loiter on top of the cage. "They've been climbing all over it!" he called. At one point Valerie, having handed up her exhausted tank, had to retreat into the cage, holding her breath as a shark thrashed across its roof over and over.

We had entered the water about 6:00, and the last diver left it at 7:30, by which time everyone of us was shaking hard with cold. In the skiff, transferring from the cages to the ship, people were shouting. The excitement far exceeded any I had seen in the footage of the greatest day off Durban; as Gimbel said, "Christ, man! These sharks are just a hell of a lot more exciting!"

The next morning, a sparkling wild day, the two sharks were still with us, and they had been joined by a third still larger. Even Ron estimated the new shark at fourteen feet, and Gimbel one or two feet more; it was the biggest man-eating shark that anyone aboard had ever seen. Surging out of the sea to fasten on a horse shank hung from a davit, it stood upright beside the ship, head and gills clear of the water, tail vibrating, the glistening triangles of its teeth red-rimmed with blood. In the effort of shearing, the black eye went white as the eyeball was rolled inward; then the whole horse quarter disappeared in a scarlet billow. "I've watched sharks all my life," Ben Ranford said, "but I've never seen anything as terrifying as that." Plainly no shark victim with the misfortune to get hold of a raft or boat would ever survive the shaking of that head.

Last night in the galley, Ron had suggested to Peter that swimming with one white might be possible, and Peter agreed. But this morning there were three, and the visibility was so limited that one could never tell where or when the other two might appear. The talk of swimming in the open water ended, and a good thing, too. In its seeming contempt for the great white shark, such a dangerous stunt could only make an anticlimax of the film's climax.

The cage will sink a foot or so beneath the surface under a man's weight—a situation to be avoided in the presence of white sharks—and the next morning, entering it, I performed with ease what I had heretofore done clumsily, flipping directly out of the skiff and down through the narrow roof hatch head first. Even before I straightened up, the largest of the sharks loomed alongside, filling the blue silence with its smile. I felt naked in my flimsy cell until Stan joined me. This shark was two or three feet longer than the next in size, but it looked half again as big, between eighteen hundred pounds and a fat ton. In white sharks over ten feet long, the increase in girth and weight per foot of length is massive; the white shark that I saw dead at Montauk, only two or three feet longer than this one, had weighed at least twice as much.

The new shark was fearless, crashing past skiff and cage alike to reach the meat, and often attacking both on the way out. Like its companions, which scooted aside when it came close, it attacked the flotation tanks over and over, refusing to learn that they were not edible. Even the smallest shark came in to sample the flotation tanks when the others were not around. I had seen one of its companions chase it, so probably its shyness had little to do with the *Saori*: unlike the sharks in the Indian Ocean the whites gave one another a wide berth. Occasionally one would go for the air tank in the corner, bumping the whole cage through the water with its snout, and once one struck the naked bars when I waved a dead salmon as it approached. Clumsily it missed the proffered fish, glancing off the bars as I yanked my arm back. Had the sharks attacked the bars, they would have splayed them. "He could bite that cage to bits if he wanted to," Valerie had said of yesterday's shark, and got no argument; for the big shark today, the destruction of the cage would be the work of moments. From below, we watched it wrestle free an enormous slab of horse, two hundred pounds or more; as it gobbled and shook, its great pale body quaked, the tail shuddering with the effort of keeping its head high out of the water. Then, back arched, it dove with its prize toward the bottom, its mouth trailing bubbles from the air gulped down with its last bite. Only one pilotfish was ever seen at Dangerous Reef; we wondered if the white shark's relentless pace made it difficult for a small fish to keep up.

Numbers of fish had come to the debris exploded into the water by the feeding, and the windstorm of the night before had stirred pale algae from the bottom. Visibility was poor, yet the sharks worked so close to the cages that the morning's filming was even better than the day before, and the cameramen worked from nine until one-thirty. By then, the ten months of suspense were over.

We were scarcely out of the water when the wind freshened, with the threat of rain. The cages were taken aboard and battened down while a party went ashore to film the *Saori* from the Reef. Then, in a cold twilight, drinking rum in the galley-fo'c's'le, we rolled downwind across Spencer Gulf, bound for Port Lincoln. Though the sea was rough, the fo'c's'le was warm and bright, filled with rock music. Valerie saw to it that the supper was cooked properly, and wine soon banished the slightest doubt that we all liked one another very much. "Is there anything more splendid," Waterman cried, "than the fellowship of good shipmates in the fo'c's'le after a bracing day before the mast?" After three weeks in the fo'c's'le, Stan had embraced the nineteenth century with all his heart.

Peter Gimbel, sweetly drunk, swung back and forth from fits of shouting to a kind of stunned suffused relief and quiet happiness. He looked ten years younger. What was surely the most exciting film ever taken underwater had been obtained without serious injury to anybody. The triumph was a vindication of his own faith in himself, and because he had earned it the hard way and deserved it, it was a pleasure simply to sit and drink and watch the rare joy in his face.

At the end of that week all the Americans returned home but myself and Cody. Stuart went into the Outback to try opal mining with Ian McKechnie, and I flew westward to East Africa. A month later, when I reached New York, Peter told me that the white-shark sequence was beyond all expectations, that the film studio was ecstatic, and that a financial success now seemed assured. How sad, I said, that his father wasn't here to see it. He grinned, shaking his head. "It is," he said. "He would have been delighted."

Already Peter was concerned about where he would go from here. Meanwhile, he had planned a violent dieting which he didn't need, and when asked why, he shrugged. "I just want to see if I can get down to a hundred seventy," he said. Perhaps I read too much into that diet, but it bothered me: the search for the great white shark was at an end, but the search was not. I recalled a passage in the letter Peter had written after the thirty-hour marathon off Durban, and when I got home I dug it out.

"I felt none of the dazed sense of awe," he wrote, "that had filled me ten days before during our first night dive. I remember wondering sadly how it could be that a sight this incredible could have lost its shattering impact so quickly for me—why it should be that the sights and sensations should have to accelerate so hellishly simply to hold their own with my adaptation to them . . . Only a week or so after having come out of the water one night to say over and over, 'No four people in all the world have ever laid eyes on a scene so wild and infernal as that,' I wasn't even particularly excited . . ."

And he continues, "I was filled with a terrible sadness that we had indeed determined precisely the limits we sought, that the mystery was at least partly gone because we knew that we could get away with anything, that the story—and such a story!—had an end."

from Savage Shore
by Edward Marriott

Edward Marriott (born 1966) is best known for his reports on dangerous adventures in far-off lands. Savage Shore recounts his trip to Nicaragua's Moskito Coast, where he learned about the bull shark—the only species known to travel inland to fresh waters. Marriott struck up a friendship with a local shark fisherman, and joined him on a fishing trip.

A t Arturo's request, I'd brought bananas—fat, ripe claws, still on the stalk—and carried them through the tropical night, down tracks I now knew well, almost able to gauge the distance by the incline, the exact crunch and give of the rubble underfoot. Down the tight alleyway to Arturo's yard, I smelled the gutterswill again, less rich now than during the day, and felt my way along the walls of houses, testing each step before moving on, doubling the length of the journey so that by the time I arrived it was past four and Arturo, to my surprise, was already up, brushing his teeth with lagoon water, not five yards from the outflow from the open sewer.

He greeted me silently, mouth afroth. Together we bailed the dugout, heaping nets and hooks high in the prow, scraping at the swollen wood with coconut halves. We worked until the boat was dry and people in nearby shacks were coughing in their sleep. In Arturo's shack, through a square of grease-smoked glass, I glimpsed his wife moving about slowly, a slight shake to her movements: too many dawn starts, I guessed, too much broken sleep. And there was, as Arturo had predicted, just the faintest breeze tickling onshore, barely strong enough to ruffle the water, detectable only in a sweet cooling of the skin.

As yet, though, we had no engine. Arturo wanted to fish further out, ten miles south, and to do that he needed an outboard. His neighbor Elias had one, and had promised to come if they split the catch, but he was nowhere to be seen. Arturo made me wait and cut round the back of his shack, muttering to himself. It was ten minutes before he returned, and in those minutes came the first intimation of dawn: a lifting of the absoluteness of night, the first edges of things rising into focus. I carried the gasoline over to the dugout, found the paddles, laid out the bananas and the bread Arturo's wife had baked, and waited.

Ten minutes later, they both emerged, Elias running apologizing after Arturo, yawning continually, dressed only in his underpants, one hand on the sagging elastic. He'd overslept, but promised we'd be out there soon. He hurried to the water's edge and began lifting away palm branches from what I'd thought was a heap of refuse, and soon was heaving the outboard clear, setting it on its back beside the tank of gasoline. He maneuvered it one-handed, with seeming ease: hard to believe an outboard that weighed so little was as quick as he boasted. I watched, feeling the first flurry of concern, uncomfortably close to my bowels. Elias looked up, grinned, hoisted his underpants. "Five minutes," he said, and was gone again.

"We'll be going soon," Arturo said, nodding, looking east across the lagoon to the bar mouth and the slowly opening sky. Dawn was edging in, nudging a slip of palest gray along the horizon, letting me stagger about less blindly. Arturo had always impressed on me the importance of a pre-dawn start, and I detected under his current resolute optimism a fear that time was running by too fast; that Elias would be a half hour, not five minutes; that the other shark fishermen were already out there working the best reaches; that we'd miss our chance and, within hours, the weather would turn again. He began to sharpen his knives, blade to blade—long, determined strokes, ending in a conjuror's flourish. The first of the cockerels awoke, bleating red-throated, tremulous.

"Where's Elias?" Arturo muttered finally, sheathing the knives. He looked at his watch, shook it, held it to his ear. "Time to go."

We did what we could—dragged the dugout to the water's edge, sat the gasoline flat in the stern, wedged blocks in the hull to serve as seats, one behind the other—and were struggling with the outboard, our feet sliding in the mud, when Elias appeared, breathless but dressed, carrying a throw net and a clutch of hooks.

"I thought we'd need some more," he said, seeming even younger than earlier, his hair now slicked back; he was chewing a clod of white bread. He walked over and took the engine from me without explanation, and he and Arturo lowered it onto the flat-backed stern, spinning tight the butterfly screws. From there to the water it took all three of us, leaning full weight, to get the dugout to move at all; it inched heavily through the mud, leaving a shallow grave into which dark water rose uncertainly.

Elias was the last, pushing off from the stern while Arturo and I weighted the prow, leaning over each other in our efforts to cast off. When we were afloat, Elias heaved himself in, mud drooling from his knees and calves, the dugout shipping gouts of water till I scrambled to midships and, finally, we lay flat in the water, with barely an inch of clearance. Behind us, the edge-dwellers were waking: an old man took to his porch and peed noisily; Arturo's wife stood in her open doorway, blank-faced. Coconut palms were stenciled against the lightening sky. Elias wound a length of twine round the starting mechanism and knelt in the hull and pulled hard. The engine sputtered soggily. I leaned back toward Arturo.

"We're not too late?" I said. Though it was a relief, at last, to be off, I was troubled by other matters—this rickety transport, for one, and whether it would withstand a larger sea—but it was clear no good would come of airing them. This question, at least, was answerable.

Arturo laughed, pounded me on the back. "You worry too much."

The engine kicked in, a single-cylinder sneeze that spat oily smoke clear to the bank. Arturo congratulated Elias, settled on his bench seat, laid the red glove flat beside him. "You'll see," he grinned, as we juddered forward, in gear at last. "The shark—he waits for us."

To a shark hunter from the West—from North America, or Australia— equipped with 300hp cruiser and air-con cabin and satellite navigator and submarine radar and high-velocity harpoon, the approach of Arturo and his kind would have seemed laughably amateur. In Nicaragua, any man with a dugout and a hand line could turn shark hunter; it was not so much a romantic calling as a means of survival, a way to feed the family, since fins commanded high prices. The attendant danger was accepted because that was the way things had always been. In richer countries, where economic hardship seldom forced men to sea to hunt sharks, shark fishermen had become heroic figures, emblematic of a braver, simpler age.

This century's best-known shark hunter was William Young, a sturdy Californian adventurer, later naval captain, who spent his life fishing shark in Australia, Florida, and French Somaliland, but who settled in Honolulu. Known to the locals as "Kane Mano," Shark Hunter, Captain Young died aged eighty-seven, having killed, by his own estimate, a hundred thousand sharks: an average day's haul was twenty or thirty. In his dotage, reminiscing over the carnage that had been his life, his callused feet cradled in sharkskin pumps, he recalled how he'd first learned the trade: he'd kill a horse, drag it to sea, slit open its belly, then harpoon the circling sharks. To him, sharks were "arrogant," "cold," "rapacious."

From photographs, Young himself appears little more, though something else is evident, too: behind those Bakelite spectacles is a hard face, with dark, animal eyes. As he stands, clad in blood-smeared overalls, behind that strung-up fifteen-foot hammerhead, the impression is of a man who has never once questioned himself, nor anything he's done.

He died in 1962, his conscience untroubled. At that point, marine biologists had not yet isolated the shark as a threatened species; then, talk was still of the "war" with sharks, and what research there was focused on the protection of man, not fish. Shark deterrents, of variable efficacy, proliferated. The "bubble fence," invented by the owner of an eastern seaboard hotel in 1960, in response to a particularly vicious attack off the New Jersey coast, carried the boast that "sharks will not even cross it to get to a juicy steak." Which would have been excellent, if true, since the bubble fence—a perforated pipe, laid on the seabed, through which compressed air was pumped, creating a rising curtain of bubbles—was certainly cheap to produce. Unfortunately, as later tests showed, sharks parted this curtain as if it were so much gossamer.

Depth-charging, attempted first in 1958 off Margate, South Africa, was equally unsuccessful: sharks possess no swim bladder, and are thus impervious to anything other than a virtually direct hit. Indeed, the vibrations from a depth charge draw sharks almost as quickly as does the scent of blood: survivors from the U.S. destroyer *Frederick C. Davis*, torpedoed in the Atlantic on 25 April 1945, told of fellow seamen torn apart by sharks attracted to the scene by the detonation of depth charges on the sunken ship.

During the first years of World War II, the lack of an efficient, portable deterrent badly undermined the fighting spirit of U.S. forces. "Reports of shark attacks on members of our combat forces have created a wartime sea survival problem that can no longer be neglected," counseled an Army Air Corps bulletin. "The possibility of attack is a growing hazard to morale."

Triggered by President Roosevelt's personal intervention, urgent research began into the possibility of chemical deterrents. In the early 1940s, at Woods Hole Oceanographic Institute in Massachusetts, no less than seventy-nine different substances were tried out. Only one—copper acetate—proved effective, and this, blended with an inky dye, became Shark Chaser, issued to all servicemen and strapped to every life raft. It was indescribably malodorous, dead-rat funky; was, in fact, the closest chemical approximation of decomposed shark ever manufactured— which, to any half-canny fisherman, made perfect sense: no shark, how- ever ravenous, will touch another that has been left to rot.

When all deterrents failed, and sharks broke through beach nets to kill sun-pinkened bathers and puppy dogs, men exacted disproportionate revenge. Two days after the fatal mauling of a fifteen-year-old Hawaiian surfer just before Christmas 1958, government officials and community leaders on Oahu called for nothing less than extermination of every shark that menaced their shores. Twenty-seven thousand dollars was raised to man and fuel a shark boat. Within the year, 697 sharks—snared on overnight half-mile lines—were captured and destroyed. They weren't even given the dignity of being mashed for fertilizer, the lowliest possible by-product: just incinerated, in great mounds, like the corpses of diseased cattle.

Yet now, four decades later, there was no figure more reviled by the marine biology establishment than the shark hunter. One in particular—a Queenslander, Vic Hislop, self-styled "Shark Man," with his shark-tooth pendant and deep-pile chest hair, his quick line in self-justification, his highly lucrative and formidably gory "Shark Show"—has become almost an outlaw in Australia. The "authorities," he believes, are engaged in a full-scale cover-up, obscuring from the public, to protect the tourist industry, the true extent of shark-related deaths off Australian coasts. In south Australia, where the great white is a protected fish, Hislop claims to have suffered police harassment, has regularly had his boat impounded. The authorities, in turn, accuse him of misleading journalists, of talking up the shark threat to keep himself and his bloodthirsty sideshow in the limelight.

In conversation Hislop comes across as garrulous, obsessed, paranoid. When I asked to meet him, he declined; when I persisted, he agreed only on condition that I pay him. I hedged; we ended up talking on the telephone. He'd grown to distrust journalists, he said: so many times he'd allowed them access to his life, had permitted camera crews to film him on the hunt, and every time he'd ended up being portrayed as a simple-minded, single-issue propagandist.

He sent me his "book," a self-published glossy brochure, in which he marshaled his arguments in full and lingered over past heroics. It was hard not to smile as the eye passed over yet another photograph of

Hislop—scrawny and diminutive, despite the Popeye posturing—leg up on yet another carcass, but there was something, some grain of the possible, in what he said. All those autopsies that read, "missing, presumed drowned"; all those swimmers and surfers whose friends had seen them sucked clean under, leaving no clue, no trace. What *had* happened to them? And what of Hislop? Had he, as he claimed, been cast out simply because his message was too unpalatable? It was not impossible.

By the time we'd reached the middle of the lagoon, still some way from the open sea, there was a slight chop on the water, the surface splintered into tiny corrugations, no longer oily-smooth. Arturo sat in the bow, I in the middle, Elias at the stern, with one hand on the tiller. We were kicking up a fine spray, which soaked us like drizzle; leaves of water spilled over the side and I bailed hard, nervous we'd founder, since we'd started with an inch in the hull and neither Elias nor Arturo seemed especially concerned.

In this spectral light I could just make out the shapes of other dories, their sails like origami triangles, inching toward the sea in the windless pre-dawn. There were twenty, perhaps more, but they made no noise, and glimmered in and out of sight, moving separately and then in convoy, floating in the pale haze as if through smoke, after a battle. When our engine died—just the fuel line coming loose, though the diagnosis took Elias a while—the voices of the other fishermen carried clear across the water, all their early-morning rumblings about cloud formations and the day's prospects, along with the hard crackle of the plastic sheeting as they roped their sails tight, the kiss of their paddles on the water, their labored breathing.

We stopped, engine off, in the lee of the mangroves at the far side of the lagoon. We needed prawns, Arturo explained, untangling the throw net: prawns would serve as bait for snapper and whitejack, which, in turn, gaffed bloody and alive, would lure the sharks. He stood in the prow, gathering the skirts of the net, taking the first corner in his teeth, laying the net in folds across his arm, then, with his breath held in, he cast it spinning over the bow. It landed a perfect circle, the lead-weighted circumference pulling the filaments down through the murk. When he pulled it up, guiding it back to the edge of the dory, it came effortlessly, shedding water from its topknot, the weights gathering the bottom shut. Only when he held it up, clear of the water, did I see that there were scores of tiny prawns in the netting, blue-gray and wriggly, snared by their whiskers.

"Ha!" Arturo said, triumphant, shaking out the net into the bottom of the boat. "A good day is coming."

The prawns spun free, bouncing off the sides of the hull; each time he repeated the maneuver they clustered more thickly round my feet, swilling about in the oily floodwater in the bottom of the hull. Arturo became ever more jubilant, convinced that their abundance was a sign—proof of the harvest to come.

As we crossed from the lagoon to the ocean, emerging from the lee of Bluff Island, the hull began to fill alarmingly. Out in this swell, the dugout, even at low revs, was shipping water over the bow and gunwales. I shouted back to Elias, pointing at my feet, which were awash to the ankles; he grinned, indicated the bailer. "A little bit of water," he said. *"Es normal."*

Here, where the lagoon met the sea, the currents boiled and surged. It took a while to breach this section, the propeller biting air in a frantic whine as we nosed off the back of each swell, but rhythm came easier once we were clear. While I bailed, just about keeping pace with the in-fill, Arturo stretched his back and massaged his knees, using the spare bailer to ladle up the prawns, sieving them through his fingers.

"Just here," he announced abruptly.

Elias, sleepy from the start, jolted upright. "Already?"

I stopped bailing. Arturo twisted round, waved a finger at both of us. "The sea horse. This is where I see the sea horse." He eyed us eagerly, as if expecting some clamorous response. I waited. Finally, when it was clear Elias wasn't planning to speak up, I said, "Sea horse?"

"Big storm day," Arturo said, nodding. He turned back to face the sea, gesturing toward the wide horizon, toward the first nudgings upward of a huge dawn sun. He threw his voice like an orator, waving wildly with a shark hook. "I see a big reeling of water and a great animal stuck out his head and was gone."

"You were out here? In a storm?"

He held the hook in front of my face, as a teacher might, growing short-tempered. "So I get up near to where it come out and when I'm there it come right out again and it's braying as a horse, same as a horse bray—'neeigh!'—and then it was gone again. It really was a sea horse—same mane as a horse, same head, same big ears." And his eyes were wide as a horse's after all this, wholly earnest, defying disbelief. Eventually, during a lull in the engine and before the next swell hit, Elias spoke.

"Arturo, *hombre*, enough. The light is coming. Can't you see?" And he heaved the boat toward the sea again and, still grinning, opened the throttle into the waves.

Further to sea, with the pelicans banking for shore, Elias leveled our course; we were running parallel to the coastline, at least two miles distant from the dark sand and wind-beaten coconut palms that formed the beachhead. Elias would watch four, five waves ahead, turning windward or away, gunning the engine or easing off, to minimize the pitch and yaw, but still we took on water, regularly, evenly, never less than inches-deep about our feet. I bailed, but less anxiously: we were out here now; the sky, now dawn had fully come, seemed to threaten nothing more than flat, absolute heat; nothing was looming; the far rim of cumulus seemed easeful, unhurried. But whenever I dropped my shoulders and, forgetting, emptied less determinedly, water filled steadily. "Eduardo!" Arturo would shout, looking round. "Your job!"

He was crouched forward in the prow, knees to his chest, backside uncomfortably on our anchor of rude-welded rods. With a scrubber of steel wool he was working through the six-inch shark hooks, concentrating on the point and barb, buffing till the steel showed through again. His equipment was aging and eclectic: the link sections, the "trace" between hook and line, which in the collection of a better-off shark fisherman would have comprised three-foot strips of tempered steel wire, were, in his case, corroded sections of chain, scavenged from other machinery.

From here, far offshore, the coast stretched to infinity: south to Costa Rica, Panama, Colombia; north to Pearl Lagoon, Cape Gracias, Honduras, the United States. It was at Pearl Lagoon, some days earlier, that the mayor, like the old logger who'd entrusted me with his letter for the Queen, had pleaded with me, as an Englishman, to mobilize my government to rid his people of "the Spaniards." If I did not, he warned, revolution was inevitable. "If these Spaniards don't stop thieving all our natural resources—all our timbers and fish—then we will have no choice but to fight. Every man here will fight."

Up those inland waterways, north from Bluefields, where once Dutch and English buccaneers hid their schooners from the Spanish overlords, where spreading mangroves and shifting sandbars constantly kept fishermen and campesinos on their guard, the bull shark lurked. Pearl Lagoon had a narrow, silted bar, dividing ocean from freshwater lagoon, and its fishermen spoke of it with dread.

Hard to imagine, traveling this coast and hearing such stories, that any shark could have ever been dismissed as "wretched" or "cowardly," but a U.S. Army manual, published before World War II, attempted just such vapid reassurance. "The shark is a cowardly fish which moves about slowly, and is easily frightened by surprises in the water, noise, movement and unusual shapes. This last point alone would be enough for a shark not to attack man." And, should one confound expectation and do just that, then all the alert marine had to do was pull a knife and "open up its stomach . . . you cause water to enter—that will kill it almost instantaneously."

Misunderstood creatures, feared and worshiped in equal measure. In the Solomon Islands, before the missionaries came, sharks were kept as captive gods, corralled in sacred caverns, appeased by regular human sacrifice. William Ellis, an early-nineteenth-century missionary, observed similar practices in the Archipel de la Société: "Temples were erected in which priests officiated, and offerings were presented to the deified sharks, while fishermen and others, who were much at sea, sought their favour."

Ancient Hawaiians, too, valued the shark, but more for its potential as entertainment: at Pearl Harbor, Hawaiian kings ordered underwater jousts between ravenous, penned-in sharks and gladiators armed only with shark-teeth swords. In the 1920s, Fijians were observed "shark-charming," a skill unheard of anywhere else. A French missionary, who'd witnessed islanders kissing sharks into submission, reported, more than a little stunned: "It's some occult power they have which I can't define, but once the native kisses it, that shark never moves again."

There were no such eccentricities with the bull shark. All the Costeños comprehended was that most basic rule, that a dorsal fin above the surface meant a hungry shark, though undisturbed calm was, conversely, no guarantee of safety. Like the great white, the bull shark as often foraged underwater, breaking the surface only at the last moment, jaws stretched to a perfect, serrated oval.

It was as stealthy as it was unpredictable, taking squid, sea urchin, crab, stingray, porpoise, whale, other shark, and each other: if one bull shark was injured in a food fight, the others would tear it to pieces in seconds. Its memory for blood was unerring, and it was impossible to read, "always inclined," according to a 1962 paper in the *Journal of the Royal Naval Medical Service*, "to be offensive . . . a particularly ferocious species which will attack large fish without apparent provocation and not for food."

Only gradually, and with the accumulation of years of data from marine biologists, coast guards, and fishermen, was a full portrait of the bull shark beginning to emerge. Off the shores of Natal, in South Africa, where once it was assumed that the near-mythical great white was responsible for most deaths, it now appeared that the pig-eyed bull shark, a good deal more compact, with its disproportionately large incisors, accounted for something like four times the number of victims. It was the hardiest of all tropical sharks, the most resilient to change, and it was able to survive many years in captivity with less stress than any other. Its depredations on the Ganges, preying on the half-burned bodies thrown from sacred ghats, were most often blamed on the Ganges shark, *Glyphis gangeticus*, but this in truth was a needle-toothed softie, a mere plankton-sifter by comparison.

As to why all this should be, there was little agreement. Certainly the bull shark's taste for both fresh and brackish water had brought it into close and regular contact with animals and men, and where the pickings are easy, so sharks make their home. A hundred years ago, Charles Napier Bell, a longtime Bluefields resident, recorded in his memoirs that "there is no harbour in the world more dangerous for sharks than Greytown"—modern-day San Juan del Norte, the settlement at the mouth of the San Juan, for which I was headed—and so it remained.

In these waters the bull shark scavenged ceaselessly, swallowing whole anything that tumbled from the bank: orange peel, empty rum bottles, stones, twigs. Along the turbid coast, and in the heavily silted rivers and mangrove waterways, with visibility often down to zero, it had developed a preternatural olfactory sense: at a hundred meters, a single drop of blood was lure enough.

And now we were heading south, to a lone cay so small it was still invisible, ancestral property of the Rama Indians, who, whenever the ocean was calm enough, would paddle across from the mainland to tend their microplantation and fish for shark. The lee of the island, Arturo said, was rich with fish, though he had discovered this only by accident, stranded late one afternoon when the wind had turned on him: the next dawn, casting from the rocks, waiting for better weather, he'd landed three big sharks. He wasn't sure why the cay had proved so abundant, what aquatic alchemy had produced such a swarming, but had made sure of one thing: he'd told no other shark fishermen, and though they had grown suspicious, and often quizzed him and Elias, none of them had an outboard and so never managed to follow the two men much further than the bar.

Ideally, he said, we should have made it there at dawn, but things had taken longer than anticipated. But he remained confident, yelling out at first glimpse of the cay—a distant thumb-smudge splintered by the heat haze—breaking off to point out flying fish, which flitted weightless across the water, flashing like chain mail. We drank luke-warm coffee from Arturo's flask, and above the noise of the engine threw out theories about what best attracted shark.

Blood, we all knew, was the surest lure, even in minute quantity; so too, Arturo held, were vomit, offal, garbage, and carrion—all rank-smelling, signaling easy pickings. Elias, who'd seen a friend taken on Bluefields bar, believed there was something in the flailings of pan-icked or inexperienced swimmers that triggered a shark's aggression: perhaps because the vibrations felt like those of a wounded fish.

From what I'd learned, it seemed that almost anything could pro-voke attack, anything unusual, particularly any large impact: more sailors, according to one breathtaking statistic, were taken by sharks in the worst World War II shipwrecks than had been killed in attacks close to shore in all of recorded history.

Sharks, so the thinking goes, have hearing acute as a trip wire, and the commotion of a ship going down or a plane scything into the sea draws them from hundreds of miles away. The torpedoing off Natal on 18 November 1942 of the English troopship *Nova Scotia*, for example, left 850 dead, from a total of 1,042; according to survivors' estimates, more than half—young men, able swimmers all, adrift in bath-warm seas—were taken by sharks.

The sinking of the Philippine ferry *Doña Paz* on 20 December 1987 was more sanguinary still: the ship, though authorized to carry only 608 passengers, was that night wedged with between 3,000 and 4,000 villagers returning home for New Year fiestas. At ten that evening the ferry was rammed portside by an oil tanker. Both vessels exploded. Those who weren't burned alive jumped into the raging sea, aslick with flame. Only twenty-five survived; over the next few days, three hundred shark-mutilated corpses were found littered on island shores, and for weeks afterward, Philippine fishermen reported finding body parts in the belly of almost every shark they landed.

• • •

In the crescent lee of the island Elias cut the engine; we drifted toward a steep, rocky beach. Though the day was near windless, there was a heavy swell, which smashed to broken foam on the red cliffs seaward. It was not much of a place—five hundred yards long, crested with stunted coconut and banana trees, with a high-ride scurf of plastic sandals and bleached aluminium drink cans and hard-dried seaweed.

"Iguana Cay!" Arturo shouted, standing upright in the prow. We nosed toward the beach, pitching in the swell, Elias behind me yelling instructions—when to jump, remember to take the rope. The water was warm here, a generous turquoise, opaque with sea life.

Grabbing the rope, Arturo jumped for shore, disappearing to his waist, paddling his arms against the suck of the swell, making it to the dry rocks soaked and breathing heavily. He beckoned me to follow, ordering Elias to stay out, drop anchor, and set the bait lines. Arturo was grinning now, as if just pleased to have made it this far. While I hesitated on the bow, wondering whether to launch off heedless, or lower myself more gently and swim for it, he held the rope loose, letting the dugout rest easy a few yards offshore. When I finally leapt forward, expecting a last-yard flounder to land, I sank to my neck. Something brushed my calf. I kicked into breast stroke, fired with panic and the certainty that, in this warm gloop, I'd get no warning of a shark, just that bleak numbness as my leg went.

"Shark," I panted as I crawled onto the beach. I struggled breathless to my feet, tried to smile.

"If you'd come two days ago," Arturo said, ignoring my flailings, giving me his hand, "you could have had this."

He pointed to the remains of a fire, set at the crest of the beach, on flat, slatelike rocks. Scattered through the cold ashes were the bones of a hammerhead, about six feet long. The head—skin stretched tight, gray-purplish in color—looked unlike any earthly living thing, an alien mutant with smoked-glass eyes set at the far edges of an airfoil skull. It would have been caught off these rocks by the Rama Indians, Arturo said, roasted and eaten the same day, its sandpapery hide cut into strips and used "to scrub the smoke from the bottom of pots." What was left of the spine—featherweight disks of ivory cartilage—would serve as counters on a homemade checkerboard. The smell, though the fish had been stripped clean and only its barest outline remained, was as potent as if from weeks of decay, sun-stewed to ulcerous softness. With a stick, I lifted the head and out of the scimitar mouth, frozen ajar, crawled fat flies, too lazy to take to the air, their wings and feet wet with feasting.

Arturo was up at the far end of the beach, trousers rolled to his knees, the material drying in streaks. He'd cut himself a spear from the bush and was sharpening one end to a pencil point.

"Iguana," he said. "Sharks eat anything, but they love iguana." This cay, he said, was thick with them, hence its name; they had been stranded here when the island split from the mainland. He grinned, confident in his mastery of history. "Millions of years ago this was the coast." He stabbed his spear into the red-clay cliff. "Come. Let's hunt."

He walked ahead, negotiating the narrow strip of dry rocks under the cliff, and I followed. We left the beach behind us as we headed for the point. Further on, the rocks became boulders, black as lead and coated with white deposit. Every few yards Arturo would stop, hold his spear above his head, and lecture me, the sea warm as tea about our ankles. For centuries, he said, the cay had been Rama property. The Indians cultivated bananas and coconuts, hunted shark and, rarer these days, the hawksbill turtle, with its perfect, mottled carapace. They'd be out here every three weeks or so, whenever the weather allowed, fishing from two or three dories, onto which they'd heap their plunder and paddle hard, on uncertain seas, back to the mainland.

Iguana Cay, Arturo believed, constituted the most abundant fishing area of the whole Miskito Bank. And, so far, it remained his and the Ramas' secret: even Maximo, when I'd asked him to name the best sharking grounds, had cited Punta Gorda, a rocky promontory some way further south. So: given all this, I wanted to know, why did the Ramas let Arturo—a Miskito with Creole blood, hardly a natural ally—fish these gold-dust waters?

"How can they stop me?" he said, spearing into the shallows, after

a darting of color. "I'm here and then I'm gone. I have an engine—
not one of them has an engine. This is the way it is. There's nothing
they can do."

Further on, as we came out of the lee, Arturo gave a little holler and fell
to his knees. "What did I say?" He was speaking as much to himself as
to me, chuckling like a happy-fed animal. As he stood up again and I
came alongside I saw he'd speared a lizard of some sort. It hung limply
and smelled poisoned, as bad as the hammerhead on the beach.

"It's dead," I said, meaning that it had been dead a while, surely too
long to be of much use to us. "It stinks. What is it?"

Arturo looked at me sorrowfully, as if amazed all over again at my
failure to learn. "Iguana."

"I thought they needed to be fresh."

"Sharks eat anything." He gripped it by the tail, lifted it off the spike,
yelled across to Elias in the dugout. "Catch this!" And with one broad
arc he slung the iguana nose-first, high into the sky. It flew a perfect tra-
jectory, diving legs out toward Elias, who waited, arms wide, a good
forty yards from our rocks. It was a near-flawless throw, missing Elias's
lap by inches, hitting the gunwale and smacking the water, waiting
there a second before coughing out bubbles and sinking into the blue.
Elias dropped his line, plunged in his arm, and caught the iguana,
water drooling from its open jaws.

"Keep it," Arturo shouted. "There'll be more."

At the point, where the high-tide mark was a spine of plastic debris and
the sea wind felt more muscular, scurrying low through the banana
trees, I came upon something far odder: a bag made from what looked
like burlap, no bigger than two cupped hands, hung from a low-jutting
root. It was weighted full, and was greasy to the touch; inside was a
honey-colored mass.

"Shark liver," Arturo said, coming from behind, knocking it with the
end of his spear.

"From the hammerhead?"

"Probably." It had been left here, some way from the carcass, to discourage rodents. Shark oil, Arturo added, setting off again across the
rocks, "cures asthma, lots of illness we don't know about."

He was relishing this chance to act the guide, to work me over with
his knowledge. Observing me balk at the very fact of garbage in a place
this remote, he turned sensitive environmentalist. "This," he shook his
head gravely, "is the modern face of paradise." He played to my weakness for shark lore, summoning wilder and ever-more-implausible stories, watching with pleasure as I gaped, incredulous. When we startled
to flight a covey of leather-winged birds, big and black as ravens, and I
asked him what they were, he led me away from the shore, toward the
banana trees, and at every step would pick up a leaf, or a seedpod, and
list its medicinal uses and aphrodisiac properties. Young coconut leaf,
he said, made fine tea. Another—"bird wine"—was "medicine for the
liver: when you drink it, your pee is like water."

In a clearing, he cut a sapling, long as a jousting lance, and lunged
upward into the canopy of a coconut palm till three coconuts thumped
to earth: hard green ovals, the size of rugby balls. He picked up each in
turn, ground their points into the base of the tree trunk, then tore away
the husks. "Who needs knives?" he said, taking a rock to the first,
naked-whiskered nut, passing it to me, holding it up like a goblet. "Go
on, drink."

This small cay, he said, had everything a man could need: palms for
roofing, a type of year-round grape, even a tangled ground cover that
produced whorls of cotton. The seaward edge was a shallow slant of
red rock, graveled with the shells of tiny crabs, up which the ocean
hissed and moaned. And at this point, growing tired, Arturo tried to
cut back to the beach, but here the plantation was at its most over-
grown, the banana trees choked with creepers and underbrush grown
hard as wire.

"The morning's getting hotter," he muttered impatiently, as if it were
somehow my fault. "We've got to get on."

As we came round the point once more, back into the lee of the island,

Elias was standing in the boat, waving and shouting. He wanted us back on board and was yelling at us to run. He waved an arm at the water immediately around him, barked a further flurry of indecipherable yelps, and Arturo, shouting something back, broke into a run, leaping from boulder to boulder.

The tide had risen steadily, making the way back to the beach treacherous, with few dry footings, but he moved fast and lightly, one hand against the cliff for balance, standing, finally, in the shallows on the beach, hauling on the anchor rope. I was slower, and less sure, and by the time I reached the beach Arturo was already aboard and Elias had restarted the engine.

We anchored mid-bay, fifty yards offshore, the westerly gradually building, pushing us hard against the anchor, making the lines sing. The bait lines were nylon, with lead sinkers, with a single-barbed hook skewered through the pale jelly flesh of two prawns. Elias and Arturo lassoed theirs out effortlessly, and it took me a little while longer to learn this, how to have the line flying weightless through the palm, how to draw it back through the water at that certain depth, how to strike—knowingly, not too fast—and, just as crucial, how to play the part of the gnarled sea dog, impassive, none too easily impressed, unchanging as the sun.

For ten, fifteen minutes, we hooked fish as fast as we could get the lines out. Even I, the novice, whom Elias and Arturo eyed uncertainly, could do no wrong; I'd strike too early, or not at all, and still would haul up catch: red snapper, whitejack, hammering their tails in the oily slop about our ankles. The snapper, Arturo said, playing in another, just feet from the boat, was Jesus' fish, the one that fed the five thousand, and still bore his fingerprints: twin dark smudges, either side of the spine, just behind the dorsal fin. And he clasped the fish between flat palms, its gills still flexing, looked hard into its bleak ballbearing eyes, and spat into its oval pout.

"That's good luck." He winked and tossed the snapper, mouthing furiously, into the squirming hull.

• • •

"When I was a kid," he said later—soaked through but beaming, big hands paying back the line as delicately as a seamstress, having just landed the biggest snapper so far—"all the creeks in Bluefields, the whole lagoon, all down this coast, all were infested with sharks. You couldn't swim nowhere. But then, in the fifties and sixties, they started to buy them for their fins and meat and the sharks started to get wild, to disappear."

"You mean the sharks somehow knew what was happening?" We'd both hauled in and were just sitting there, growing stiff on our haunches, rocking in the swell, the sea knocking hollow against the hull. "They understood?"

Arturo held up a finger. "In certain ways," he said, turning to check on Elias's line, then testing mine too, "they are smart animals. They have a way to survive just like we do. Whenever you kill the animal, and it bleeds, it never goes to that place again."

"But here?" He'd returned to this cay many times: why had the sharks not yet worked this out?

"Some places"—he tapped a finger against his nose—"they will always come back to." Iguana Cay, with its unique confluence of marine life, the way the undersea shelf rose up here, delivering abundance and variety on a scale unknown anywhere else along the Miskito Coast, would always prove irresistible. He leaned forward. "Let me tell you something. Listen to this, then tell me what you think."

He talked, keeping his line taut. "A few months ago, I was out here, in this very spot, with Elias." He nudged Elias with his mahogany fish club; Elias, looking down, smiled. Arturo was baiting up again as he spoke, and as he stood to cast his line I noticed dark movement beneath the surface, midway between us and the shore, working transverse, closing on us.

"Arturo," I said, wanting him to look too, but he was warming to his story, and would not be diverted.

"So we were here, four in the morning, we'd spent the night on the cay. Very dark, the moon was new." He was watching his line now, but dreamily, only half focused. "And all of a sudden, after an hour of nothing, we hook a shark of a hundred and fifty pounds. Big enough, I tell you, but not a monster. I've got it on the rope, it's hooked well and good, and it fights a big fight. I'm on my knees, Elias is keeping the boat steady. . . ."

At the edge of my vision I saw the dark shape again, and this time nearer the beach; Elias, whose line was paid out that way, jolted upright and started round. Arturo, oblivious, talked on.

"Did you see that, Arturo?" I blurted.

Arturo stopped still, let his line hang loose in his hands. "What?"

"A big fish. Shark?" I pointed to where I'd seen the movement, but now there was nothing; now I was seeing shadows everywhere, the surface of the water splintered into sky, beach, red cliff, its own deep turquoise.

"Shark?" Arturo repeated, looking across my head to Elias. "Shark?"

Elias nodded. "*Creo, pero no estoy seguro.* I'm not sure."

"*Muy bien,*" Arturo said, softening. "So we haul in. We've got enough bait." There was a sudden shimmy on his line, a guitar-string quiver, but he continued at the same pace, hand over hand, and started where he'd left off, playing out the story as he wound in his line: unhurried, deliberate, conscious.

"So, after fifteen minutes, perhaps twenty," he went on, "I'm getting the shark close to the boat. I can see him down there, diving and fighting, but I know he's getting tired. I've got the rope, I'm sitting down, he's getting closer and closer. And then—" He clapped his hands together, opened his palms to the sky; his voice rose, rapturous. "Then the water gets BIG, I can't see what's happening, everything goes white and churned up and when it calms down the line's gone slack." He paused. Elias was motionless, turned toward Arturo, his line loose over his knees, mouth open.

"So what do I do?" Arturo continued, his eyes enormous. "I can feel weight, but no movement. What's happened to this shark?" Again, that pause. "Only one way to find out: pull on the rope, hard as God allows." He grinned at Elias, who snorted into the back of his hand. "It comes up fast, oh my God too fast, and the sea turns from blue to red and at the last moment, just when I realize, just when it's too late, the whole thing is flying out of the water toward me."

"The whole shark?"

"No! Just the head! The whole rest of it was bitten off. Just the head is left on my hook, just the head flies out of the water and lands in my lap."

Elias was shaking with silent laughter. "Just the head," he repeated, in a hoarse whisper. "Just the head." He reached across, knuckled Arturo in the ribs.

At that moment, no more than ten yards ahead of us, the sea turned to milkshake. Arturo, in the middle, jolted forward, threw an arm against the gunwale to steady himself; his bait line sprang free of the water, loosing drops all down its length. Then it snapped. No whip crack, no dramatic high note, just a tangle of soggy nylon thread, half in the boat, half out. The water, still again momentarily, broke one last time: a sharp, dark outline cut free, then disappeared into foam of its own creation, like a diver's flippers, giving one last kick.

"*Sangre de Dios,*" Arturo breathed. "Get those shark lines out."

Yet for the next half-hour, with all three lines baited with snapper, all was quiet. We said little, Arturo and Elias convinced a strike was imminent. Arturo laid his red glove over the gunwale in front of him, and from time to time touched it with reverence.

"Arturo?"

"*Sí?*

"What happens if we hook a three-hundred, four-hundred-pound shark? What good's your glove going to be then?"

"My glove," he sighed, "is so the rope don't burn my hand. A big shark will haul the canoe round and round as he looks for deep water." He smiled, guardedly. "We're going to have to play him really hard." We'd fight it to the beach, land and kill it there; after that, somehow, we'd heave it into the dugout and make for the mainland.

Two pelicans were circling us, almost colorless against the sky, cutting low over the cay and back again, making an odd clicking sound; they moved their wings little, setting and readjusting to the warm updrafts, passing between us and the sun, maintaining their distance.

It was getting hotter: I had only a baseball cap for shade and kept shifting the peak round, trying to protect my neck. Unused to such intense direct sun, my face and neck liquid with sweat, I tried to scoop up seawater to cool me down, but at the surface it was almost blood temperature and the salt when it dried made me even thirstier. Arturo, seeing me struggle, offered coffee from his flask: "Hot is good, it cools you down." Which was fine in theory, but didn't take into account the quantity of sugar he'd stirred in; so I sipped, and thanked him, and handed it quickly back.

Arturo speared the iguana onto an extra hook, its belly splitting easily as soaked paper, a guff of bad-egg air as the innards bulged through. He threw it from the bow and it hit the water heavily, floating tail-up for a few seconds before sinking abruptly, in a cough of bubbles. He looped the line around the plank on which he sat.

"It's really going to go for that?" Here, where there was no shortage of fresh snapper and succulent whitebait?

Arturo turned, smiled. "Well, we'll see."

In my imagination, the monster I'd glimpsed out there in the shallows would have had no problem with a putrefying iguana, could indeed, if the mood struck it, have swallowed the dugout, all three of us, the outboard and gas tank, whole, with one dilation of its industrial-sized gullet.

Ever since childhood I had feared and been drawn to the ocean, its unseen depths, and when long ago had learned of *Carcharodon megalodon*, the prehistoric shark, this fear seemed nothing less than reasonable. Here was a fish whose fossilized teeth were six inches long; whose gape, face on, measured a good ten feet in diameter; whose length, nose to tail, reached well over a hundred feet. Or "reaches," rather, since it is argued that *megalodon* is no more extinct than "megamouth," a soot-colored plankton sifter unknown to science until 1976, when a fourteen-foot specimen was snagged in netting by a U.S. Navy research boat. The evidence for *megalodon*'s continued existence is inconclusive, but certainly plausible: early in this century, some four-inch incisors were dredged from the bottom of the Pacific—"real" teeth, not fossils—which could not have been down there for long, since early dredging equipment was only robust enough to scrape the shallowest trench. So, I imagined, somewhere down there, beyond the tropical cays and reefs and turtle grounds, the great fish lurked still, seldom surfacing from the very deep, and only then for swift, spectacular meals: whole lines of shrimp pots, half a seal colony.

However, neither Arturo, gazing out across the water, nor Elias, lying back against the engine with his cap pulled low over his face, seemed to share any of my sense of foreboding. This was Arturo's livelihood and, over the decades, as shark had become scarcer and the price of fins had risen, he'd turned ever more wily, lying to the other fishermen when they'd pressed him for his favorite spots, setting deliberately misleading trails, dropping clues that led his rivals in the exact opposite direction from the one toward which he was headed. And as the business had changed, so had the fishermen: in the 1960s, when fins were plentiful and were off-loaded for a mere twenty-five cents a pound, they all worked together, secure in the knowledge that there was enough for everyone. Now, with fins scarcer, and fetching upwards of thirty-five dollars a pound, the fishermen operated alone, suspicious of one another, jealously protective of whatever special knowledge they had acquired, drying their catch in secret, smuggling the fins to Maximo under cover of darkness.

With the heat of the sun and the slop of machine oil and rotten water, the fish in the hull were beginning to smell; the snappers were blanching, their eyes gone puffy, tiny whorls of excreta trailing out behind. Arturo, in a low murmur that had almost sent Elias to sleep and was close to achieving the same effect on me, was reminiscing about the old days of plenty, mentioning names I'd never heard, places I'd never been.

It filled me with sadness, this downward curve in fortunes that had been his working life, this struggle to eke a living from ever-diminishing resources, but whenever I started to offer sympathy, he shook his head, stopped me with an upheld hand. Just listen, his silent gesture instructed me. Hear me out.

Suddenly, with a yelp, Elias was awake. He'd tied his line round his wrist and now, desperately, was struggling against pressure to work it free. "I've got one, I've got one," he jabbered, the line tight toward the beach. Eventually he managed to untie it and throw it loose, but the slack disappeared in an instant. He wrapped the engine rag round his hand and braced himself, the line flexing into deep water off the stern, so tight it shivered the surface.

"What is it?" I was leaning over, trying to catch its shadow. But Elias didn't seem to hear; he was focused, taking line as the fish stalled, paying out again as it cut underneath us. When it surfaced—Elias arched against it, his back bowed with the strain—it came very fast, thrashing against the side of the boat: sinewy, black, a big cobra's jaw, straining at the hook.

"Barracuda!" Elias shouted, jubilant. He ordered me to stay back, and he and Arturo wrestled it aboard. It was three or four feet long, thick as a fire hose, with a wolf's fangs and a menacing underbite. Its tail pounded our legs; its teeth snapped at the air. Arturo gripped the club, about to complete the kill, but seemed suddenly as mesmerized as I, immobile, watching the great fish slowly die. It seemed unlike anything I'd ever seen or imagined, an unholy hybrid of serpent and mile-deep sightless groper, distorted almost to humanness by its great vampire mouth.

As it lay there, sucking in ever slower, its gill leaves breezing smaller and smaller flutters, I felt my line tug once, then twice: persistent, heavyweight fumblings.

"Arturo . . . ," I said, testing the tension, unsure. "What's this? What do I do?" Strike? Leave alone?

Arturo, up in the prow, didn't answer. He was holding his line between thumb and forefinger and concentrating hard. I saw his hand clench, unclench, and he reached for the glove, forced in his fingertips and yanked it on with his teeth.

"Shark?" I said, speaking as much to myself as to him. I'd had a heavier take, then a deadweight, not what I expected it to feel like.

"Possibly." He grinned, toothy as the barracuda. "Oh, yes, just possibly." His line was running fast through his glove, slack spooling from his lap. And then again, harder this time, I felt my line go, burning my skin as it ripped away.

"Let it run!" Arturo shouted at me, still focused hard on his own. "Let it take it and tire itself out."

I tore off my cap, forced it flat into my hand as protection, but in the half-second it took to change grip I lost my last five meters of line and it sprang hard against its backstop, the plank seat, out of my hand.

"What now?"

"Take it up," Arturo said, doing the same himself, hand over hand. "It won't take long."

Mine played erratically—compliant, then brutish, sometimes almost teasing. Shark, Arturo said: we must have hit a number, all hunting, all at the same time. We'd have got three if Elias hadn't been struggling to untangle his line. I wondered about his diagnosis, though: I was no strongman, yet was able to fight it with my own hands.

Elias, in the stern, had dropped his line and was instructing me, miming the necessary actions, how much pressure I should be applying, when to tighten up and when to play it easy. He ran salt water through his hair, pasted it flat to his skull, and leaned close to me; I could feel his heat, the smell of last night's beer and frijoles.

"There!" He pointed off the stern, no more than ten yards: a pale racing of color, like a seal's back, just below the surface.

"That's it." Arturo beamed. "What did I say?" His fish was hard by the boat now, his line plumbing vertically into the sun-slanted water. I stole glances at him, realizing this might be my only lesson, but every time I did so I lost grip of my own line, letting run too much slack so that the fish dived fast the next moment and slammed hard against the gunwale. Arturo seemed able to watch both at once— checking on me, following his own weaving line as he drew it ever nearer—and when he swept his fish into the boat it was with a simple, unbroken movement.

It hit the bottom writhing: a four-foot shark with filmy cat's eyes and a tail that smashed about wildly, soaking me with fish-scaly water. The extra weight sank us perilously low and at every swell now we were shipping water. Elias grabbed the bailer; the water he slung out was dark, smeared with prawns and entrails of snapper and tubercular clots of engine oil.

"You, now," Arturo said, ignoring his own shark, which lay agasp in the hull, hook still through its bottom jaw.

"What do I do?" It felt as though it was directly below us, switching direction like a caged animal.

"It's getting tired." He leaned forward, shielded his eyes from the sun. "Bring it up. Slowly."

I could have drawn in quicker, but I could feel my muscles cramping. Arturo was right: the fish did seem to be slowing, and only once did it draw away strongly enough for the line to pull through my hand. As I brought it closer, it seemed almost to be cowering from us, pulling the line back under the hull as it stuck to the boat's shadow.

"Bring it in now," Arturo said, hands braced on the edge of the boat.

"But I can't see it."

"It's there. Lift it out."

I half stood, just enough to see where the line entered the water. The shark was there, split lengthways by our shadow, hanging motionless as if it knew exactly the way this was going. I could feel it trembling down the wire, and knew it could feel me too, both of us new to this, both anxious rookies. After all my dreams of hooking a monster, this one seemed disappointingly small, something of a consolation prize, docilely waiting.

I wrapped the line round both hands and pulled hard. The shark was heavy, and its head tilted stiffly, rucking creases across its back. It was so still, and the underside of its throat and belly was pale as linen in the sunlight just below the surface. The hook glittered as I hoisted the fish toward vertical.

"Finish it quickly," Arturo muttered. "Get it out."

But I couldn't. I leaned harder against it, my knees on the gunwale, but could bring it no further than the surface. Maneuvering it underwater, weightless, had been easy: hauling it aboard, fighting its true weight, felt impossible. The shark itself, half comatose, did nothing to help: basking in the warmth, sun on its back, bewildered and exhausted by the struggle, it was resting against me, its weight against the hook.

"Give me a hand," I said, but Arturo, anticipating, was already at my shoulder, ordering Elias to the other side of the boat.

"Come on," he said. "Now! You pull!" And he knelt in the boat, in the blood and oil and fish scales, and plunged his arms into the water. With his face almost submerged he grabbed the shark round its middle, shouted at me to lift and together we hoisted it clear of the water. "Now in the boat!" he shouted. "Quick!"

Halfway over, the shark hammered sideways, knocking me to the floor. Arturo still had a hold on its tail, but it was flailing crazily now, its jaw locked open, strips of snapper caught in its teeth. I tried to stand, but the boat was rocking and taking water and I was dizzied by the knock, so I stayed where I was, certain they were both about to land on me. The shark was corkscrewing through Arturo's grasp, like a too-big child not wanting to be dressed. Arturo trod backward and slumped into the prow and the mess of netting and, forced back by the weight of the fish, sat down heavily, the shark kicking away from him. For a second, it lay still on the bottom of the boat. Elias, looking up from bailing, hooted.

"Bastard," Arturo breathed, his chest heaving.

"How are we going to get back?" Elias said. The stern was leaking fast. Left much longer, the shark would have been able to swim free.

"Take in the anchor," Arturo snapped. We'd pull onto the beach, off-load nonessentials. "Where's my club?" He groped behind himself, through the heap of netting, scooped a hand through the hull-slop. I saw it before he did: floating near Elias's feet, half-submerged, clean and dark as a bone. I hooked it with my foot and lifted it out.

Arturo knelt in the hull between the two sharks. His, landed ten minutes earlier, had stilled; mine, startled momentarily on capture, was now beating about wildly again, one arching muscle, drumming the side of the boat. Its head was up, showing the hook and the bloodless wound through its underjaw, torn ragged by its fighting. It shouldered forward, then slid back toward the stern, and its skin against my calves was like emery paper.

"Hold it there," Arturo ordered, twisting round to get an angle on its skull. I tried to steady it round its middle, leaning my whole weight forward, but it surged and pounded. Arturo forced his knee onto its back until only its tail was moving and struck it on the snout, between the eyes; through its body I felt a shiver of electricity. Again and again he clubbed it, until and beyond the point when it was clearly dead and had ceased to even twitch. There was no blood, nothing to suggest pain, no rolling of the eyes, just a soft indent where he'd hammered it repeatedly. He closed his eyes halfway through, and when he handed back the club, his head was still bowed. He lay back in the bow, on the rubbish and bottles and netting, pulled his cap down over his eyes and folded his arms tight across his chest. His hands were shaking.

We left the anchor buried in undergrowth and drained the dugout on the beach as best we could. It was after midday now, and too hot to continue fishing. Yet, just off the cay, heading for the mainland, Elias hooked another. He'd been trailing his line experimentally, using the last, most fetid snapper as bait. The shark he hauled in was bovine, almost comatose, though a good foot longer than the other two. It was a nurse shark, Arturo said—the color of the seafloor, freckled with pale spots. Arturo reached over the side and he and Elias heaved it aboard.

He shook his head, disappointed. "Not dangerous. He lives in the rocks, eats lobster, crabs." Yet, stranded at our feet, half the snapper still in its mouth, it clung on longer than the other two, its gills whispering in and out until we were almost home. Seeing it there, purblind, helpless, I wished we'd put it back, since its seal-soft fins were worthless and its meat was fatty and cloying, but Arturo wanted to show it to his neighbors' children, let them tug its fleshy whiskers and run their fingers along its milk teeth, so we wedged it in the hull. Arturo sharpened his knife on its side, flipping the blade in the sunlight, his eyes unfocused, shoulders heavy.

It was hard to imagine, having witnessed the ease of Arturo's baited-hook technique, that shark fishermen had ever practiced anything else, but in Micronesia, until midway through this century, hunters used snares woven from plant fibers. Tied like a noose, the snare was lowered from a canoe, and seashells were rattled in the water to draw the shark, which was then teased through the loop by the lure of bloody meat. It took time, this method, and patience too, since any panicky movements startled off the fish: slowly, with a steady hand, the noose was drawn over the head, and was tightened as it passed the gill slits. Maoris, who prized unchipped center teeth as earrings, perfected the method: hooks, they knew, wreaked dental mayhem.

Early hooks were of bone or wood. Hawaiian chieftains bequeathed their skeletons for the carving of hooks, although, throughout the islands, bones of great fishermen were judged equally propitious. To prepare wooden hooks, young ironwood branches were lashed into tight Us, and released only when they'd hardened into shape. And always, whatever their constituent materials, the hooks were speared with the oiliest and bloodiest bait fish. Sharks can sniff food at five hundred meters—one part mammal blood, according to researchers, in a hundred million parts water—and even their eyesight, once thought weaker than that of most fish, was, in poor light, a good ten times more sensitive than man's.

We took a different way back, a shorter route to shore, heading for the south entrance to the Bluefields lagoon. We rode with the swell, which had strengthened since we'd been fishing and now tipped us firmly back, with a sense of barely contained power. In part this change of route was of necessity, since to return northward would have meant taking the swell side-on, but in part it was because Arturo wanted to fish for prawn alongside the mangroves again, and these southern mangroves were the best.

Pelicans followed us, watching for floundering fish where the water shallowed and boiled. With each swell, each shove toward shore, the sea lost its luminous turquoise and became darker and muddier.

Arturo, up in the bow, was shouting back orders to Elias: keep straight, hard left now, that's it, steady. The shallower we got, the more opaque the water became. Arturo tried to avoid riding the waves, but at points this was impossible, and we'd crest with a great howl as the outboard reared out of the water. And then, beyond the bar, in an instant the water was deep again and I smelled the dirt of the warm land, saw once more the grackles overhead above the forest and felt relieved, more than I'd ever guessed I'd feel, to be heading for the safety of streets and buildings.

Through the lagoon mouth, into the lagoon itself: the water was a mile wide here, and with forest so brightly green the color looked painted on. Above the canopy towered spikes, like outsize telegraph poles—all that remained of the coconut palms that had survived the hurricane, a decade earlier.

"Everything you see," Arturo said, indicating the new forest, the way it crowded the water's edge, "all of it has pushed up since the big storm."

"Even the mangroves?" They seemed so sturdy, immovable, their claw roots thick as a man's legs.

"When the hurricane came," he answered, turning back to face the front, "everything went down. Only five houses in Bluefields remained standing. And the forest—all that was destroyed. From the town you could see straight out to sea—no roofs or walls stood in your way."

Ahead I noticed three dories, smaller than ours, struggling under tarpaulin sails. They scarcely seemed to be moving at all, and their sails sagged motionless.

I watched all this half-dreaming, aware that soon I'd be moving on, tracking the bull sharks south, to the San Juan River, and beyond. I wanted Arturo to join me—had wanted this, in fact, ever since he'd said he had family there. San Juan del Norte, the settlement at the river mouth, was by all accounts a pirate town, not much different now than it had been two and a half centuries before, and I figured Arturo could ease my way. He'd intimated more than once that he'd been planning just this trip for a few years now, but the opportunity had never arisen. I suspected something else: a wound, some rift let fester. As we closed on the dories I asked again. How about it, I said, casually as I could manage, why not? Here's the chance you never had. He knew I'd help with the travel—that much we'd discussed already.

He turned back to face me, smiled as if he hadn't heard. "See those boats?" He hooked a thumb across the bow. "Rama Indians."

They looked a scanty lot, in tattered clothing, sitting two to a canoe. They stopped their paddling to watch us approach.

"Morning," Arturo called out, in English. Elias cut the engine and we coasted level. One of the Indians reached out a hand to grab our boat; the dories slid together, swollen timbers creaking. Two of their boats were empty, but in the furthest, a slug-fit in the hull, was a considerable-sized shark, half on its side, its long-muscled tail fin dragging in the water. It was the color of clay shot with lead, and its mouth, ripped sideways by the hook, was clamped shut: ugly, pitiable, like a prize-fighter being stretchered from the ring. In a final show of disrespect they'd heaped their netting and old bait on top, and sat with their feet up on its hide.

"Some shark," Arturo said, kneeling up to see better, his eyes wide. "Where did you catch it?"

They glanced from one to another, suddenly fidgety. "Out there," one said.

Arturo grinned. "Out where?" He scanned their faces, acting blithe, as if it was all a big joke.

"To sea." This was the first man talking, the one who'd pulled us alongside. He rested his jaw in his hand.

"To sea—that so? We've been out all morning. Never saw you all." Arturo was sizing up the big shark, muttering to himself. No one answered him; I could sense them steal glances our way, comparing the catches.

"Iguana Cay? You been out there?" The Rama was smiling as he said this, chewing something in his cheek.

"No, no," said Arturo, too quickly, but they were all eyeing him now, hands on their paddles, laid flat across their dugouts. "What you going to do with the shark?" he added, flustered. "Take it to Maximo?"

"Take it home first." The Rama laughed and was echoed by the rest: mouthfuls of broken teeth, blackened, holed, mostly missing. He picked up his paddle and dug the surface. "Show the ladies."

I asked Arturo why he'd lied, especially since, by his own admittance, the Rama well knew he fished their cay, but he did not answer. We rode the hour back in silence, and not until we reached the wet mud landing at his house, and were unloading the sharks in front of the children, did I try him again.

"How long," I began, as we dragged the dugout from the water, into the same mud furrow from which it came. "How long's the weather going to last? How long will it be good for?"

He straightened, leaving mud prints on the gunwale. "Have fun today? Consider yourself a shark fisherman now?" Elias, fuel tank in one hand, gas line in the other, was mumbling good-bye, ignoring Arturo.

"Yes," I said, to them both. Elias turned to go. "I'm off too," I said to Arturo. "Perhaps tomorrow. As soon as I work out how to get to San Juan del Norte." He was leaning over the sharks, measuring them in hand spans. I spoke to his back. "And you, Arturo? You coming?"

"Ah," he said. "The question." He laid a hand on my shoulder, pushed us out of the sun, under an overhang. He screwed up his eyes, roused phlegm in his throat, spat noisily at a garbage pail. "You don't worry about me. I'll be there."

Shark Dive
by Tim Cahill

Tim Cahill (born 1944) travels the world in search of danger and discomfort, then goes home to write about it. His sense of humor keeps us guessing: Just how worried should we be?

This," Jack McKenney said, "is your shark club." It was a broom handle with a nail in the end and I was supposed to use it underwater, while scuba diving, to whap the menacing sharks we hoped to attract and thus convince them, Jack explained, that we weren't to be considered appetizers. I said that a broom handle seemed somewhat fragile for the task at hand.

"Well," Jack said reasonably, "you won't have to use it if you don't get out of the cage."

We were standing on the stern of a dive boat called the *Atlantis*, which was drifting out in the channel between San Pedro Harbor and Catalina, near a place called 14 Mile Bank. The water was glassy blue, under blue skies on a nearly windless day. Off half a mile in the distance, dense clouds of sea birds were whirling and diving above several city blocks' worth of ocean that seemed to be in full boil. Tony, the captain of the *Atlantis*, figured that bait fish were being driven to the surface by marauding sharks. I was looking at an acre or so of pure terror.

The shark cage sat on the deck. It was tied to a boom that would lower it ten feet into the water. I had always supposed that such a cage would be constructed of heavy metal, that it would be made of wrist-thick prison-type bars. The contraption in question, however, was constructed, for the most part, from wire, the kind of stuff used as bedsprings in cots.

"How many sharks will we get?" I asked Jack.

"Hard to tell," he said. "I don't think we'll be skunked. If we're lucky, we could have as many as twenty."

"Oh boy," I said with a singular lack of enthusiasm that seemed lost on Jack McKenney.

"Yeah," he said, "it could be a good one. Problem is: it's too nice a day."

"Just our rotten luck, all right."

"If we only had some wind," Jack said. We had been adrift for a little less than an hour and hadn't seen any sharks yet. We were chumming for them, sending out little invitations: come to the feeding frenzy. Sitting on the deck, near the shark cage, were several boxes of mackerel: about four hundred pounds of foot-long frozen fish. As soon as Tony cut the engines, Jack and his son John put fifteen pounds of the fish into one of those plastic mesh boxes designed to carry milk cartons. They wired a second such box onto the first—open end to open end—and dropped it over the side on a rope so that the box was half in and half out of the water. The rocking of the boat maserated the defrosting fish, and I could see oil and blood and bits of mackerel floating away from the boat in a snaking line.

A cruising shark that crossed the chum line would turn and follow it to the boat. To attract the maximum number of sharks, we wanted to spread that line out across a mile or so of sea. With the boat dead in the water, the chum tended to sink to the bottom. We couldn't motor, though: engine noise and fumes would confuse the sharks. We needed a stiff wind to push the boat along and spread out the chum line.

I was going through a final check of my dive gear when Tony mentioned, rather cavalierly I thought, that "we got one." It was a six-foot-long blue shark, and it had rolled over onto its back and was chewing, half-heartedly, on the milk boxes full of chum. It rolled slightly and one flat black eye looked up at the faces peering at it over the side of the boat. The shark rolled again, like a jet fighter doing a barrel roll, and disappeared under the boat.

In the distance, about a hundred yards off, I could see another fin, gliding along the snaking path of chum toward the boat. Beyond that was still another fin coming in our direction along the same meandering path. It was early in the morning, and the sun was low in the sky, so that the water seemed cobalt blue, but the wake behind the shark fins was an odd emerald color that glittered on the surface of the glassy sea. There was a muffled thump as the shark hit the chum box a second time.

Jack McKenney said, "Let's get the cage in the water and go diving."

Canadian-born Jack McKenney, who lives in Los Angeles, is a legend in the diving industry; a filmmaker, photographer, and adventurer. He has filmed whale sharks and ridden manta rays in the Sea of Cortez; he has made more dives on the *Andrea Doria* than any other person. Hollywood has paid him to learn a lot about different kinds of sharks. He was a stunt double in both *The Deep* and *Shark's Treasure*, two movies in which he also filmed some of the underwater sequences.

Jack and his twenty-six-year-old son, John, were making their first video production for the home market: it would be a documentary about shark diving, which they hoped to sell in the scuba magazines. The production would show that a shark dive can be "a safe and enjoyable" experience . . . when done properly.

On hand to coordinate the dives were Bud Riker and Susan Speck, co-owners of Divers West, a dive shop in Pasadena. For the past two years, Bud and Susan have been sponsoring four or five shark dives a year. The trips are open to advanced open-water divers with "a lot" of open-water experience. Previous shark-diving experience is not necessary.

The video documentary would concentrate on three novice shark divers: Paul Bahn, a musician; Laine "Buck" Scheliga, a bartender; and

Pam McKenney, a flight attendant. These were the people who were going to experience "safe and enjoyable" diving in the midst of a feeding frenzy.

Also on hand for the experience were Bonnie Cardone, the executive editor for *Skin Diver* magazine—it would be her second planned shark dive—and Chip Matheson, a stunt man "trainee" whose work you may have seen on *Riptide*. Chip has been diving with sharks for seven years.

I have been diving and writing for various scuba magazines for a decade, and in that time have found myself in the water with tiger sharks on the Great Barrier Reef, with hammerheads off Central America, with Caribbean nurse sharks, with black tip and white tip reef sharks, with carpet sharks, sand sharks, and lemon sharks. None of this was intentional. These sharks just appeared, entirely unwanted, like ants at a picnic. The idea of purposely getting into the water with a dozen or so man-eaters seemed silly, suicidal, dumb as rocks. Still, Jack McKenney had asked me to participate, and Jack knows what he's doing. It was Jack McKenney, doubling for Nick Nolte, who made a free ascent through that shark feeding frenzy in *The Deep*. No long-time diver would pass up an opportunity to dive with Jack McKenney, just as no pilot would turn down an invitation to fly with Chuck Yeager.

McKenney had also invited Marty Snyderman to appear in the video. Marty is a well-known underwater photographer from San Diego. About ten years ago, it occurred to him that people weren't paying proper attention to his photos: all those shots of corals and "scenic" fish, of sponges and nudibranchs in blazing color. It was the time of *Jaws*, and the public was interested in sharks. "So I became good at shark diving and shark photography," Marty told me, "and, when people know that, somehow they seem to find my other photos infinitely more interesting and beautiful."

Since Snyderman spends so much time in the water with sharks, shooting stills and filming television documentaries, he has also seen fit to spend $5200 on a custom-made Kevlar and chain mail shark suit.

In this suit, he told me, he has been "nipped" by sharks "literally hundreds of times." McKenney hoped to get some good footage of sharks nibbling away on Marty Snyderman.

The real stars of McKenney's video promised to be the sharks themselves. There are 250 or more species of sharks—research is still being done on the matter—and not all of them are dangerous to man. In Australia, for instance, I have been diving with a small, sleek, pretty little fish known as an epaulette shark because of the white-rimmed spots it carries above its pectoral fins. It is a timid beast, the epaulette shark, and it flees the approaching diver in what appears to be a frantic subaquatic panic. Like the ostrich, the epaulette shark considers itself hidden if it can't see you, and the fish can often be found with its head wedged into some small coral cave while the rest of its body is completely and ludicrously visible. This shark, incidentally, has no teeth at all, and Australian divers refer to it as a "gummie." Dangerous sharks, man-eaters like tigers and great whites, are called "munchies."

Some fishermen and boating enthusiasts believe that blues are not munchies, that they are virtually harmless, but there are documented cases of blues attacking human beings. Don Wilkie, Director of the Scripps Institution of Oceanography at UCSD, says flatly that "blues are potentially dangerous, but it is unusual for them to be involved in an unprovoked attack." Setting out a chum line, Wilkie said, "is a clear provocation."

Blues are common in the deep waters between Los Angeles and Catalina: they are fast, slim-bodied sharks with pointed snouts and saw-edged teeth. They can grow to twelve feet in length—man-eaters become dangerous at three or four feet—and often follow boats, feeding off of discarded garbage. Sometimes called blue whalers, these sharks are noted for the speed with which they materialize around slaughtered whales and for their piranhalike feeding frenzies.

"If there's only six or seven down there," McKenney, told me, "it'll be pretty calm. If we get twenty or more, they can get a little aggressive. I suppose it's competition: when there's a lot of them, they have to move fast to get their share. Also, when there's more than two or three, it's hard to keep track of them. They can come up behind and nip you."

Which, I imagined, would be like getting "nipped" by a Bengal tiger, only underwater.

We had fifty feet of underwater visibility and everything down and up and all around was blue, including the sharks milling around the cage and chum bucket. Their bodies were brighter than the sea water and their bellies were a contrasting white. The cage was positioned ten feet below the chum bucket. Little white bits of mackerel were dropping down through the bed springs. The divers brushed the stuff off their shoulders, like dandruff. I could see five blue sharks outside the cage. They were swooping lazily through the water like eagles soaring over the prairie on a blue summer afternoon.

Just getting into the shark cage had been an adventure. You don't get to go down with it on the boom. Bed springs won't hold the weight of several divers. No, you have to swim to the cage.

"Go now," Bud Rilker had told me, as I sat with my legs just out of the water. The command meant that there weren't any sharks in my immediate presence, and I reluctantly slipped into the water beside the chum bucket. In a shark dive, you don't want to roll or jump off the boat because the bubbles you create obscure the view for ten or fifteen seconds, during which time a guy could get "nipped." Not incidentally, the bubbles also attract curious sharks.

So I sat on the swim step, edged into the sea, broom handle in hand, and rocketed through the blue water and blue sharks to the open cage door in ten seconds flat. Paul was already in there, along with Buck. Bonnie hovered just above the door, taking photos. Above, the boat was rocking in some gentle swells that had just come up, and the cage, which hung from the boom by a ten-foot line, echoed that rocking. I kept banging my head or knees on the wire and the temptation was very great to hold on to the side of the cage, but that meant that part of my hand would be outside, in the open sea, where the sharks were, and Jack had warned us that holding on to the cage in this manner was "a good way to get nipped."

The five sharks were milling around, aimlessly cutting sine curves in the sea. Occasionally, one would swim up to the chum bucket and nudge it with its snout. Then, with a figurative shrug of the shoulders, it would drop down to join the other sharks. They seemed curious and a little confused, these milling blues.

Above, along the chum line, I could see another shark accepting our invitation. The new guy was big, ten feet long at a guess, and he was moving purposefully toward the chum bucket, which he hit without hesitation. Nothing for him there but a mouthful of mackerel-flavored plastic. He dropped down to join the other sharks and they all made several passes by one another just outside the cage door.

If sharks can be thought of as having a conversation—which of course they can't but never mind—the newcomer looked as if he were saying: "What's going on here?"

"Dunno," another replies. "It's weird."

"What are those funny-looking things there?" The big blue was twenty feet off, looking at us.

"Potential breakfast."

He came at us then, this new shark just off the chum line, but he was swimming slower now, and moving toward the cage at an oblique angle. I revised my estimate: up close this shark was a good twelve feet long. It coasted slowly by the cage, apparently staring off into the distance and not interested in us at all, but it passed within inches of the wire and I could see its near eye—perfectly round and flat black with a small circle of white all around the pupil—and that eye swiveled back as the shark passed.

I've done pretty much the same thing: you're walking along a city street and see a cop handcuffing some guy who's shouting obscenities. A crowd of street folk has gathered, and you walk right on by, staring straight ahead but glancing surreptitiously at the scene out of the corner of your eye. You're curious but you sure don't want to get involved in any trouble.

That was something of the message I got from the sharks cruising by the cage: If you're weak and bleeding and helpless, they seemed to be saying, we'd be happy to rip you to shreds. But, hey, we just came here for breakfast. We don't want no trouble.

In two days I logged over seven hours in the water with sharks. We took goodie bags full of mackerel down with us and hand-fed the sharks as they cruised by little gunsight windows in the cage. (Hold the fish by the tail and shake it outside the cage. Keep your hand inside, of course.) The sharks do not roll over onto their backs when feeding, as one myth has it. They'll eat in any attitude at all.

As the shark's mouth opens, a kind of lower eyelid—a white, nictitating membrane—covers the eye so that, at the moment of munch, the animal is effectively blind. This protects the shark's eyes from its prey. Several times, out of curiosity, I offered the fish, then yanked it away while the fish was blind. Ha-ha, shark. Neener neener neener. The phrase "open your mouth and close your eyes" kept running through my head. Presently, I began feeling a little guilty about teasing the man-eaters. They had these large, sadly surprised-looking eyes that never blinked . . . except at the moment of the kill.

On my second dive, I began to find the cage confining, and decided to go outside where Jack and John and Marty were filming. I had had, in my mind's eye, a vision of sharks as swift predators, torpedoes rocketing in for the kill, and that is the way they came up the chum line. But once they hit the chum box and began milling around as if confused, you could track them as they came toward you, as they made their studied, nonchalant passes.

Off forty yards in the distance, Jack McKenney was shooting a sequence in which his son John swam alongside a shark and pushed it around with a broom handle. The shark, a six-foot-long male, seemed mildly annoyed. It put on a slight burst of speed and came gliding in my direction. I had a full ten seconds to get my own broom handle in position, and when the shark was within a foot of me, I whapped it a good one on the snout. Its body twisted away from me—a snakelike gesture of avoidance—and the shark dived at a gentle angle, disappearing into a cobalt blue that purpled down into the blackness of abysmal depths.

I turned and saw another shark approaching from the rear and I beaned him as he made his pass. It seemed clear that the mildest show of aggression put these fellows off their feed. The broom handle was handy when a shark was coming at you with its mouth open and eyes closed, but, in general, you could send them skittering off into the distance with a casual backhanded gesture, the sort of motion you'd use to shoo a pigeon off some picnic table in the park.

Conversely, the sharks hit anything that didn't move. Marty Snyderman, in his chain mail shark suit, was shooting stills of the divers in the cage watching half a dozen sharks swooping by. He was kicking slightly, but his upper body was motionless and the camera was steady. A shark came up behind him: the mouth opened, revealing saw-edged teeth, and the eyes closed. The shark hit Marty in the upper left arm. He elbowed it in the snout, the shark swam away, and Marty never even looked at it. He was busy shooting pictures and getting nipped was an annoyance. Marty's shark suit cost more than my car and I wanted one.

Jack McKenney didn't have a shark suit, and either Chip or John swam above him: safety divers who swung their shark clubs over the filmmaker's motionless upper body. Jack wanted to get lots of sharks in the same frame, and he tended to hang around the chum line, where they were the most dangerous. On the second day, late in the afternoon when the night-feeding blues were getting aggressive, one came up from below and hit Jack in the finger. He was not wearing gloves, not when he had to constantly adjust focus. The bite, truth to tell, had been really just an experimental "nip," and the wound was a small jagged tear, less than an inch long: the sort of thing that might happen to you if you brushed your hand over some barbed wire. A small bit of blood rose from the cut and floated toward the surface. The blood, in this blue water, looked green. (I know. Blue and red don't make green, but that's the way it looked.)

The sharks did not go into a feeding frenzy. Everything was as it was before, and Jack kept on filming.

These little nipping incidents I saw tended to make me extremely alert when I chose to be out of the cage. It wasn't that you had to watch just your backside: the sharks could come at you from every point of the sphere. You lost them at about fifty feet and they would circle around and come at you from another angle. When there were more than three around, you could never keep track of them all. Bonnie told me that she got a picture of me concentrating on a shark that was coming at my chest. "Did you know there was another one just behind your head?" she asked.

"Of course," I lied.

After that, whenever I was out of the cage, and there were no sharks in sight, I swung the broom handle over my head, just in case. In general, a diver's arms and legs are moving, but he tends to be motionless from the shoulders up and that is where he is likely to be hit: right in the back of the head.

It took a tremendous amount of concentration to swim around outside the cage, and I found that fifteen minutes was about all I could take before a kind of numbing fatigue sent me shooting back to the safety of the bed springs. Jack, John, Marty, and Chip never got in the cage. They were pros and their discipline amazed me.

Marty Snyderman and I were sitting in the galley, drinking coffee and discussing what is likely to be the most talked-about sequence in McKenney's video. Jack had been shooting Marty hand-feeding several large sharks. One six-footer rose to the bait, and when it closed its eyes, Marty thrust his whole forearm in the animal's mouth. The shark ragged at his arm for a full sixty seconds. Marty was jerking the man-eater around in the way that you'd play with a dog.

"What about the jaw pressure?" I asked. "Doesn't it bruise you?"

Marty showed me his arm. There was no bruise: only a slight redness there. "They calculate jaw pressure from the point of one tooth," Marty said, "but I had my whole arm in the mouth and that spread the pressure out. And then the chain mail tends to distribute the pressure over a larger area."

The Neptunic Shark Suit is custom-made for each diver by Neptunic, Inc., a San Diego company headed up by the inventor of the suit, Jeremiah Sullivan. The underlayer is a Velcro-covered wet suit. Twenty-three Kevlar pads—they look like shoulder-pad material—fasten onto the Velcro. The chain mail forms the outer layer. It is made of 400,000 stainless steel links and weighs twenty pounds.

"I put my arm in a shark's mouth the first day I had the suit," Marty told me. "I needed to know if it would work."

"You're right-handed."

"Yeah."

"You put your left arm in the shark's mouth, then?"

"Well, I didn't know if it would really work."

"What does it feel like?" I asked.

Many grabbed my forearm and squeezed, careful not to dig his fingernails into my flesh. I calculated that he was squeezing at about three quarters of his full strength. "It feels like that," he said.

Out on the deck, John McKenney shouted, "Hey, shark wranglers, we got four or five more blues coming up the chum line."

We were, all of us, suited up in less than ten minutes: eight fools in dorky-looking rubber suits, one fool in a dorky-looking chain mail suit, each of us ridiculously eager to get in the water and battle man-eating sharks with broom handles. An outsider, someone who hadn't been down there with us, would have to think we were brave as hell. Or dumb as rocks.

A twelve-footer was gnawing away at the chum box. I could see at least a dozen sharks milling around the cage. "Let's go diving," Jack McKenney said.

A Shark in the Mind of One
Comtemplating Wilderness

by Terry Tempest Williams

Terry Tempest Williams (born 1959) writes about nature and people and connections between the two. Here she considers our concepts of "shark" and "wilderness" in the contexts of art and nature.

A shark swims past me in a kelp forest that sways back and forth with the current. It is deliberate and focused. I watch the shark's sleek body dart left and right as its caudal fin propels it forward. Its eyes seem to slice through the water in a blood gaze as the gills open and close, open and close. Around and around, I watch the shark maneuver through schools of fish. It must not be hungry. The only thing separating me from the shark is a tall glass pane at the Monterey Sea Aquarium. Everything is in motion. I press my hands on the glass waiting for the shark to pass by again and when it does, I feel my own heart beating against the mind of this creature that kills.

In the enormous blue room of the American Museum of Natural History, I stare at the tiger shark mounted on the wall of the second floor. Its surface shines with the light of taxidermy, creating the illusion of having just left the sea, now our own natural-history trophy. I see how out of proportion its mouth is to the rest of its body and wonder how many teeth hung from its gums during its lifetime, the rows of teeth, five to twenty of them, biting and tearing, thrashing and chomping on flesh, the teeth constantly being replaced by something akin to a conveyor-belt system. Somewhere in my mind I hold the fact that a shark may go through 20,000 teeth in a life span of ten years. I imagine the shark sensing the electrical field of a seal, swimming toward the diving black body now rising to the surface, delivering with great speed its deadly blow, the jaws that dislocate and protrude out of its mouth, the strong muscles that open, then close, the razor teeth that clamp down on the prey with such force that skin, cartilage and bone are reduced to one clean round bite, sustained over and over again. The blue water now bloody screams to the surface. Even in death, I see this shark in motion.

Sensation. I enter the Brooklyn Museum of Art to confront another tiger shark, this the most harrowing of all the requiem sharks I have encountered in a weeklong period. Requiem sharks. They say the name is derived from the observation that once these large sharks of the order *Carcharhinid* attack a victim, the only task remaining is to hold a requiem, a mass for the dead. *Galeocerdo cuvieri.* It is neither dead nor alive, but rather a body floating in space, a shark suspended in solution. Formaldehyde. To preserve. What do we choose to preserve? I note the worn, used sense of its mouth, shriveled and receding, looking more manly than fish. The side view creates a triptych of head, dorsal fin and tail, through the three panels of glass in the frame of white painted steel. I walk around the shark and feel the charge of the front view, a turquoise nightmare of terror that spills into daylight. Sensation. Damien Hirst is the creator of *The Physical Impossibility of Death in the Mind of Someone Living* (1991).

I do not think about the shark. I think about myself.

> *I like the idea of a thing to describe a feeling. A shark is fright-*
> *ening, bigger than you are, in an environment unknown to you.*
> *It looks alive when it's dead and dead when it's alive. . . . I like*
> *ideas of trying to understand the world by taking things out of*

the world. . . . You expect [the shark] to look back at you.
(Damien Hirst)

As a naturalist who has worked in a museum of natural history for more than fifteen years, how am I to think about a shark in the context of art, not science? How is my imagination so quickly rearranged to see the suspension of a shark, pickled in formaldehyde, as the stopped power of motion in the jaws of death, an image of my own mortality?

My mind becomes wild in the presence of creation, the artist's creation. I learn that the box in which the shark floats was built by the same company that constructs the aquariums of Brighton Sea World. I think about the killer whales kept in tanks for the amusement of humans, the killer whales that jump through hoops, carry humans on their backs as they circle and circle and circle the tank, day after day after week after month, how they go mad, the sea of insanity churning inside them, inside me as I feel my own captivity within a culture—any culture—that would thwart creativity: We are stopped cold, our spirits suspended, controlled, controlled sensation.

Tiger shark, glass, steel, 5 percent formaldehyde solution.

Damien Hirst calls the shark suspended in formaldehyde a sculpture. If it were in a museum of natural history, it would be called an exhibit, an exhibit in which the organism is featured as the animal it is. Call it art or call it biology, what is the true essence of shark?

How is the focus of our perceptions decided?

Art. Artifact. Art by designation.

Thomas McEvilley, art critic and author of *Art & Otherness*, states,

> The fact that we designate something as art means that it is art for us, but says nothing about what it is in itself or for other people. Once we realize that the quest for essences is an archaic religious quest, there is no reason why something should not be art for one person or culture and non-art for another.

• • •

Wild. Wilderness. Wilderness by designation. What is the solution to preserving that which is wild?

I remember standing next to an old rancher in Escalante, Utah, during a contentious political debate over wilderness in the canyon country of southern Utah. He kicked the front tire of his pickup truck with his cowboy boot.

"What's this?" he asked me.

"A Chevy truck," I responded.

"Right, and everybody knows it."

He then took his hand and swept the horizon. "And what's all that?" he asked with the same matter-of-fact tone.

"Wilderness," he answered before I could speak. "And everybody knows it, so why the hell do you have to go have Congress tell us what it is?"

Damien Hirst's conceptual art, be it his shark or his installation called *A Thousand Years* (1990)—where the eye of a severed cow's head looks upward as black flies crawl over it and lay eggs in the flesh that metamorphose into maggots that mature into flies that gather in the pool of blood to drink, leaving tiny red footprints on the glass installation, while some flies are destined to die as a life-stopping buzz in the electric fly-killing machine—all his conceptual pieces of art, his installations, make me think about the concept and designation of wilderness.

Why not designate wilderness as an installation of art? Conceptual art? A true sensation that moves and breathes and changes over time with a myriad of creatures that formulate an instinctual framework of interspecies dialogues; call them predator-prey relations or symbiotic relations, niches and ecotones, never before seen as art, as dance, as a painting in motion, but imagined only through the calculations of biologists, their facts now metamorphosed into designs, spontaneously choreographed moment to moment among the living. Can we not watch the habits of animals, the adaptations of plants, and call them performance art within the conceptual framework of wilderness?

To those who offer the critique that wilderness is merely a received idea, one that might be "conceptually incoherent" and entranced by "the myth of the pristine," why not answer with a resounding yes, yes, wilderness is our received idea as artists, as human beings, a grand piece of performance art that can embody and inspire *The Physical Impossibility of Death in the Mind of Someone Living* or *Isolated Elements Swimming in the Same Direction for the Purpose of Understanding* (1991).

Call it a cabinet of fish preserved in salt solution to honor the diversity of species, where nothing is random. Or call it a piece of art to celebrate color and form found in the bodies of fishes. Squint your eyes: *Imagine a world of spots.* Colored dots in the wilderness. *They're all connected.* Damien Hirst paints spots.

"Art's about life and it can't really be about anything else. There isn't anything else." Tell us again, Damien Hirst, with your cabinet of wonders; we are addicted to wonders, bottles of drugs lined up, shelf after shelf, waiting to be opened, minds opened, veins opened, nerves opened. Wilderness is a cabinet of pharmaceuticals waiting to be discovered.

Just as we designate art, we designate wilderness, large and small, as much as we can, hoping it begins a dialogue with our highest and basest selves. We are animals, in search of a home, in relationship to Other, an expanding community with a mosaic of habitats, domestic and wild; there is nothing precious or nostalgic about it. We designate wilderness as an installation of essences, open for individual interpretation, full of controversy and conversation.

"I always believe in contradiction, compromise . . . it's unavoidable. In life it can be positive or negative, like saying, 'I can't live without you.' " Damien Hirst speaks again.

I cannot live without art. I cannot live without wilderness. Call it *Brilliant Love* (1994–95). Thank the imagination that some people are brave enough, sanely crazy enough, to designate both.

"Art is dangerous because it doesn't have a definable function. I think that is what people are afraid of."

Yes, Damien, exactly, you bad boy of British art who dares to slice up the bodies of cows, from the head to the anus, and mix them all up to where nothing makes sense and who allows us to walk through with no order in mind, twelve cross-sections of cow, so we have to take note of the meat that we eat without thinking about the topography of the body, the cow's body, our body; we confront the wonder of the organism as is, not as a continuum but as a design, the sheer beauty and texture of functional design. We see the black-and-white hide; there is no place to hide inside the guts of a cow sliced and stretched through space like an accordion between your very large hands. You ask us to find *Some Comfort Gained from the Acceptance of the Inherent Lies in Everything* (1996).

We have been trying to explain, justify, codify, give biological and ecological credence as to why we want to preserve what is wild, like art, much more than a specimen behind glass. But what if we were to say, Sorry, you are right, wilderness has no definable function. Can we let it be, designate it as art, *art of the wild,* just in case one such definition should arise in the mind of one standing in the tall grass prairies of middle America or the sliding slope of sandstone in the erosional land-scape of Utah?

Wilderness as an aesthetic.

Freeze. Damien Hirst brought together a community of artists and dis-played their work in a warehouse in England, these Neo-Conceptualists who set out to explore the big things like death and sex and the meaning of life. Wilderness designation is not so dissimilar. In your tracks, *freeze,* and watch the performance art of a grizzly walking through the gold meadows of the Hayden Valley in Yellowstone. In your tracks, *freeze,* a constellation of monarch butterflies has gathered in the mountains of Mexico. No definable function except to say, wilderness exists like art, look for an idea with four legs, with six legs and wings that resemble fire, and recognize this feeling called survival, in this received idea of wilder-ness, our twentieth-century installation as Neo-Conservationists.

A shark in a box.

Wilderness as a box.

Wilderness as *A Thousand Years* with flies and maggots celebrating inside the corpse of things.

Q: What is in the boxes?

A: Maggots.

Q: So you're going to put maggots in the white boxes, and then they hatch and then they fly around . . .

A: And then they get killed by the fly-killer, and maybe lay eggs in the cow heads.

Q: It's a bit disgusting.

A: A bit. I don't think it is. I like it.

Q: Do you think anyone will buy it?

A: I hope so.

(Damien Hirst interview with Liam Gillick, Modern Medicine, 1990)

Do I think anyone will buy the concept of wilderness as conceptual art? It is easier to create a sensation over art than a sensation over the bald, greed-faced sale and development of open lands, wild lands, in the United States of America.

I would like to bring Damien Hirst out to the American West, let him bring along his chain saw, *Cutting Ahead* (1994), only to find out somebody has beat him to it, creating clear-cut sculptures out of negative space, eroding space, topsoil running like blood down the mountainsides as mud. Mud as material. He would have plenty of material.

The art of the wild is flourishing.

How are we to see through the lens of our own creative destruction?

A shark in a box.

Wilderness as an installation.

A human being suspended in formaldehyde.

My body floats between contrary equilibriums. (Federico García Lorca)

When I leaned over the balcony of the great blue room in the American Museum of Natural History, I looked up at the body of the Blue Whale, the largest living mammal on earth, suspended from the ceiling. I recalled being a docent, how we brought the schoolchildren to this room to lie on their backs, thrilled beyond words as they looked up at this magnificent leviathan who, if alive, with one quick swoosh of its tail would be halfway across Central Park.

I only then noticed that the open spaces below where the children used to lie on their backs in awe was now a food court filled with plastic tables and chairs. The tables were crowded with visitors chatting away, eating, drinking, oblivious to the creatures surrounding them. How had I missed the theater lights, newly installed on the balcony, pointing down to illuminate the refrigerators humming inside the showcases with a loud display of fast foods advertising yogurt, roast beef sandwiches, apples and oranges?

The Blue Whale, the Tiger Shark, Sunfish, Tunas, Eels and Manta Rays, the Walrus, the Elephant Seals, the Orca with its head poking through the diorama of ice in Antarctica, are no longer the natural histories of creatures associated with the sea but simply decoration.

Everything feels upside down these days, created for our entertainment. Requiem days. The natural world is becoming invisible, appearing only as a backdrop for our own human dramas and catastrophes: hurricanes, tornadoes, earthquakes and floods. Perhaps if we bring art to the discussion of the wild we can create a sensation where people will pay attention to the shock of what has always been here *Away from the Flock* (1994).

Wild Beauty in the Minds of the Living.

The Shark's Parlor
by James Dickey

Novelist and poet James Dickey (1923–1997)

often wrote about encounters with death. This

poem explores man's impulse to control nature,

and where that impulse can lead.

Memory: I can take my head and strike it on a wall   on Cumberland Island
Where the night tide came crawling under the stairs came up the first
Two or three steps   and the cottage stood on poles all night
With the sea sprawled under it   as we dreamed of the great fin circling
Under the bedroom floor. In daylight there was my first brassy taste of beer
And Payton Ford and I came back from the Glynn County slaughter house
With a bucket of entrails and blood. We tied one end of a hawser
To a spindling porch pillar and rowed straight out of the house
Three hundred yards into the vast front yard of windless blue water
The rope outslithering its coil   the two-gallon jug stoppered and sealed
With wax   and a ten-foot chain leader   a drop-forged shark hook nestling.

We cast our blood on the waters   the land blood easily passing
For sea blood   and we sat in it for a moment with the stain spreading
Out from the boat   sat in a new radiance   in the pond of blood in the
      sea
Waiting for fins   waiting to spill our guts also in the glowing water.
We dumped the bucket, and baited the hook with a run-over collie
      pup. The jug
Bobbed, trying to shake off the sun as a dog would shake off the sea.
We rowed to the house   feeling the same water lift the boat a new way,
All the time seeing where we lived rise and dip with the oars.
We tied up and sat down in rocking chairs, one eye or the other
      responding
To the blue-eye wink of the jug. Payton got us a beer and we sat

All morning sat there with blood on our minds   the red mark out
In the harbor slowly failing us   then   the house groaned   the rope
Sprang out of the water   splinters flew   we leapt from our chairs
And grabbed the rope   hauled   did nothing   the house coming subtly
Apart   all around us   underfoot   boards beginning to sparkle like sand
With the glinting of the bright hidden parts of ten-year-old nails
Pulling out   the tarred poles we slept propped-up on   leaning to sea
As in land wind   crabs scuttling from under the floor   as we took
      turns about
Two more porch pillars   and looked out and saw   something a
      fish-flash
An almighty fin in trouble   a moiling of secret forces   a false start
Of water   a round wave growing: in the whole of Cumberland Sound
      the one ripple.
Payton took off without a word   I could not hold him either

But clung to the rope anyway: it was the whole house bending
Its nails that held whatever it was   coming in a little and like a fool
I took up the slack on my wrist. The rope drew gently   jerked   I lifted
Clean off the porch and hit the water   the same water it was in

I felt in blue blazing terror at the bottom of the stairs and scrambled
Back up looking desperately into the human house as deeply as I could
Stopping my gaze before it went out the wire screen of the back door
Stopped it on the thistled rattan   the rugs I lay on and read
On my mother's sewing basket with next winter's socks spilling from it
The flimsy vacation furniture   a bucktoothed picture of myself.
Payton came back with three men from a filling station   and glanced at me
Dripping water   inexplicable   then we all grabbed hold like a tug-of-war.

We were gaining a little   from us a cry went up   from everywhere
People came running. Behind us the house filled with men and boys.
On the third step from the sea I took my place   looking down the rope
Going into the ocean, humming and shaking off drops. A houseful
Of people put their backs into it   going up the steps from me
Into the living room   through the kitchen   down the back stairs
Up and over a hill of sand   across a dust road   and onto a raised field
Of dunes   we were gaining   the rope in my hands began to be wet
With deeper water   all other haulers retreated through the house
But Payton and I on the stairs   drawing hand over hand on our blood
Drawing into existence by the nose   a huge body   becoming
A hammerhead   rolling in beery shadows   and I began to let up
But the rope still strained behind me   the town had gone
Pulling-mad in our house: far away in a field of sand they struggled
They had turned their backs on the sea   bent double   some on their
       knees
The rope over their shoulders like a bag of gold   they strove for the ideal
Esso station across the scorched meadow   with the distant fish coming up
The front stairs   the sagging boards   still coming in   up   taking
Another step   toward the empty house   where the rope stood straining
By itself through the rooms   in the middle of the air. "Pass the word,"
Payton said, and I screamed it: "Let up, good God, let up!"   to no one
       there.
The shark flopped on the porch, grating with salt-sand   driving back in
The nails he had pulled out   coughing chunks of his formless blood.

The screen door banged and tore off   he scrambled on his tail   slid
Curved   did a thing from another world   and was out of his element
          and in
Our vacation paradise   cutting all four legs from under the dinner table
With one deep-water move he   unwove the rugs in a moment
          throwing pints
Of blood over everything we owned   knocked the buck teeth out of my
          picture
His odd head full of crushed jelly-glass splinters and radio tubes
          thrashing
Among the pages of fan magazines   all the movie stars drenched in
          sea-blood.
Each time we thought he was dead   he struggled back and smashed
One more thing   in all coming back to die   three or four more times
          after death.
At last we got him out   log-rolling him   greasing his sandpaper skin
With lard to slide him   pulling on his chained lips as the tide came
Tumbled him down the steps as the first night wave went under the
          floor.
He drifted off   head back   belly white as the moon. What could I do
          but buy
That house for the one black mark still there   against death   a fore-
          head-
toucher in the room he circles beneath   and has been invited to wreck?
Blood hard as iron on the wall   black with time   still bloodlike
Can be touched whenever the brow is drunk enough: all changes:
          Memory:
Something like three-dimensional dancing in the limbs   with age
Feeling more in two worlds than one   in all worlds the growing
          encounters.

from The Lonely Crossing
of Juan Cabrera

by J. Joaquín Fraxedas

In J. Joaquín Fraxedas' first novel, three Cuban men tie three inner tubes together and set out to cross ninety miles of ocean to Florida. In this passage only two remain alive after riding out a hurricane.

The colors of the sky grew softer after sunset. A few trailing cloud ribbons flushed pink as they raced northward over the western horizon. Above these flat, tenuous clouds, a thin crescent moon was beginning to glimmer in the fading light, and a gentle breeze blew over the water.

Juan and Raúl were shivering as they pulled themselves up on the raft. They lay on their backs, shaking violently, with their arms folded across their chests.

"Juan, are we still in the Stream?"

"Yes, we have to be."

"Why does the water feel so cold?"

"Don't know. Maybe the hurricane drew the heat from the sea."

"You think it blew us into the Gulf?" Raúl asked.

"No, the trailing edge blew us to the northeast, so we should be closer to the Keys."

"Are you sure?"

"Yes. Why are you so worried? It's not like you to be worried."

"Just had a bad feeling all of a sudden."

"Like what?"

"I felt I was never going to see land again."

"But the worst is over, Raúl. We made it through."

"I know, it was just a strange feeling."

"You're just hungry. That's what Andrés would have said."

"I must be. I'm beginning to think weird thoughts, like I always do when I get hungry. But it sure was strong."

"What was strong?"

"The fee . . . Never mind, I'm just hungry. That's all. I'm hungry as hell."

Along with everything else, the storm had taken the three paddles Andrés had carved from a single twelve-foot length of pine board. The loss of the paddles bothered Raúl even more than the loss of the food and the water. Raúl was a practical, physical man, at ease in the everyday world of objects. No matter how remote or bleak the place, or how dismal the circumstances, he always found structure and meaning in his universe as long as he held a machete or a shovel or an ax or any other tool securely in his hands. The very *act* of digging a trench or cutting a path through the jungle brought him comfort.

Even though, like Juan, he was a stranger to the sea, Raúl made himself at home in this new world and, paddle in hand, attacked the waves as he had, at other times in distant places, conquered the jungle with his machete and broken the earth with his shovel.

Unlike Juan, who had taught physics and astronomy at the University of Havana, Raúl was not comfortable in the ethereal world of ideas. He was, without pretension, a *guajiro*, a man of the earth, and he distrusted those things he could not touch and hold in his hands. How can a man, without ever touching it, weigh and measure a star? Raúl could not understand it, and he did not completely believe it.

Now, adrift, without anything to do and without a tool to do anything, Raúl felt, for the first time in his life, truly lost. His soul was restless as disturbing thoughts raced through his mind. He felt resentment toward Juan, who, never having been at sea, spoke with assurance about the speed and direction of the currents; who always pointed the way they should go, day or night; who could barely tie a decent knot, but who regularly announced their location on the black, trackless water by measuring the height of the North Star, stretching out his arm and aligning the bottom of his closed fist with the horizon. A closed fist was ten degrees, *he* said. A finger's width was two-point-five degrees, *he* said. Now they were twenty-four degrees north latitude, better than halfway there, *he* said. Why should he believe Juan, who, after all, was a damned liar and a coward? No, he didn't even want to *think* about that, or about the things Juan had done, not now.

Raúl resented Juan and his knowledge acquired from books, and he resented his own reliance on that knowledge.

"Juan, are you *sure* we didn't get blown into the Gulf of Mexico?"

"Yes, I'm sure."

"Why?"

"We were too far to the east by the time it hit us, and the tail end must have blown us closer to the Keys."

"How far do you think we are?"

"Around forty miles south of Key West."

In the dark water, they saw bright green phosphorescent streaks as unseen fish darted, like meteors, under the inner tubes. Pangs of hunger gnawed at Raúl, and he thought about the tasty fish swimming beneath them and he imagined that he was frying them now on a big cast-iron frying pan over the open flame of a campfire under the stars. He could smell the onions and the green peppers and he could hear the pan sizzle as he squeezed lime juice, plenty of lime juice, over the delicious blackened fillets, and his mouth watered.

"Do you think we might be able to catch a fish?" he asked Juan.

"How?"

"Don't know, just thought you might have an idea."

After midnight, Juan saw the constellation of Orion rise majestically in the east and he showed it to Raúl. Then he lay on his back, looking at the stars until he fell asleep.

He dreamt that Orion the hunter, the son of Neptune, was walking on the sea, as he used to do before he was killed. In his dream, the good giant Orion came walking sadly on the surface of the sea and passed him in the darkness and did not see him but walked on by, without disturbing the waves, and disappeared forever in the west amid a crowd of stars.

The morning was bright and calm. Great patches of yellow sargasso weed covered the sea around the raft. Tiny crabs and shrimp crawled around the little air sacs that kept the seaweed afloat. Sleek blue and gold dorados swam in the shade under the seaweed, waiting for the smaller fish that fed on the miniature crustaceans.

Raúl picked up a clump and saw the colorful half-inch crabs scurrying around the thickly matted branches. He reached in, searching with his fingers, and pulled one out. He held it between his thumb and forefinger as the tiny pincers opened and closed grasping the air. He threw it into his mouth, cracking the salty shell between his molars. It tasted better than he thought it would. He tried another and then another, chewing them and letting the juices run over his tongue.

"These taste good, Juan. Here, try one."

Juan chewed a crab and then tried one of the shrimp. They *are* tasty, he thought. It had not occurred to him that they would taste this good uncooked.

Raúl's spirit was lifted by his discovery, and he began to think how he might catch one of the dorados swimming under the inner tubes. The shrimp and crabs were good, but they were not sufficient. If he could only figure out a way to capture a big dorado, they would eat well, very well, he thought. Then their only problem would be fresh water, and he had already thought of a way to collect rainwater, using the remnants of the deflated inner tube. All he needed was rain, and it was bound to rain. Of course it would rain. It always rains, he thought.

An idea then began to form in his mind about how he would capture a dorado. He reached into the water and undid the two eight-foot lines he had lashed to the raft at Guanabo. He took the end of one line and made a big S. He then took the end of the other line and tied it across the top curve of the S to make an enclosure. He continued making S's with the first line and tying the second one straight across, and then, after a while, he came back, tying knots along the center part of the S's, and made a number of rows like that until he began to see something that looked like a net.

When he first started thinking about his idea, he thought he would have to cut the lines in many places, and that it would be laborious and take a long time. Thinking about that, he reached down and felt around the zippered pocket of his army trousers for his pocket knife and confirmed it still was safely tucked in there. But as he began to work with the lines, he realized that he hardly had to cut them at all, and that it was easier than he thought it would be. But when he had used up the lines, he saw that the size was not adequate, and he was surprised at how small a net sixteen feet of line made. He then noticed that the quarter-inch nylon rope he was using was actually made of four separate smaller strands twined together. He undid what he had done, unraveled the individual strands, and repeated the process using the smaller strands. He also took the lashings that had held the remnants of the deflated inner tube to the other two and used them to get more strands. He saved the rubber remnants to make a container for rainwater; he would figure out the exact details for that project later.

In a few hours, after several attempts using different knots and approaches, he had what looked like a decent net, about four feet by four feet when he stretched it out. The problem now was to wait for a dorado to come swimming under his inner tube and trap it in the net. He did not expect immediate success—that was not his nature, and he had lived long enough to know that success was hardly ever immediate. Sometimes it was, but that was luck, and he did not trust luck. He did trust his perseverance and he knew he had plenty of that in reserve. But he was not sure exactly how he would go about capturing his dorado. He figured he would try the first thing that came to mind, and if that didn't work, he would keep modifying his technique until he found one that did. It is not important to know exactly how to do something, he thought. It is only important to know that you are going to do it. And he knew he was going to catch his dorado or—at worst—another fish that was not so fast. But he hoped it would be a big, tasty dorado.

The sun was high, and shone down into the water that was now a deep dark blue. The hurricane had churned the water and made it look greenish and strange as it passed. But the powerful currents of the Gulf Stream had swept all that water away during the night, and now it was blue again and warm like before. The rays of the sun penetrated deep into the water, and the men could clearly see the different fish as they swam by under the raft.

Raúl lay on his stomach across the inner tube, with his head and upper body hanging over the side. He gathered two corners and the middle of one side of the net and held them with his teeth, making a sort of scoop. He then held the two remaining corners in his hands and stretched his long arms as far as he could under the raft. As soon as he did that, he thought that he should have gathered some of those little shrimp and crabs and dropped them under the raft to attract smaller fish that would then get the attention of the dorados. It was too late now, though. He had gone to some trouble getting one end of the net just right in his mouth to make a scoop, and now he was in this awkward position and he decided to wait and see if it worked before he tried anything else.

After a while he saw a greenish golden shape rise from the deep and approach the raft, sparkling as it moved in the sunlight. Then it came under the raft and hung suspended in the shade. It was a male dorado, about ten pounds. With his eyes close to the water, Raúl could see the fish as it inspected the underside of the raft. He could see it gradually adjust its position, slowly moving its pectoral fins. Then he saw it as it began to bump the bottom of his inner tube with its prominent forehead. The magnificent colors of the living dorado amazed Raúl. He had seen dorado before, but always at the docks, as fishermen flung the dead fish on the rough concrete. Even there, stiff and lifeless, and stripped of all dignity, they were beautiful fish. He could tell the males from the females by their high foreheads, tapering back to the forked, swallowlike tails. But he had always thought their color in life was the same dull gray they displayed in death, and when he was a boy, he wondered, without ever bothering to ask anyone, why the fishermen called them *dorados*, which in Spanish means "golden ones." He had later decided that the name probably had more to do with the spirit of the fish than with its true color, since he had heard fishermen describe them as great fighters. But after a while he grew up and stopped wondering about this and other inconsistencies.

Now, as he watched the fish in the full splendor of life, he could see the deep blue of its back, which started out at the top almost purple, like the Gulf Stream. As the blue came down its sides, he noticed how it gradually grew lighter and lighter until it began to blend with the gold along the middle. The mixture of the blue and the gold produced an exuberance of greens from deep emerald to the most delicate color of the freshest spring. Then the green, farther down, yielded to the gold, which, like the blue, started out in deep hues. At first it was like tarnished brass, with dark spots. Then it descended through all the possible shades of gold so that the belly of the fish looked almost silver. But even there, at the very bottom, there were specks of gold. And, as the fish turned in a shaft of light, all of those colors, all of them at once, exploded in a fantastic burst of brilliant tones of gold. Seeing that, Raúl remembered the stiff, dull bodies on the dock and he knew what no one who is a prisoner of the shore would ever know. He knew why the fishermen of his boyhood called them dorados, the golden ones, and why the name had such a sad and distant sound whenever they pronounced it.

Raúl lay still now, with his outstretched arms in the water, and held his breath as the dorado edged closer and closer to the suspended net. The water magnified the fish like a lens, and it looked huge to him as it poked its head over the open end of the net. He could hear his heart beating so loudly that he was afraid it would scare away the fish, and he could feel the pounding of his blood inside his head. Raúl waited until the entire fish was over the net, and then raised his arms against the inner tube and brought them together in one quick motion.

The upper half of his trunk was already hanging over the side, and this movement was so violent and sudden that he plunged headfirst into the sea, grasping the net under the water and thrashing the surface with his feet. In the blurry, bubbling confusion he saw a quick flash as the dorado turned and disappeared in the purple water like a glittering bullet.

Juan was laughing as Raúl pulled himself onto the raft, with streams of water running down his beard. Raúl laughed too, and was not discouraged. They then discussed different ideas about how to capture a fish, and they decided that the best way was to take some of the leftover strands from the lines and tie a four-foot length to each corner of the net. That way each man could hold one strand in either hand and, with their backs to each other, they would lower the net until it hung in the water, several feet under the raft, weighed down with Juan's belt buckle, which they tied at the center. This idea seemed to have a number of virtues; one of the chief ones was that it allowed them to sit in a comfortable position while they waited for the fish.

As the clumps of sargasso floated by, they picked them up and shook out the little crustaceans over the holes at the center of the inner tubes. Then they began to put some of the seaweed there to make it more realistic and enticing for the fish. After a while, schools of pinfish gathered under the raft and began feeding. Raúl encouraged them by picking out little crabs, cracking the shells between his teeth, and spitting them into the water.

Above them, a frigate bird looked down on the raft as it glided in wide circles, barely flapping its long, elegant black wings. Juan and Raúl did not notice the bird. They squinted as they looked into the water with great concentration. The sun was lower now, and its light more subdued. A warm breeze blew from the south and it felt soft and pleasant.

Under a drifting island of sargasso, Raúl saw another dorado. It was a female and not as big as the first one. Still, it looked over two feet long, and Raúl could see its flank glistening in the slanted light of the afternoon. He tensed as the yellow island floated near the raft.

"Don't move, Juan. There's one under those weeds. Maybe she'll pay us a visit."

They slowly lowered the net even farther, to make sure there was plenty of room between the net and the bottom of the raft for the fish to swim in, should it decide to come over and inspect. The dorado appeared to be in no hurry to go anywhere, and for a moment it looked as if it was going to stay in the shade of the passing sargasso. But as the floating island drifted away, the dorado suddenly turned and darted under the inner tubes. With the fish suspended under them between the hanging net and the bottom of the raft, they argued in whispers whether it would be better to raise the net in one quick motion or to bring it up gradually until the penultimate moment. They decided that even their quickest action would be no match for the explosive speed of the dorado.

Then, with great patience, Juan and Raúl began to raise the net gradually, almost imperceptibly, while they kept an eye on the fish through the gaps between the clumps of sargasso that they had placed in the holes at the center of the inner tubes. The fish nibbled on the miniature animals in the sargasso unaware of—or unconcerned about—the approaching net.

"Do you think she can see that the net is coming closer?" Raúl whispered.

"Don't know."

"She seems so damned calm and unruffled—almost cocky, like she's taunting us."

"Wouldn't you be, if you had her speed?"

As the net was about to brush against the dorado's tail, Raúl yelled, "Now!" and they quickly yanked up the four corners of the net, pressing it tightly against the bottom of Raúl's inner tube. At the same time, still holding on to the lines, Raúl threw himself across the inner tube, covering the hole in the middle with his huge chest. All hell broke loose as the fish desperately tried to escape. The dorado leaped out of the water and bounced off Raúl's chest. It then shot straight down and pushed against the net. Coming back up, it swam in frantic circles around the inside rim of the inner tube, beating the water into a froth with its tail as small clumps of sargasso flew all over the place.

"Grab her, Juan! Grab her!" Raúl yelled.

"How? I can't let go of the lines!"

"See if you can hold two in one hand! But, whatever you do, don't let the net go slack!"

Juan held both of his lines tightly against the inner tube with his left hand, and reached in for the fish with his right. Again and again he grabbed at the fish, but each time the fish slipped between his fingers.

"Grab the gills! See if you can grab her by the gills!" Raúl yelled.

The dorado leaped again, and as it hit Raúl's chest, Juan managed to get his hand around the bottom of the fish and slip his fingers under the gill covers. He squeezed with all his strength and felt the delicate structures inside the gills break and the blood begin to run on his hand and drip down into the water. The fish, feeling the pain, shook violently and Juan pinned it against Raúl's chest and held it there. He could hear the tail slapping against Raúl's body, and in his hand he felt the spasms of the fish in its death struggle. After a while the convulsive shaking stopped, and then Juan felt a gentle tremor as life left the dorado.

"We got her, Raúl! Your net worked!" said Juan. "And what a fish! Look at those colors!"

Juan handed the fish to Raúl, his hands trembling. He then pulled the net from the water and folded it across his lap, and they laid the dorado on it. Even as they were admiring it, the colors began to fade and in moments turned into an ugly gray, almost as dark as charcoal at the top, and lighter, but just as dull and lifeless, along the sides.

Raúl took the knife from his pocket and slit the fish's belly, and a handful of fish eggs spilled on Juan's lap. As Juan held the fish, Raúl scooped up the clumps of roe, letting only a few shiny yellow eggs dribble into the water. Raúl ate the roe slowly, savoring each salty lump, first rolling and then squashing the tiny eggs between his tongue and the roof of his mouth. Reaching into the cavity with two fingers, Raúl cleaned out the remaining eggs and shared them with Juan. He then made the slit bigger, thrust his whole hand into the belly of the fish, and began to pull out the organs. They ate the liver and all the other soft parts and found most of them good and sweet except for a few bitter pieces, which they spit into the water.

Then Raúl carved a fillet of white meat from one side, starting at the top next to the dorsal fin, and cutting down along the ribs. He cut the meat in little chunks and they ate their fill, finishing all the meat from one side. Feeling strong and full of life now, with the essence of the fish coursing through his veins, Raúl cut out the meat from the other side in one big slab more than a foot long and almost an inch thick at the top. He dipped it in the water to clean off the blood and, without scaling it, he secured it to the inner tube using two strands from the rope.

When he finished with the fish, he watched the disk of the sun descend toward the western horizon. And as the last shining remnant of the uppermost rim vanished into the sea, Raúl saw the quick flash of green light that sometimes comes at sunset on very clear evenings when the air has been cleaned and purified by the passage of a great storm.

A heavy jolt awoke Juan. At first he thought they had struck rocks, and he sprang up and sat stiffly, peering into the dark water. But he saw no rocks. The surface of the water was smooth and unbroken. Everything was still, and the only thing he heard was the muffled sound the inner tubes made against the water as they moved slightly when he shifted his position to look over his shoulder.

He shook Raúl, who was already awake.

"Did you feel that, Raúl?"

"Yes, what was it?"

"Don't know, felt like we hit a rock."

"See anything?"

"No."

The blow came again, and this time it was followed by a wet

squeaking sound as the back of a shark rubbed against the underside of the raft. The skin of the shark was solid and rough, and it felt as though the inner tubes were being dragged over barely submerged rocks or concrete pilings. In the darkness, the shark did not feel like a living thing.

An arm's length away from the raft, Juan saw a swirling phosphorescence as the shark passed under them. The glowing whirlpool lingered on the surface of the water while the full length of the shark slipped beneath the raft. Then he saw the edge of a fin moving away, cleaving the still water. His eyes followed the thin line and saw it turn broadside twenty feet from them. The outline of the fin showed ghostly white in the starlight as it began to cut a circle around them on the surface of the water.

The shark circled twice, and then the dorsal fin dipped lower and disappeared. It was a tiger shark with a very broad, squared-off head. At either end of its shovel-shaped snout it had large, wide-open nostrils that looked more like the nostrils of a horse than the usual small nostrils that most sharks have, and they were covered by ugly flaps of skin that fluttered as the shark moved through the water. It was sixteen feet long and must have weighed over a thousand pounds. Its jaws were a foot wider than a man's shoulders and were filled with rows of serrated teeth that were notched on one side and angled on the other, like the comb of a rooster. It had a ravenous appetite and was one of the few sharks that, like the great white, sometimes attacked boats and other things floating on the water.

Juan could not see it now as it moved toward the raft, several feet under the surface. But soon he felt another bump. This one was more tentative, almost gentle, then the shark turned away and slid deeper into the water.

"Is he gone?" Raúl asked.

"There!" Juan yelled. "See? There's the fin! No, over *there!*" he said, pointing toward a dark shape moving on the surface.

Then they heard a rippling sound as the shark gained speed and the dorsal fin raised spray, splitting the water. Juan followed the dim white spray circling the raft.

"You think he can smell the fish?" Raúl asked.

"What?"

"The fish, the fish I tied to the inner tube."

"No, well . . ."

As he said that, Juan yanked the slab of dorado from under the ropes lashed around Raúl's inner tube, and flung it at the shark. It splashed a few feet in front of its snout, but the shark, paying no attention to the piece of fish meat, kept circling.

Again and again it circled them and then, suddenly, Juan saw it turn and head straight toward them before it disappeared once more into the dark water.

"He's coming at us, Raúl! He's coming straight at us! Look!" Juan yelled as he watched a green phosphorescent streak rushing toward them about eight feet under the surface.

The shark came under the raft at speed and, without slowing, arched its body and shot straight up. The flat snout crashed against the bottom of Raúl's inner tube, flipping the raft and tossing them through the air. It then turned on its back, showing its pale belly just under the surface, and bit into Raúl's inner tube, tearing it to pieces.

Treading water a few feet away, Juan could see the one good inner tube, still inflated and lashed to what remained of Raúl's, dragging back and forth across the surface enveloped in a cloud of spray as the shark jerked its head from side to side in violent spasms, all the while clicking its huge jaws and tearing chunks of rubber from the deflated inner tube.

"Let go, you bastard! Let go!" Raúl yelled.

As he shouted, Raúl began to swim toward the inner tube that was still throwing up walls of spray each time the shark jerked it across the water.

"Stop, Raúl! Stop! He'll kill you!" Juan called.

"If he tears the other one up, it'll be over anyway!" Raúl yelled back.

In his rage, Raúl swam toward the shark. When he was halfway between Juan and the shark, the inner tube stopped moving. The surface of the water became still again, and everything turned quiet.

Raúl stopped in mid-stroke, letting his legs drop under him, and his motionless body hung suspended for a moment in the water. He then began to adjust his position, moving his legs like scissors, as he scanned the surface of the water around him looking for a sign of the shark.

The sea was like a sheet of glass. Thirty feet away from him he could see the silhouette of the inner tube against a patch of stars hanging low over the eastern horizon.

A few minutes passed, and then Juan whispered, "Do you see him?"

"No."

"Can you reach the inner tube?"

Raúl did not answer as his eyes skimmed the surface of the water. The inner tube was now drifting away from him, and Raúl began once again to swim toward it in a smooth breaststroke. With his head high above the water, he kept looking all around him while he swam.

A light breeze ruffled the water now and blew the inner tube farther away. Raúl picked up his pace as the breeze teased him, pushing the inner tube out of his reach whenever he came close.

Then the breeze blew stronger and Raúl broke into a crawl, chasing after the tube. His big arms came down hard, beating the water with each stroke, and his legs churned the water, leaving a frothy trail behind him.

Raúl was now within reach of the inner tube, and he gave a few powerful strokes and lunged toward it. As his right hand grasped a line, the water under the inner tube exploded and the head of the shark burst out in front of him. Raúl let out a scream as the snout struck his chest and pushed him back, whirling through the water, out of the way of the massive animal. The shark's momentum carried it past him, and for a moment Raúl could see the back of the shark just under the water, speeding away from him into the darkness. Then he saw the dorsal fin, as wide as a door at the base, turn around and head toward him, slicing the surface and throwing up spray.

Raúl saw the water bulge before him, and as the shark came upon him, he stretched his arms out, trying to fend off the attack, and jammed a finger deep into the fleshy nostril on the left side. The shark turned its head away from the offending finger, and Raúl saw its black eye turn white as the nictitating membrane closed over it. Then the shark circled back and flipped on its side as it came toward him. And Raúl saw the blurry outline of the jaws as they opened beneath him, showing the enormous, all-devouring black cavity against the pale underbelly.

Juan had followed Raúl, swimming behind him. And now, as he moved closer, he felt something that does not carry a name. Something that had lingered like a vapor in the secret memories of his childhood. Juan could not explain it and he did not understand it because there was nothing to understand, nothing to explain. He had been afraid and now he was not. And how do you explain such a crossing? From darkness to light, from death to life. How do you explain such a thing?

Raúl turned toward Juan and shouted, "¡Atrás! Go back!"

But Juan swam closer, closer, until he sensed the swirl and bulge of the water ahead of the onrushing shark. As the shark came at Raúl, Juan grasped a pectoral fin and struck the gills hard with his fist before reeling back from the force of the moving shark.

Then he saw the strange, broad teeth thrust out and the jaws close around Raúl's waist, ripping the flesh and sinking deep into his abdominal muscles. And he saw Raúl lifted clear above the surface and shoved down headfirst into the water, only to be raised again as the shark shook its head back and forth, back and forth.

In the starlight Juan saw the rippling lateral muscles of the shark as its whole body convulsed and he saw Raúl struggling, striking the shark, his dark blood staining the white underbelly every time the shark raised its head out of the water. Then Juan heard the crunching sound of bones snapping as Raúl's ribs and spinal column cracked, and the noise the bones made when they snapped was louder than Juan ever imagined such a sound would be. And he saw the jaws open very wide and then shut tight, severing Raúl's body in half.

The bloody severed torso fell from the mouth of the shark and floated on the surface for a moment before the shark opened its mouth again and swallowed what remained of Raúl in a single bite.

Then the shark dove back into the depths and the ripples on the water faded until the surface was flat again and there was only silence and the light of the stars reflected on the sea.

Numb with shock, Juan swam to the remaining inner tube that was floating nearby, grabbed a line, and towed it back to the spot where he thought Raúl had last been. But there was no way of really knowing that the place he swam back to was the exact spot, and even in his confused state, he was aware that he could not know.

Still, he imagined that he was back at the place in the sea where Raúl had been, because he felt a great need to be there—as if all the fear and all the death and all the duplicity of the last thirty years had been swallowed in that place, had vanished in that place.

Then he thought that even if he had come back to the same place where Raúl had been, the current was carrying him away from there, and it made him anxious and for a moment he started swimming against the current. But then he thought that the current carried everything with it, just as it had carried him and the raft together as he swam toward it, keeping their relative positions the same as it swept them along, and the only thing that made a difference was the wind. But there was no wind now, so everything must be moving together, even the exact spot, which had to be moving with him now, right with him, and below him, and all around him.

The thought that both he and the place where Raúl had been were flowing together in the Gulf Stream brought him a mysterious comfort—filled him with a confidence that he was sure came from Raúl. And even as he felt the comfort and the confidence, he knew that it made no sense.

Then he thought that he might be going crazy, but he realized in a flash that he was aware of the strangeness of the ideas that filled his mind, and this meant that he was not mad. And that very realization almost brought him back to his old world, but he saw the door begin to open and he caught a glimpse of the horror behind it and he knew that he did not want to face it. So he shut the door and thought that the water felt warmer over the place, and he even reached out and touched the other water outside the place and felt that it was, indeed, colder, which meant that he was still where he was supposed to be.

Under the Deck Awnings
by Jack London

Jack London (1876–1916) had little patience for civilization, which tends to corrupt or otherwise harm the characters in his stories.

C an any man—a gentleman, I mean—call a woman a pig?"

The little man flung this challenge forth to the whole group, then leaned back in his deck chair, sipping lemonade with an air commingled of certitude and watchful belligerence. Nobody made answer. They were used to the little man and his sudden passions and high elevations.

"I repeat, it was in my presence that he said a certain lady, whom none of you knows, was a pig. He did not say swine. He grossly said that she was a pig. And I hold that no man who is a man could possibly make such a remark about any woman."

Dr. Dawson puffed stolidly at his black pipe. Matthews, with knees hunched up and clasped by his arms, was absorbed in the flight of a gunie. Sweet, finishing his Scotch and soda, was questing about with his eyes for a deck steward.

"I ask you, Mr. Treloar, can any man call any woman a pig?"

Treloar, who happened to be sitting next to him, was startled by the abruptness of the attack, and wondered what grounds he had ever given the little man to believe that he could call a woman a pig.

"I should say," he began his hesitant answer, "that it—er—depends on the—er—the lady."

The little man was aghast.

"You mean . . . ?" he quavered.

"That I have seen female humans who were as bad as pigs—and worse."

There was a long pained silence. The little man seemed withered by the coarse brutality of the reply. In his face was unutterable hurt and woe.

"You have told of a man who made a not nice remark and you have classified him," Treloar said in cold, even tones. "I shall now tell you about a woman—I beg your pardon—a lady, and when I have finished I shall ask you to classify her. Miss Caruthers I shall call her, principally for the reason that it is not her name. It was on a P. & O. boat, and it occurred neither more nor less than several years ago.

"Miss Caruthers was charming. No; that is not the word. She was amazing. She was a young woman, and a lady. Her father was a certain high official whose name, if I mentioned it, would be immediately recognized by all of you. She was with her mother and two maids at the time, going out to join the old gentleman wherever you like to wish in the East.

"She, and pardon me for repeating, was amazing. It is the one adequate word. Even the most minor adjectives applicable to her are bound to be sheer superlatives. There was nothing she could not do better than any woman and than most men. Sing, play—bah!—as some rhetorician once said of old Nap, competition fled from her. Swim! She could have made a fortune and a name as a public performer. She was one of those rare women who can strip off all the frills of dress, and in simple swimming suit be more satisfying beautiful. Dress! She was an artist.

"But her swimming. Physically, she was the perfect woman—you know what I mean; not in the gross, muscular way of acrobats, but in

all the delicacy of line and fragility of frame and texture. And com-
bined with this, strength. How she could do it was the marvel. You
know the wonder of a woman's arm—the fore arm, I mean; the sweet
fading away from rounded biceps and hint of muscle, down through
small elbow and firm soft swell to the wrist, small, unthinkably small
and round and strong? This was hers. And yet, to see her swimming the
sharp quick English overhand stroke, and getting somewhere with it,
too, was—well, I understand anatomy and athletics and such things,
and yet it was a mystery to me how she could do it.

"She could stay under water for two minutes. I have timed her. No
man on board, except Dennitson, could capture as many coins as she
with a single dive. On the forward main-deck was a big canvas tank
with six feet of sea-water. We used to toss small coins into it. I have
seen her dive from the bridge deck—no mean feat in itself—into that
six-feet of water, and fetch up no less than forty-seven coins, scattered
willy-nilly over the whole bottom of the tank. Dennitson, a quiet
young Englishman, never exceeded her in this, though he made it a
point always to tie her score.

"She was a sea-woman, true. But she was a land-woman, a horse-
woman—a—she was the universal woman. To see her, all softness of soft
dress, surrounded by half a dozen eager men, languidly careless of them
all or flashing brightness and wit on them and at them and through
them, one would fancy she was good for nothing else in the world. At
such moments I have compelled myself to remember her score of forty-
seven coins from the bottom of the swimming tank. But that was she, the
everlasting wonder of a woman who did all things well.

"She fascinated every betrousered human around her. She had me—
and I don't mind confessing it—she had me to heel along with the rest.
Young puppies and old gray dogs who ought to have known better—
oh, they all came up and crawled around her skirts and whined and
fawned when she whistled. They were all guilty, from young Ardmore,
a pink cherub of nineteen outward bound for some clerkship in the
Consular Service, to old Captain Bentley, grizzled and sea-worn, and as
emotional, to look at, as a Chinese joss. There was a nice middle-aged

chap, Perkins, I believe, who forgot his wife was on board until Miss
Caruthers sent him to the right about and back where he belonged.

"Men were wax in her hands. She melted them, or softly molded
them, or incinerated them, as she pleased. There wasn't a steward,
even, grand and remote as she was, who, at her bidding, would have
hesitated to souse the Old Man himself with a plate of soup. You have
all seen such women—a sort of world's desire to all men. As a man-
conqueror she was supreme. She was a whip-lash, a sting and a flame,
an electric spark. Oh, believe me, at times there were flashes of will that
scorched through her beauty and seduction and smote a victim into
blank and shivering idiocy and fear.

"And don't fail to mark, in the light of what is to come, that she was
a prideful woman. Pride of race, pride of caste, pride of sex, pride of
power—she had it all, a pride strange and wilful and terrible.

"She ran the ship, she ran the voyage, she ran everything, and she
ran Dennitson. That he had outdistanced the pack even the least wise
of us admitted. That she liked him, and that this feeling was growing,
there was not a doubt. I am certain that she looked on him with kinder
eyes than she had ever looked with on man before. We still worshiped,
and were always hanging about waiting to be whistled up, though we
knew that Dennitson was laps and laps ahead of us. What might have
happened we shall never know, for we came to Colombo and something else happened.

"You know Colombo, and how the native boys dive for coins in the
shark-infested bay. Of course, it is only among the ground sharks and
fish sharks that they venture. It is almost uncanny the way they know
sharks and can sense the presence of a real killer—a tiger shark, for
instance, or a gray nurse strayed up from Australian waters. Let such a
shark appear, and, long before the passengers can guess, every mother's
son of them is out of the water in a wild scramble for safety.

"It was after tiffin, and Miss Caruthers was holding her usual court
under the deck-awnings. Old Captain Bentley had just been whistled
up, and had granted her what he never granted before . . . nor since—
permission for the boys to come up on the promenade deck. You see,

Miss Caruthers was a swimmer, and she was interested. She took up a collection of all our small change, and herself tossed it overside, singly and in handfuls, arranging the terms of the contests, chiding a miss, giving extra rewards to clever wins, in short, managing the whole exhibition.

"She was especially keen on their jumping. You know, jumping feet-first from a height, it is very difficult to hold the body perpendicularly while in the air. The center of gravity of the male body is high, and the tendency is to over-topple. But the little beggars employed a method which she declared was new to her and which she desired to learn. Leaping from the davits of the boat-deck above, they plunged downward, their faces and shoulders bowed forward, looking at the water. And only at the last moment did they abruptly straighten up and enter the water erect and true.

"It was a pretty sight. Their diving was not so good, though there was one of them who was excellent at it, as he was in all the other stunts. Some white man must have taught him, for he made the proper swan dive and did it as beautifully as I have ever seen it. You know, headfirst into the water, from a great height, the problem is to enter the water at the perfect angle. Miss the angle and it means at the least a twisted back and injury for life. Also, it has meant death for many a bungler. But this boy could do it—seventy feet I know he cleared in one dive from the rigging—clenched hands on chest, head thrown back, sailing more like a bird, upward and out, and out and down, body flat on the air so that if it struck the surface in that position it would be split in half like a herring. But the moment before the water is reached, the head drops forward, the hands go out and lock the arms in an arch in advance of the head, and the body curves gracefully downward and enters the water just right.

"This the boy did, again and again, to the delight of all of us, but particularly of Miss Caruthers. He could not have been a moment over twelve or thirteen, yet he was by far the cleverest of the gang. He was the favorite of his crowd, and its leader. Though there were a number older than he, they acknowledged his chieftaincy. He was a beautiful boy, a lithe young god in breathing bronze, eyes wide apart, intelligent and daring—a bubble, a mote, a beautiful flash and sparkle of life. You have seen wonderful glorious creatures—animals, anything, a leopard, a horse—restless, eager, too much alive ever to be still, silken of muscle, each slightest movement a benediction of grace, every action wild, untrammeled, and over all spilling out that intense vitality, that sheen and luster of living light. The boy had it. Life poured out of him almost in an effulgence. His skin glowed with it. It burned in his eyes. I swear I could almost hear it crackle from him. Looking at him, it was as if a whiff of ozone came to one's nostrils—so fresh and young was he, so resplendent with health, so wildly wild.

"This was the boy. And it was he who gave the alarm in the midst of the sport. The boys made a dash of it for the gangway platform, swimming the fastest strokes they knew, pell-mell, floundering and splashing, fright in their faces, clambering out with jumps and surges, any way to get out, lending one another a hand to safety, till all were strung along the gangway and peering down into the water.

" 'What is the matter?' asked Miss Caruthers.

" 'A shark, I fancy,' Captain Bentley answered. 'Lucky little beggars that he didn't get one of them.'

" 'Are they afraid of sharks?' she asked.

" 'Aren't you?' he asked back.

She shuddered, looked overside at the water, and made a *moué*.

" 'Not for the world would I venture where a shark might be,' she said, and shuddered again. 'They are horrible! Horrible!'

"The boys came up on the promenade deck, clustering close to the rail and worshiping Miss Caruthers who had flung them such a wealth of backsheesh. The performance being over, Captain Bentley motioned to them to clear out. But she stopped him.

" 'One moment, please, Captain. I have always understood that the natives are not afraid of sharks.'

"She beckoned the boy of the swan dive nearer to her, and signed to him to dive over again. He shook his head, and along with all his crew behind him laughed as if it were a good joke.

" 'Shark,' he volunteered, pointing to the water.

" 'No,' she said. 'There is no shark.'

"But he nodded his head positively, and the boys behind him nodded with equal positiveness.

" 'No, no, no,' she cried. And then to us, 'Who'll lend me a half-crown and a sovereign?'

"Immediately the half dozen of us were presenting her with crowns and sovereigns, and she accepted the two coins from young Ardmore.

"She held up the half-crown for the boys to see. But there was no eager rush to the rail preparatory to leaping. They stood there grinning sheepishly. She offered the coin to each one individually, and each, as his turn came, rubbed his foot against his calf, shook his head, and grinned. Then she tossed the half-crown overboard. With wistful, regretful faces they watched its silver flight through the air, but not one moved to follow it.

" 'Don't do it with the sovereign,' Dennitson said to her in a low voice.

"She took no notice, but held up the gold coin before the eyes of the boy of the swan dive.

" 'Don't,' said Captain Bentley. 'I wouldn't throw a sick cat overside with a shark around.'

"But she laughed, bent on her purpose, and continued to dazzle the boy.

" 'Don't tempt him,' Dennitson urged. 'It is a fortune to him, and he might go over after it.'

" 'Wouldn't *you*?' she flared at him. 'If I threw it?' This last more softly.

"Dennitson shook his head.

" 'Your price is high,' she said. 'For how many sovereigns would you go?'

" 'There are not enough coined to get me overside,' was his answer.

"She debated a moment, the boy forgotten in her tilt with Dennitson.

" 'For me?' she said very softly.

" 'To save your life—yes. But not otherwise.'

"She turned back to the boy. Again she held the coin before his eyes, dazzling him with the vastness of its value. Then she made as to toss it out, and, involuntarily, he made a half-movement toward the rail, but was checked by sharp cries of reproof from his companions. There was anger in their voices as well.

"'I know it is only fooling,' Dennitson said. 'Carry it as far as you like, but for heaven's sake don't throw it.'

"Whether it was that strange wilfulness of hers, or whether she doubted the boy could be persuaded, there is no telling. It was unexpected to all of us. Out from the shade of the awning the coin flashed golden in the blaze of sunshine and fell toward the sea in a glittering arch. Before a hand could stay him, the boy was over the rail and curving beautifully downward after the coin. Both were in the air at the same time. It was a pretty sight. The sovereign cut the water sharply, and at the very spot, almost at the same instant, with scarcely a splash, the boy entered.

"From the quicker-eyed black boys watching, came an exclamation. We were all at the rail. Don't tell me it is necessary for a shark to turn on its back. That one didn't. In the clear water, from the height we were above it, we saw everything. The shark was a big brute, and with one drive he cut the boy squarely in half.

"There was a murmur or something from among us—who made it I did not know; it might have been I. And then there was silence. Miss Caruthers was the first to speak. Her face was deathly white.

"'I . . . I never dreamed,' she said, and laughed a short, hysterical laugh.

"All her pride was at work to give her control. She turned weakly toward Dennitson, and then on from one to another of us. In her eyes was a terrible sickness, and her lips were trembling. We were brutes— oh, I know it, now that I look back upon it. But we did nothing.

"'Mr. Dennitson,' she said, 'Tom, won't you take me below?'

"He never changed the direction of his gaze, which was the bleakest I have ever seen in a man's face, nor did he move an eyelid. He took a cigarette from his case and lighted it. Captain Bentley made a nasty sound in his throat and spat overboard. That was all; that and the silence.

"She turned away and started to walk firmly down the deck. Twenty feet away, she swayed and thrust a hand against the wall to save herself. And so she went on, supporting herself against the cabins and walking very slowly."

Treloar ceased. He turned his head and favored the little man with a look of cold inquiry.

"Well," he said finally. "Classify her."

The little man gulped and swallowed.

"I have nothing to say," he said. "I have nothing whatever to say."

from Close to Shore
by Michael Capuzzo

New Jersey beach resorts in 1916 were begin-ning to attract more people who wanted to try ocean swimming, a newly popular leisure activity. A series of freak events—which sixty years later would inspire a different summer phenomenon: the blockbuster movie—made the water less appealing. Here author Michael Capuzzo describes the first incident.

C harles stood knee-deep in the shallow surf, feet planted on the soft golden sand, the outgoing tide gently swirling about his calves. His feet were pale from indoor work and fully visible in the cool, clear water. The breeze was mild, the sun pale and forgiving in the late hour, the ocean bottom free of seaweed. This was why people from the great West, as far as St. Louis, rode the Pennsylvania Railroad to the bather's paradise of the Jersey shore. It was a place of legendary beauty, a place to feel *alive*. Even with calm weather and high blue skies, Charles could feel the whisper of an undertow, the faint rocking motion of distant waves, the immense tug of the sea. He looked out at the flat surface of the ocean, which con-cealed the softly sloping coast for which South Jersey was famous. Ahead bobbed the diving platform Robert Engle had installed in front of his hotel for the new season; in the distance floated a line of salmon clouds. The water was chilly, but in a few moments Charles would be used to it. Behind him he could hear the dog splashing and paddling toward him. It was a red Chesapeake Bay retriever, the only American breed in the American Kennel Club, a rugged, tireless seventy-five-pound bird dog. Charles recognized the breed on sight, for any man who handled a rifle—and Charles had been a member of the gun team at the university—admired the beautiful water hunter of the vast Maryland bay. The Chessie had the steadiest of retriever personalities, sound of judgment, biddable but not silly, a stout worker bred to partner with man. He and Charles bonded instantly. There really was no way, once the dog bowed deep into its front paws to signal play, that the dog could be prevented from following him into the water. Or that Charles could resist the charms of the Chessie. He had grown up with dogs and longed to have one again.

The dog was paddling hard now, approaching fast. Charles could hear the splashing and knew without looking—an instinct all mammals share—that something was bearing close, and he reacted instinctively and dove to stay ahead of the dog: two species playing, communing across the waves. With a rush of coolness along his torso, the man swam, joining the blissful tumble of the deep, falling into the master stroke of the nineteenth century, which he was taught was the most natural form in the water, an imitation of the frog: the breaststroke. It was fashionable in Charles's time to celebrate the effortless, instinctive nature of being in the water, the first human home. It was said that the ocean flowed in the veins, that blood was nearly the consistency of seawater. In the ocean a man escaped the Industrial Revolution and rediscovered his eternal self, was fully human again. After a few strokes, as he adjusted to the water, Charles stretched into a crawl, the master stroke of the new century, recently popularized for its speed and power. The dog followed.

As man and dog swam out in a line, they joined the sweeping canvas the ocean offers the shore, the portrait of white-tipped sea that stirs feelings the Romantics believed only artists and poets could experience. The ocean swelled to meet them, waves lifted them up and rolled on toward the coast, where they broke on the sands and withdrew with a prolonged hiss. Charles closed his eyes as his face turned rhythmically into the sharp, cold brine, feeling the rush of coolness along his torso, eyes stung with saltwater as he stroked in measure with the cadence of the swells. The dog kicked with all four legs beneath the surface, a force that lifted its head above the waves and left its shaggy tail floating in a trail of froth. At the same time, unseen beneath the surface, other waves traversed the shallows and the deep, waves of differing lengths and speeds but all of the same flawless contour and pattern of the breakers—underwater waves shooting across the spectrum in multichannel cacophony.

Far out at sea, swimming steadily, the young shark received a faint signal. Currents were washing against the thin steel cable that rooted the diving platform of the Engleside Hotel to the bottom, causing it to vibrate and issue infinitesimal waves of sound from its anchorage one hundred feet from the beach. These waves exploded seven miles out to sea in less than eight seconds, moving at more than three thousand miles an hour, rhythmic, constant, reaching a sensitive line of nerves embedded in the head of the fish, the head that turned slowly side to side to improve the chances of favorable reception. The faint sound waves grew stronger, more regular, and the shark made a tiny adjustment in direction. The great fish swam directly into the wave of sound, which broke and scattered over its huge pyramidal head, as it began, ever so slightly, to move faster.

Emerging from the deep, in perhaps fifty feet of water, the shark sensed something different. Long, powerful, irregular noises began to batter its conical head, a wild mixed signal. A suprahuman detective, it cruised at fifteen miles an hour while instantly processing information across the spectrum. An image appeared in its brain, an electronic projection, a pulsing outline of two objects moving near the surface. The shark could detect microscopic urine particles in the water: *Mammals.* Each movement broadcast sounds and scent and an electronic trail, an aura of impulses.

Charles was the strongest swimmer in the water now, his arms and legs indicating one thing to the shark: *Large prey.* Then there was the dog. It is now known that a man who swims in shark-infested waters with a dog greatly enhances his odds of being attacked by a shark nearby, according to ichthyologist George Burgess, who directs the International Shark Attack File, a compilation of well-known shark attacks. "The irregular swimming actions of animals are extremely attractive to sharks. The front paws doggy-paddling, creating a maximum splash, the rear legs bicycle-pedaling, four rapidly moving legs making a blending motion at the surface couldn't be a whole lot more attractive." In 1987, off Panama City, Florida, a man jumped from his boat to go swimming. His girlfriend lowered his poodle into the water, and within moments a large bull shark removed much of the man's leg, killing him instantly. The Shark Attack File is filled with accounts of sharks drawn to human victims by the erratic thrashing of a paddling dog. That afternoon in 1916, sound waves from the seventy-five-pound dog drummed on the great fish's head with feral intensity, a jagged, broken signal of distress.

The shark swam nearer, preparing to launch its signature attack—sudden, surprising, relentless. Charles stroked smoothly and happily, unaware he was being profiled. The great white was closing in.

A small crowd on the beach watched as Vansant, a strong swimmer, stroked out beyond the breakers. They were as a group in that moment, standing on the edge of time in 1916, wise in ways moderns are not, educated in the classics and myths, more in touch with the sea. Sperm whales were the oil fields of their time, the ocean the highway. But these people lived before modern oceanography, before radio and television, and were no more prepared to witness the first man-eating shark in American history rise from the waves than to see Captain Nemo's *Nautilus* surface from the abyss. Who could blame them if they saw a "sea monster"?

There were other ghosts of antiquity the Edwardians saw along the beach that evening, visions that enchanted them in the pleasing form of a young man and dog at play in the simple theater of the sea. The virile young athlete was an Edwardian icon. Dorian Gray, *The Wind in the Willows, Peter Pan*, and the Boy Scouts revealed the cultural worship of Pan, who "is not dead," Robert Louis Stevenson declared. In reaction to industrialism and Victorian repression, the young man who never grows old led "the whole earth in choral harmony." Charles was eager to prove his vitality, and there was no finer place to do so than at the beach, his form and vigor on display in society as they were nowhere else. "The surf," according to beach historians Lena Lencek and Gideon Bosker, "emerged as an area in which the strong were separated from the weak, where young males played out the drama of natural selection before the eyes of discriminating females."

In the late afternoon of July the first, Charles was swimming the Atlantic to see how far he could go. Long-distance swimming was an adventure that enthralled the public. Charles did not slow his stroke when he and the Chesapeake retriever had passed all the swimmers in the water. This earned a small cheer from shore. Unknown to Charles, he had entered a wilderness, and his desire to set himself apart led him to violate a fundamental rule of nature: Stay with the group. A lone mammal, exposed and vulnerable, invites a predator. In a study of great white shark behavior by George Burgess and Matthew Callahan using data from the International Shark Attack File, no other humans were within ten feet of the victim in 85 percent of the attacks. As Charles was being feted and admired from the beach and boardwalk, he was being observed, as well, underwater.

Fifty feet away, in deeper water, the great white was mulling whether to attack. Far from our image of a mindless killer that overwhelms its victims, the great white takes no chances when challenging prey. Once a great white decides the odds favor it, the decision is beyond appeal, the attack relentless.

As the crowd on the beach studied the tableau of man and dog, suddenly, with no apparent reason, the retriever turned back toward shore. Witnesses thought the dog tired out, simply swam too far. Charles was the victor in the amusing play.

Charles turned around, too, treading water, and called out to the dog, enticing it to return. But the retriever, climbing onto the beach, shook itself off and remained on the sand, looking out at the man in the water. On the boardwalk and beach, people waited for a resolution to the drama. The Vansant girls saw Charles give up the game. He was coming in.

But as Charles swam toward shore, a bystander on the beach noticed something odd. A dark fin appeared in the water behind the young man. At first it was mistaken for a porpoise, a sight people were accustomed to then. But porpoises were known to roll in schools parallel to the coast; this fin was alone and moving swiftly toward shore in the direction of the young man. Someone on the beach cried across the waves, "Watch out!" As the fin approached, the chorus grew: "Watch out! Watch out!"

But Charles could not hear the warnings. He was turning his head in and out of the water in a rhythmic crawl. The great white could see his prey now moving underwater with startling clarity, making what followed even more unusual. For in the great majority of shark attacks on humans, sharks are hurtling through roiling, cloudy water in which they must strike quickly to seize their prey. The flash of a pale foot resembles the darting of a snapper, a belt buckle winks in the sun like a fish scale, and the shark bites. But the great white saw Charles Vansant clearly and kept coming. In the last instant, some researchers have suggested, it detected the final confirmation of mammal: the blood pounding through Charles's veins. *The thumping of his heart.*

In that moment, an awful feeling swept over Vansant as the continued cries, louder now, "Watch out!" rang from the beach. Seconds before the attack, a shiver traveled down his spine—humans are gifted, as are all large mammals, with the instinctive ability to detect that they are being hunted. As the creature's shadow merged with his on the bright, sandy floor of the sea, Charles experienced an adrenal explosion, the overpowering natural urge to live. He was in only three and a half feet of water, close to shore. Safety was at hand. But it was too late.

The great jaws rose from the water, a white protective membrane rolled over the eyes, fifty triangular teeth closed with more than six tons of pressure per square inch, and man and fish splashed in a spreading pool of blood. One bite. One massive, incapacitating bite tearing into the left leg below the knee. Charles screamed in mortal agony, a scream that resonated to the beach and tennis courts and veranda. The attack had taken less than a second, but now time began to slow down. His parents and sisters and the crowd of onlookers stood transfixed in horror and disbelief.

Charles still screamed, numb with terror, trying to free himself from the vise of fifty large serrated teeth, but he, too, had little idea what was happening to him. He went into shock, and even as shock subsided, despite the gruesome wound, he felt, incredibly, a minimum of pain. As strange as it seems, it is common for shark attack victims to experience "painless torture"—to greatly underestimate the severity of their wounds. Some experts suggest the first bite produces massive nerve damage or somehow numbs the victims of pain. One neuro-physiologist calls this phenomenon "non-opiate stress-induced analgesia." A body of anecdotal evidence compiled over many years suggests that under great stress, soldiers, athletes, and other people don't seem to "feel" pain—perhaps, experts say, because pain in the most life-threatening situations is not advantageous for the survival of the species.

People onshore had no frame of reference for what was happening. "The young man was bathing in only three and a half feet of water," remembered W. K. Barklie, a Philadelphia businessman on the beach that day. "We thought he was joking until we saw the blood redden the water."

Charles fought valiantly, but his struggle to free himself only tightened the shark's grip on his femoral artery: the great teeth ground down to the bone. Witnessing their son being devoured by a predator, Dr. and Mrs. Vansant were numb with shock and pain that would shadow them for the rest of their lives. But Louise, the middle sister, kept her wits about her as she witnessed a sight she would never forget: "Everyone was horrified to see my brother thrashing about in the water as if he were struggling with some monster under the surface," Louise recalled. "He fought desperately, and as we rushed toward him we could see great quantities of blood."

Then, as if a spell were broken, men entered the water to rescue the young man as shouts arose from the beach.

What followed baffled shark researchers for decades: The great white backed off in the red-tinged surf, pieces of Charles Vansant's calf and femoral artery in its mouth, and appeared to be waiting. Twenty years later, in the summer of 1936 in Buzzards Bay, Massachusetts, a great white provided a clue to the shark's behavior in Beach Haven in the summer of 1916. That summer, a fourteen-year-old boy swimming in shallow water was savagely bitten by a great white. As the boy screamed and floundered in a balloon of blood, the shark was observed "standing off in the blood-reddened water but a few yards away, seemingly ready to make another attack—and why it did not is inexplicable."

The reason is brutally simple, according to John E. McCosker, director of San Francisco's Steinhart Aquarium. The great white employs a classic predatory technique once practiced by the saber-toothed tiger. The extinct tiger hunted the woolly mammoth by biting it once and standing back. So, too, soldiers are trained to make an easy shot for the stomach instead of the trickier shot to heart or head. The sure, deadly shot echoes the primitive logic of the massive first bite and retreat. Avoid needless confrontation. Expend no more energy than necessary. Take no chances.

The great white was waiting for Vansant to bleed to death.

First to reach the surf line was Alexander Ott, an exceptional swimmer, who later became a champion and a swimming showman with Johnny Weismuller in the 1920s. His decision to enter bloodied water where a shark was taking its prey took extraordinary courage. Ott swam swiftly, but by the time he reached Vansant in waist-deep water, the fight was over. The young man was struggling not to drown in a cloud of his own blood. The shark had vanished. Quickly Ott hoisted Vansant under the arms and began to tow him to shore. It was then that Ott felt a powerful tug in the opposite direction, and realized with horror that the shark had hit Vansant again and fastened to his thigh. The shark and Ott were in a tug-of-war with Vansant's body. The shark appeared to Ott to be black, ten feet long, and five hundred pounds. It was unimaginably strong, he thought. He cried for help.

More men rushed into the water and formed a human chain with Ott, frantically trying to free Vansant from the jaws of the shark. Vansant was still conscious, struggling to escape, but the great teeth held fast; the creature was an eating machine of inconceivable power. The human chain had succeeded in pulling Charles nearly to the beach—but the great white followed, its massive conical body scraping the sands. The monster was *coming onto the beach*. Then, suddenly, it was gone, a whirl of foam trailing the dark fin as it submerged. "The shark held on until it scraped bottom," Barklie recalled, "then it let go and swam away." Profound shock had momentarily seized the people on the sands. They had no context for what had happened; there was no way for them to know that sharks, in other times and other lands, followed their human victims right up onto land. It was unthinkable, alien, awful confirmation of a Darwinian truth the Victorians had long denied: Nature was "red in tooth and claw." There was no way for them to know that the popular new sport of recreational swimming, fueled by expanding wealth, industry, and human population, had brought the nightmare of centuries of sailors to shore.

Charles lay crumpled on the beach, bleeding profusely. Men and women rushed to his side, some out of love, others out of morbid curiosity; still others, unable to look, turned away.

Louise Vansant, who had kept composure during the attack, almost fainted when she approached her brother. "The terrible story was revealed," she said. "His left leg had been nearly torn off."

Dr. Eugene Vansant flew down the boardwalk steps, onto the sand, and rushed to the fallen figure of his son. Ott and Barklie moved aside to make room, and Eugene kneeled on the beach and took Charles's hand. The young man was lying on his back, his left leg a bloodied mass, blood pouring from the wound and pooling with the soft, receding tide. His face was a ghastly white, and he moaned in pain, reeling toward unconsciousness. Eugene put his fingers to his son's wrist; the boy's pulse was weakening. His eyes signaled that he recognized his father. There was little time.

Dr. Vansant removed his jacket and vest, rolled up his sleeves, and ordered that no one touch the wound. Germ theory was one of the principal findings of Dr. Vansant's lifetime, and Vansant operated in sterile whites instead of a black business suit, as he had once done. But no modern supplies were available now. The doctor's mind raced as he was thrown back on his training in nineteenth-century medicine. He had never seen such a wound. What in the Lord's name had caused it? Was it suffused with animal poisons? It appeared like a wound of war, but it was a bite. He recalled the wisdom of his teachers—men who were legendary doctors from the Crimean War, the Civil War, and the Spanish-American War. His mentor, Dr. Samuel David Gross, wrote *The Manual of Military Surgery* in 1861 at the request of Lincoln and Ulysses S. Grant. It became the classic Union guide to amputations on the battlefield, using chloroform and a bone saw. Confederate doctors used it too, adding a sip of brandy to soften a man's will for the procedure. But now there was little available but brandy, and nothing could be done, Dr. Vansant realized, until the bleeding was stopped.

Alexander Ott, the heroic swimmer, tore strips of fabric from a woman's dress to use as a tourniquet, but the rush of blood barely slowed. Soon Dr. Herbert Willis, a future mayor of Beach Haven, joined Dr. Vansant at his son's side, along with Dr. Joseph Neff, former director of public health in Philadelphia. The three medical men inspected the wound and conferred. A fish bite of such magnitude was outside their experience. The bleeding was so profuse that the doctors feared Charles wouldn't survive an automobile ride to the nearest hospital in Toms River, thirty miles northwest.

Engle suggested they move the young man back to the hotel, where there was water, soap, and bandages. Dr. Vansant helped carry his son to the hotelier's office. There the men quickly unscrewed the hinges of Engle's office door and laid it across two desks as an operating table, a familiar sight to Dr. Vansant, for it resembled the legendary old wooden operating table in the Jefferson Hospital operating theater. But little else during the crisis was familiar, and it was soon evident that in the hour of his son's direst need, Dr. Vansant wasn't quite sure what to do. This pained him terribly, both as a father and as a physician, dredging up memories he would rather never have re-encountered. For many years, it was suspected by his peers in nineteenth-century medicine that Vansant wasn't properly trained to handle an emergency. The criticism may have been unfair, but it weighed heavily on him since his main critic was the legendary Dr. Gross, the venerable "father of American surgery."

Gross was immortalized in the most famous medical painting of the nineteenth century, Thomas Eakins's masterpiece *The Gross Clinic*, in which the renowned professor stands in black street clothes, raising a bloody scalpel to make a lecture point, having made an incision in a young man's leg without sterilization procedures, which were unknown. In the gloom of the operating theater—lit only by skylight— a black-cowled woman, apparently the boy's mother, covers her face in agony.

Vansant heard the grandiose white-haired professor's admonitions in his dreams. Gross had warned that to leave the ranks of legitimate practitioners for a narrow specialty was to forgo the proper education of a medical man, to risk inability to recognize general problems in the major organs and extremities of the body, to be helpless in a crisis. Gross once introduced the most distinguished laryngologist of the nineteenth century, Dr. Jacob da Silva Solis-Cohen, to a lecture hall as a man "who devotes most of his time to a cubic inch of the human anatomy," adding, "Someday I suppose we will have specialists confining themselves to diseases of the navel."

The sight of his son also recalled and magnified the feelings of doubt and helplessness Dr. Vansant had suffered upon the sickness and death of his other sons, Eugene Jr. and William. In Engle's office, Dr. Vansant assisted in cleaning and bandaging the wound, but the bleeding remained profuse. He discussed with the other doctor transporting Charles to a hospital by motorcar, but the wound was so severe, they agreed he would not reach the hospital in time. Half a century later,

Vansant's wound would have been considered relatively minor for a shark attack, medium-severity arterial damage, which "the victim usually survives if correct (modern) treatment is administered on the beach," according to South African doctors D. H. Davies and G. D. Campbell in *The Aetiology, Clinical Pathology and Treatment of Shark Attack.* But that evening, at 6:45, an hour after he entered the water for a swim, Charles Epting Vansant died of shock and massive hemorrhaging on Robert Engle's office door. Dr. Eugene LaRue Vansant looked on helplessly as his son died.

Within a year, grief would age him terribly, turn his hair completely white, and leave him a stooped and beaten man.

That evening a hush fell over the Engleside dining room. But after dinner, hotel guests cornered fishermen and baymen and other wizened veterans of the shore who drifted on and off of the veranda all night long. The red trails of pipes and cigars waved in the night, and the number of people who had witnessed the attack seemed to grow by the hour. Robert Engle tried to remain stoic and calm as reporters from Philadelphia newspapers scuttled about the lobby and veranda, questioning his guests. Disagreements and arguments broke out, until finally a consensus emerged of suspects in young Vansant's death: a giant tuna, a shark, but most likely a great sea turtle, which had the power, the fishermen said, to snap a man in half. The attending physician had a different opinion. He recorded the primary cause of death on Vansant's death certificate as "hemorrhage from femoral artery, left side," with the contributory cause being "bitten by a shark while bathing." It was the first time a shark bite had appeared as an official cause of death in U.S. history. Seeking to reassure his guests, Engle stood and declared bathers had nothing to worry about—the next morning, the hotel would erect a netting around the beach strong enough to block German U-boats. Swimming in the clear, paradisal waters of the Engleside would go on as usual.

But a somber mood pervaded the Engleside that evening as one by the one the hundreds of room lights that cast out over the shore winked out. A new and nameless fear had seized the guests, a fear of the unknown as well as a fear of the sea. Even those who watched the attack had little notion of what they had witnessed, except to agree, as W. K. Barklie told whoever would listen, "Mr. Vansant's death was the most horrible I ever saw."

from Cousteau's Great White Shark
by Jean-Michel Cousteau

Jean-Michel Cousteau (born 1938) began a career in marine exploration aboard his father Jacques's research ship Calypso. His 1988 search for the great white was part of an attempt to portray the animal honestly, without the sensationalism of some other films about the species.

I t is virtually impossible to find a great white shark in the obscurity and vastness of the sea. Arrangements must be made for the shark to find *you*.

We would prefer to slip unobtrusively into the white shark's milieu and watch the creature go about its business undistracted by our presence. The purity of such observations in the wild would be priceless. But the chances of encountering a great white shark through happenstance are incalculable.

We would have to attract great whites to *Alcyone* through some kind of baiting process. This would mean that the water space into which we drew whites would be polluted by a concentration of tastes and odors unlikely in the natural world. The behavior we studied might, therefore, be both abnormal in itself and further compromised by our presence, but there was no alternative. We would have to do as others have done in order to come eye-to-eye with a great white shark.

What others have done is to create the deception that their ship is a wounded whale. The artifice is twofold: by anchoring a vessel one presents an image that arriving sharks might mistake for a dead or dying whale along the surface; by pouring blood and other animal matter into the water one simulates bodily fluids leaking from the whale.

Before the decline of whaling, and the imposition of stringent marine-mammal protection laws, Australians who sought great whites used whale meat and oil to attract the sharks. There is evidence that white sharks in some parts of the world relish whale meat. In the north Atlantic, whites have been observed feeding on the floating carcasses of dead whales, and bite marks found on whales suggest they may even gouge meat from living animals. Many years ago, when whaling vessels routinely pulled into Durban, South Africa, anglers were able to catch great whites commonly from piers at the entrance to the harbor. Presumably, the whites were attracted to the remains cast off the whaling vessels, perhaps following the ships into the harbor. When whaling dwindled in the sixties, and eventually ended, the catches of great whites also declined.

We heard reports that some Australians who hope to film or capture whites still retain a clandestine supply of whale products, but we were bound by conscience to avoid such bait. To concoct a recipe likely to entice great whites we sought the help of a man who has attracted, and surely observed, more great white sharks than anyone in the world. During the past three decades, Australian Rodney Fox has led some thirty-five major expeditions to film or to study great white sharks off South Australia. Although he is not a trained scientist, Rodney has been a devoted diver and a keen observer of the undersea world since childhood. But his fascination with the great white shark comes not from any abstract whim. While diving nearly thirty years ago, Rodney was attacked by a white shark in such dramatic fashion that his survival was miraculous, and his story is forever fixed in the lore of the great white shark. Some would have forsworn diving in the aftermath, but Rodney's curiosity was fueled and he has spent most of his life trying to learn more about the creature that nearly killed him.

When I met Rodney I avoided asking him to relate the details of his attack. There would be plenty of time later to hear his story. I wanted to know if he would consider joining our expedition and I described our purpose. He is a soft-spoken man with a lively intelligence, and I saw his eyes light up with excitement.

Rodney told me he had begun to feel somewhat guilty about the menacing image of the great white. He had served as a guide and consultant during the filming of live-action scenes for the movie *Jaws.* He now considers it the worst job he ever took.

"I didn't know it would be a horror film," he told me. "Now I find that many people have given up diving and swimming after seeing the film. It was a fictional story, but people believed it. And it isn't only *Jaws.* All the film companies I've been involved with for the past twenty years have portrayed the great white smashing into cages and biting baits, emphasizing their most savage look. Nobody portrays them normally—just swimming beautifully through the water. The world has seen the nasty side of the great white and not the good side."

With Rodney's help, we would try to capture an honest portrait of an animal elevated to the role of demon in the public's mind.

We began our quest mid-April 1989, loading *Alcyone* under the cool breezes of the austral autumn in Port Adelaide. After filling our freezer and our below-deck pantry with food, stowing the crew's gear, and hauling aboard the new cylindrical LEXAN cage—built in Adelaide under Rodney Fox's supervision—we headed across Gulf St. Vincent and Spencer Gulf to Port Lincoln, a small fishing village that would serve as our staging area.

Here, an already crowded deck came to resemble a miniwarehouse. In addition to a Zodiac and an aluminum dinghy, electric scooters, Comsat satellite antenna, and assorted piles of diving, scientific, and deck gear, we had to find room for the two antishark cages and half a dozen shrimp boxes. Rented from the Port Lincoln fishing fleet, these four-foot-square containers would serve as bait boxes for Rodney's special shark-attracting *bouillabaisse.*

The arrival of a melange—more than a ton in all—of various kinds of chum marked a change in our life aboard *Alcyone* that would persist throughout the expedition. We would live with a noxious stench. We would not only imitate a dead whale, we would smell like one. To bring the bait aboard, we formed a chain of crewmen from the wharf down the gangplank to the deck, and as the chum was passed along the line, I watched faces turn sour, eyes roll, heads shake in disbelief. The mixture was formidable: the recipe consisted of fish heads, minced blue fin and skipjack tuna, as well as whole fishes and tuna oil, containers of both wet and dried blood, and raw horsemeat. Dried blood, we learned from Rodney, is commonly used as fertilizer and also as a foaming agent in firefighting chemicals. The horsemeat, obtained from a pet food company, peaked our curiosity. Why horsemeat? Rodney smiled. He had no idea why, but it was markedly superior to beef in attracting sharks.

The excitement of searching for great white sharks was quickly tempered by the repugnance of the gifts we would offer them. In the days to come we would endure sickening gusts of foul odor swirling about us in the breeze and would wince as blood streaked *Alcyone*'s white decks.

Our spirits were lifted, however, when several Port Lincoln fishermen sailed by to express support for our mission, and to welcome us to the area with presents of fresh tuna, not for the sharks but for our own consumption.

Before embarking, we welcomed aboard the final essential tool, a scientific mind capable of assessing shark behavior. Months earlier I had invited an old friend, Don Nelson, to accompany us on the shark search. Nelson is a professor of biology at California State University, Long Beach, where he researches the behavior, ecology, and sensory biology of sharks and rays. Whenever time permits, Nelson and his students study their subjects in the field, and his published papers appear in the most prestigious journals and books. Nelson is famous among his peers for a series of innovative studies of gray reef sharks, *Carcharhinus amblyrhynchos*, considered the boldest, most aggressive shark around the coral atolls of Polynesia and Micronesia. He and colleague Richard H. Johnson were the first to study in detail a type of threat display common to gray reef sharks in the moments before they launch an attack. When cornered, the sharks arch their backs, raise their snouts, and lower their pectoral fins. With aides, Nelson developed a one-person, fiberglass shark observation submersible, enabling his team to witness attacks at the closest possible range—from within a tiny submarine as it became the object of a gray shark's apparent anger. Years ago Nelson had shown me film taken from within the sub, which was attacked some ten times, sustaining minor damage from the sharks' lightninglike strikes.

Nelson's curiosity about white sharks stemmed from an incident several years ago in the Florida Keys when he came upon one unexpectedly during a dive. The great white immediately fled. Nelson suspects that most white shark attacks on people are not the result of aggressive behavior such as defending territory, but rather that they are merely investigative bites by a hungry animal.

Aboard *Alcyone*, Don could team up with Rodney to provide us with experienced eyes; they would be sensitive to shark behavior patterns our crew might not notice.

On the afternoon of April 19, we set out on a southeasterly course from Port Lincoln, arriving at dusk along the two tiny plots of land known as Dangerous Reef. As one of our staff members in the United States wrote when faxing *Alcyone*, the name sounded like a setting in a Hardy Boys adventure. Yet the name had nothing to do with great white sharks. It was bestowed by early sailors who saw in these low, rocky mounds a peril for ships during rough or foggy weather.

No one is quite certain why great whites can be found here. Rodney's years of searching have identified Dangerous Reef as the most likely site in South Australia to find them. He always begins here, then moves to other islands if none appear. He describes the reef as a calling place for the whites, and suspects that whether they are traveling northward to the shallower water of the gulfs, or southward toward deeper water, they tend to congregate at Dangerous Reef.

There is a more tangible explanation, and we could hear it as we approached the islands. A colony of Australian sea lions, *Neophoca cinerea*, lives on Dangerous Reef, one of the few havens left for the animals, which have been vastly reduced in number by human hunting. There may be only about 10,000 in existence. They are a handsome species with smooth, palomino coats. The conventional wisdom assumes that white sharks seek out Dangerous Reef to prey upon these sea lions and their pups when they enter the water.

We anchored along the lee side of the islands, where the water was only about eighty feet deep. One factor in the decision was safety. Should an accident occur during our diving—such as the snapping of a cage cable—the equipment and personnel would be within easy rescue, even if they dropped to the bottom.

Immediately Rodney began creating his plume of blood and tuna oil in the water off the stern. He also tossed a few lines out with a tuna head and a balloon tied to the end of each. The balloons act principally as warning devices. When they suddenly disappear from the surface, one can surmise that a shark has taken the bait. The bait trail would be maintained through the night and until it bore results. Peering down into the stained waters, I watched the arrival of hundreds of small silver fish, cousins of the Australian salmon known locally as tommy roughs. Perhaps when a white shark came along they would disperse, but until then the ocean ceiling was raining a feast of fish fragments, sending them into a ravenous swarm.

Captain Dourassoff posted a schedule of four-hour watches for the crew, tacking up alongside it the directions for mixing the chum, or burley, as Australians call it. To their regular routine of checking the anchored ship for leaks, fires, drifting off course, approaching vessels, and weather developments, the team would soon be accustomed to the tedium of steadily pouring a malodorous mixture into the sea.

My experience has been that the ocean is ever deceptive. Whatever one expects when setting out on an expedition will prove to be a misjudgment, as if there was a mind at work in the waters maliciously disappointing or confusing those of us along the surface. Rodney had told us it could take several days to attract whites and we arrived at Dangerous Reef prepared for a long wait. We were surprised almost immediately by their appearance and then, when hopes were high, by their disappearance.

Shortly after dawn on our first morning at the reef, Rodney's normally subdued voice boomed out "Shark! Shark!" Paul Martin rang the dinner bell—our prearranged signal to alert the crew to the presence of a shark—and every bunk on the ship emptied quickly. By the time we had all reached the stern, Rodney was pointing to a dun-colored, torpedolike shape in the water. The creature was moving slowly in a great circle, gliding beneath *Alcyone* and then surveying the chum-saturated waters at the stern. Rodney estimated the length at about eleven feet, but couldn't see if the shark had the telltale male sexual organs called claspers behind the anal fin, the only obvious marks of gender. The shark had my attention, of course, but I couldn't help noting that the little tommy roughs seemed unconcerned about its presence. They continued to lurch through the chum.

Then suddenly the white swept upward easily to engulf an entire three-foot-long tuna from a bait line, and the tommy roughs briefly parted along its path. For a moment the shark thrashed its head from side to side, pulling the fish free, and then quickly dived out of sight toward the bottom.

I turned to Louis Prezelin, who was holding his light meter up to the emerging sunshine. He shook his head. The light would not be sufficient yet for filming underwater. Antoine Rosset arrived with the surface camera, and Prezelin spent a few minutes trying to capture shots of the shark emerging from the gloom to lunge for bait. Our strategy was determined by Rodney, who suggested we allow arriving sharks to take a bait or two. In his experience, this immediate success and the lack of apparent danger encouraged sharks to hang around, sometimes all day. But to avoid wasting bait or satisfying the creatures, we would then try to pull away the bait lines just in advance of succeeding strikes, the marine equivalent of a carrot-and-stick routine.

This time, the strategy failed. By the time we had enough sunlight to descend in the cages to film, the shark was gone. Nevertheless, we had indeed seen our first great white shark, and a momentous decision faced us. As is customary aboard Cousteau vessels, animals under study receive nicknames. What should we call our first visitor? Someone jokingly suggested that we name the creature after our founder—as the employees of a corporation might—and our first great white shark was accordingly dubbed *JYC.*

By the time it was certain that *JYC* had vanished to wherever white sharks go, we had already proceeded with our preparations to film him. With the crew suited up and the cages ready to be lowered, we decided to make two test dives. We would check out the equipment, become accustomed to it, and hope that, perhaps intrigued by the activity, *JYC* might return to observe the commotion. He did not.

We returned to the surface and went through the hour-long process of cleaning and stowing the gear. Just as we finished, the dinner bell rang out. Rodney was pointing to another great white off the stern, estimating its length at thirteen feet. We raced about again, madly reassembling ourselves as underwater shark filmers, but the creature lingered only for a few minutes. By the time we were again prepared to dive, the second shark had followed the first into the endless haze of the undersea horizon. In light of the criterion used to name the first shark, the second was christened *Jean-Michel.* It is a rather odd feeling, knowing that somewhere in the sea there is a great white shark bearing your name. But the honor was soon forgotten. We never again saw either *JYC* or *Jean-Michel.*

Yet our spirits soared. In only twelve hours of chumming we had already attracted two sharks. This was easy stuff, after all. We turned again to the drudgery of chumming and scanning the horizon, waiting for the next great white to appear at any moment. In fact, the next one would not arrive for six days.

During our second night on Dangerous Reef, the wind rose and the seas kicked up. South Australia is at the mercy of storms propelled northward from the Antarctic, and weather forecasting can be a dicey business. We had elected to leave our cages in the water, but by morning on the second day we were forced to secure them to the deck. The immense strain exerted on the cage lines by *Alcyone*'s heaving could break a cable. We continued to chum, but Rodney was not optimistic. He believes great whites dislike storm-swollen surface waters as much as humans do, and that when the water is choppy they retreat to the more tranquil waters near the bottom.

The next few days wore on, gray and windy and surging with heavy swells. Out of frustration, the crew turned to those maintenance tasks set aside for spare time at sea. Australian Capkin Van Alphen, our newest diver and deckhand, patrolled the ship with the sanding and painting tools of rust prevention. At six-feet-five inches tall and twenty-two years of age, he was the biggest, strongest, and youngest aboard. A diver since the age of ten, he roamed *Alcyone* with the bounding enthusiasm of a giant child playing on an immense new Christmas toy. Our only problem with Capkin was that his restless muscles and herculean frame burned fuel at a high rate. His resultant appetite was as outsized as his personality, forcing Bruno Gicquel to prepare fifteen meals for a crew of twelve.

Wandering the ship, I watched each man tending to his special responsibilities. Chief diver Steve Arrington spent hours sorting through the medical supplies aboard, noting which drugs or bandages were old or in short supply. Aboard *Calypso* there is room for a doctor, but on *Alcyone* we rely on a crewman with extensive first-aid knowledge. With fourteen years as a bomb-disposal frogman in the U.S. Navy, and years of experience supervising a recompression chamber, Arrington meets our qualifications. In his California home there is a Naval Commendation Medal bestowed for saving five lives during his service career.

To our engineers, Paul Martin and Joe Cramer, *Alcyone* is a floating machine shop, and they busied themselves tuning the generator engines and the outboard motors. Cramer, like most of us, retires to his quarters during off hours to read or write letters home, but Martin leans across the stern life raft for hours at a time with a rod and reel, helping to supplement our food supply with fresh fish. I've eaten meals caught by Paul from Gibraltar to the Amazon.

The absence of sharks has little bearing on the continual work of the captain and the navigator, Dourassoff and Stern. The log must be kept, the weather reports monitored, the duties assigned. There are slow times, however, during which they inventory the charts or supervise the restowing of the line locker, where mooring lines and fenders are kept.

Yet we were not in the South Seas for ship's maintenance. We were here to study sharks. After two more days of waiting at Dangerous Reef, we decided to try other locations, and followed Rodney's directions north to islands in the Sir Joseph Banks Group, to no avail, then south to the Neptune Islands. Anchoring off South Neptune at dinner time, we again created an "odor corridor" of chum off the stern, then gathered for one of Gicquel's four-star meals.

I sensed boredom as I looked around the table in the *carré*, so I asked Rodney to regale us with the story of his near-fatal white shark attack. For an hour we sat in rapt attention, enthralled not only by the story but by Rodney's fluid way of telling it.

In 1963, Rodney was a newly married twenty-two-year-old, making a living as an insurance salesman but consumed by his passion for diving and for spearfishing. He was the reigning male spearfishing champion in Australia, and the favorite to win the South Australian Championship, which was held December 8 at Aldinga Bay, about thirty miles south of Adelaide.

Four hours into the event, Rodney was free-diving about a thousand yards offshore. Some forty other spearfisherman were hunting, and since a great many fish had been taken there was blood in the water. No one had speared as many fish as Rodney and he appeared likely to win. Seeing a dusky morwong—a large, perchlike bottom fish— Rodney approached for the kill that would ensure victory. With his left arm raised for stability, he aimed the gun to fire.

"All of a sudden," Rodney told us, "a huge thump hit me in the chest. It knocked the gun out of my hand and the mask off my face, and I was just hurled through the water at great speed. That was my greatest impression at first, that I was traveling faster through the water than I ever had. I quickly realized that it must have been a shark, and that the shark was holding me as a dog holds a bone, so I gouged around its head, knowing that its eyes would be the only vulnerable spot. As I tried to poke its eyes, it suddenly pulled back. I thrust my right hand at its face to ward it off, and my hand disappeared over its teeth, ripping my hand so badly that it would eventually be closed by ninety-seven stitches.

"Quickly, I pulled my hand out before it could be chewed off, and I thought: I'll grab it in a bear hug. So I put both arms around it—away from its head so that it couldn't bite me. But I was snorkeling, and I simply ran out of air. I knew that I would drown any second, so I pushed off from the shark and kicked myself upward to the surface with all my strength. I took two or three very big gulps of air, and then I looked down."

Rodney paused, looking about the faces at the table, shaking his head. "What I saw was the nightmare we all worry about, and I cannot ever forget it. There below me the water was all blood red, and a huge head with its mouth open was coming up to eat me. That was the terrifying moment of the experience.

"I kicked at the shark as hard as I could, and the shark spun around. Instead of biting me again, it swallowed a nylon buoy that I was towing behind me with one fish on it. As the shark continued its circle, it came to the end of the buoy cord, which was attached to my belt, and suddenly I was being towed downward through the water. The shark went faster and faster, and I was swirling uncontrollably behind him. I tried to grab my quick-release belt to free myself, but the release had slipped around to my back, out of reach. Again I was about to drown, or to die from the wounds, and I had given up, when all of a sudden the buoy cord snapped. Apparently, when the shark had first bitten me, he had cut halfway through the cord. Now, under great pressure, the line broke and I was free. I managed to drift up to the surface, and when I emerged I yelled out, 'Shark! Shark!' as hard and as loud as I could."

Miraculously, a rescue boat had spotted the clouds of blood and was heading in Rodney's direction to investigate at the moment he surfaced. He was quickly pulled in, with blood pouring from his wetsuit, and rushed to shore. There, while a stranger held his intestines in place, he was transferred to a car, which was soon met by an ambulance, and he was admitted to a hospital for emergency surgery within an hour of the attack. The teeth of the white shark had left gaping holes in Rodney's torso, revealing his stomach, lungs, and ribs, many of which were cracked. The circle of punctures extended up his left arm, which was open to the bone. The wounds required 462 stitches, but Rodney survived. In fact, he and a partner won the team spearfishing championship only a year later, and soon Rodney was making his living as an abalone diver in waters known to harbor great white sharks.

"I don't feel any malice toward the white shark," Rodney said. "I'm not very happy with the one that bit me, but I don't believe they're man-eaters. I think they cause problems by biting people now and again by mistake, but it's no reason to kill them off."

"But why would you care?" I asked. "After all, a white shark nearly killed you."

"I think they're beautiful animals," he said, "and I believe we must try to understand them better. I feel sorry for them. I don't think we should kill off a species just because we fear them."

Throughout Australia, where beaches are a way of life and sharks are a pervasive worry, Rodney's attack dominated the news and he was an instant celebrity. People stopped him on the street, eager to see his scars.

"The media still ring me up at the beginning of each summer here, and they say: 'We've heard that the gulfs are full of sharks this year. Would you like to make a comment?' And if I tell them the truth, that white sharks seem to be declining, they don't report it. If I say: 'Oh, there could be a few more this year,' then the story escalates into a major front-page warning."

So concerned are Australians with the threat of sharks roaming their beaches that the country instituted an unprecedented protection program more than fifty years ago. Prior to 1937, Australia had the highest incidence of shark attacks in the world. To calm public fears, the New South Wales government devised a system of shark netting—also called meshing—that was set up at intervals along the beaches of Sydney, Newcastle, and Wollongong, where most of the attacks had taken place. Held to the bottom by lead weights, the nylon gill nets are about 500 feet long and 20 feet deep. They are set parallel to beaches about a thousand feet offshore, sometimes farther. Though there are many gaps between the nets, and the lowering of the nets is done periodically, the system has proved remarkably effective. In the twenty-one years prior to meshing, there were twenty-seven shark attacks along New South Wales beaches. In the fifty years since, there have been two. This record of success prompted the introduction of similar meshing programs in Durban, South Africa, in 1952 and in Queensland, Australia, in 1962. To date, no other beaches in the world are similarly protected by extensive netting.

Yet there are problems with the system. Some researchers believe that the nets succeed by depleting the shark populations in the region to near extinction. And the captured sharks, most of which are dead, are not treated as a resource but are casually dumped at sea, eliminating the possibility for scientific studies. The greatest problem may be that the nets are not discriminatory; other harmless animals are trapped and killed in them. Since 1962 in Queensland alone nets have caught 468 dugongs, 2,654 turtles, 317 dolphins, and two whales.

Relatively few great white sharks end up in the nets. Between 1949 and 1990, only about eleven have shown up in the nets each year, and nearly all were immature. In fact, catches of great whites have steadily declined since the introduction of meshing. No one can say whether this is a result of the net captures or other factors, but it is disconcerting to those who, like Rodney, believe that the whites are disappearing.

These records increase our doubts about the reputation of great whites. Throughout the world, whites are blamed for more attacks on humans than any other species. Yet often no clear identification of the attacking sharks has been made. Further, most attacks occur in tropical waters where great whites are rarely sighted. Many of these incidents may actually involve bull and tiger sharks, which are common in the tropics and are known to have attacked people and boats.

Moreover, great white attacks on humans are rarely fatal. Along the coast of California and Oregon, some 33 white shark attacks on humans have been recorded in the past 53 years. Of these, only four proved fatal, and in each case the victim was not eaten but died from loss of blood after being pulled from the water. The most likely explanation is that white sharks bite humans by mistake and withdraw, or bite simply to inflict a major wound and then back off to wait while the victim grows weak. Many researchers believe that such a strategy could enable whites to disable large prey such as sea lions without risk. A struggling pinniped could bite and harm a shark during a sustained battle, but a wounded sea lion would likely be incapacitated by the loss of blood after a period of time, making it easier to consume.

By the morning of April 26, the storm had abated and our spirits rose. There were no sharks at the bait lines, but the sea was relatively flat off South Neptune Island, and we decided to break the monotony with another test dive in the cages. Dourassoff supervised the preparation of the cages, Van Alphen the diving gear. Just when all was ready, we heard Thierry Stern shouting and pointing at one of the bait lines. It was severed and drifting on the surface with neither bait or balloon. Then came the cry we had awaited for days. "Shark!" yelled Stern, pointing to a dark shape passing beneath our aluminum dinghy. Rosset passed our new 35mm underwater camera to Prezelin, who leaped into a cage. Our plan was to send a lookout diver with the cameraman at all times. Armed with a plastic billyclub, the lookout would provide another set of eyes while the cameraman was busy filming. For this first shark dive, Arrington would act as lookout, and when he climbed in, the cage was quickly lowered.

From above, we were able to identify the shark as a young male about ten feet long. He seemed cautious, swimming in wide circles, probably perplexed by the arrival in his world of a square-shaped object emitting clouds of bubbles. Eventually, he approached the stern again and with slow but powerful tail strokes slid upward to gulp a two-foot tuna in a single bite.

Below, Prezelin and Arrington had a different impression. Though young, the white seemed enormous. Rodney had warned us that divers are always unprepared for the size of a white shark. Older sharks, especially, seem extraordinarily wide. It is believed that their growth pattern changes at some point, that they may not continue to grow longer but increase in girth, so that an older shark has a tremendous chest.

As the minutes passed and the shark maintained his distance from the cage, Prezelin gave three tugs on a rope that acted as a messenger line to the surface. The cage was lowered fifteen feet farther. Seemingly more confident, the white now came closer to investigate the strange apparatus hanging before him. He headed toward the observation gap in the cage, where Prezelin held his camera, then suddenly veered upward and tried to bite one of the two metal floats fastened to the top of the cage. The strike was neither rapid nor ferocious, and the white quickly turned away. Yet his curiosity seemed piqued. For several minutes he swam back and forth directly over and within inches of the cage.

Now Prezelin, eager to capture a close shot of one of these sorties, poked his head, arms, and camera through the cage port. From the beginning of our expedition planning, we had wondered about the possibility of a small shark managing to slip into the cage through this space. Rodney had assured us that he had seen no white sharks that small in these waters. But now Prezelin encountered an unanticipated problem. Suddenly the shark glided downward on a direct line toward his head. Arrington grabbed the cameraman in warning, and Prezelin began to draw back into the cage. Ever the professional filmmaker, Prezelin wore his underwater light meter like a necklace around his neck, and as he lurched back to safety, the light meter caught on the metal bars of the cage. As the shark passed, Prezelin's head was left protruding into the water like bait. The shark passed without apparent interest.

On the deck above, Don Nelson tossed a special bait line into the water. He had encased within the body cavity of a tuna a transmitter that puts out 40 kilohertz pulses, producing a characteristic pinging sound. Using an underwater telemetry receiver, the pulses can be picked up as far as a mile away. Similar experiments with other species of sharks have shown that the animals are not hurt by the device and eventually regurgitate it. If Nelson could encourage the white shark to swallow the transmitter-laden tuna, we could attempt to track the shark and gather clues about its daily movements and habits.

Rodney poured a cloud of blood into the water near the special bait and, after several passes, the shark took the tuna, triggering a volley of cheers from the team on deck.

With such a cooperative subject on hand, Nelson rushed to assemble another experiment. He had recorded artificial sounds resembling the erratic and intermittent noise produced by a struggling fish or one that is enveloped in a feeding frenzy. By playing the tape through an underwater speaker, he had successfully attracted species of reef sharks, as well as a mako shark, a close relative of whites. Yet the experiment had never been attempted before with great whites.

Unfortunately, the watery environment at our stern, crowded with equipment and flushed with blood, afforded a poor test area. The shark seemed uninterested in the speaker, passing stolidly at a distance without investigating. Nelson was not surprised, since the variety of demands on the animal's sensory system—smells, tastes, new sights, new sounds—probably represented a confusing circus of stimuli. Yet an odd thing occurred. Some twenty minutes after Nelson had given up and turned his tape machine off, the shark approached the stilled speaker and nudged it. Coincidence, or a latent curiosity about sounds heard from the speaker earlier? "Who knows," said Nelson.

For nearly two hours the shark remained near our stern, giving us ample time to consider a name for him. Since it was a male, I was moved to christen him *Philippe*, after my late brother. Philippe Cousteau grew up fascinated by sharks, and deeply appreciated their grace and beauty in the sea. His love for the animals was evident in the underwater footage he captured of them, and in the eloquence of his 1970 book *The Shark*. Were he alive today Philippe would be holding the camera in the cage below us, thrilled by his proximity to the greatest of all sharks.

As the late afternoon light waned *Philippe* could be seen turning from *Alcyone*, heading away. Nelson and I carried telemetry equipment into the dinghy and gave chase. While I steered the boat, Nelson donned head-phones and lowered a pole-mounted hydrophone into the water. By swinging it from side to side, he could detect the peak intensity of the transmitter's pings, and when he pointed in a direction, I set out slowly in pursuit. For several hours, as darkness settled around us, we were able to track *Philippe*. Eventually the pulses grew weak and we lost him. It is pos-sible, Nelson thought, that with larger sharks such as whites we would have to attach transmitters to the exterior of the body, since the ingested transmitter seemed to relay an insufficiently strong signal.

Again buoyed by a shark encounter, we set about chumming the next morning with high expectations. The skies were clear, the sea was glassy, the chum was redolent. And nothing happened. There was no sign of a white shark all day, nor the next day. When a third sharkless day passed, we returned to Port Lincoln for provisions, spent a night docked at the fishing wharf, and returned to the Neptunes. In three days our bait attracted nothing but tommy roughs, so we sailed to Dan-gerous Reef, anchored, reestablished an odor corridor for three days, and still no shark arrived.

By May 14, nearly a month after the mission had begun, we called a temporary halt and returned to Port Lincoln again. We had seen only three white sharks and had filmed only one underwater. The mood aboard was glum. I decided we would take a break, look for some other filming opportunities, and return for one last chumming session.

The next day we sought out a man named Howard Tidswell, who makes his living as a professional abalone diver. Our interest was not so much in his work, or in abalones, but in a device he uses while diving. We had heard, and Tidswell confirmed, that many abalone divers in South Australia go to extreme means to protect themselves from white sharks. Accompanying Tidswell for a day, we filmed him as he descended to the sea floor in an ingenious device—a small, one-man mobile shark cage. Fitted with buoyancy tanks and hydraulic power, the cage acts as a kind of open submarine and work station. A breathing rig to the surface gives Tidswell unrestricted bottom time, and a hot water hose attached to his wetsuit as an umbilical keeps his body warm, extending his time in the cold water. The price of the mobile cage—about $12,000—would make the device a luxury item if it were designed merely for convenience. As Tidswell attested, its purpose is to prevent his demise in the jaws of a white shark.

Such cages began to appear following a fatal white-shark attack on a South Australian abalone diver in 1974. Just off Cape Catastrophe, only fifteen miles southeast of Port Lincoln, diver Terry Manuel was struck by a white shark with such force that he was lifted from the water. The shark took off one of Manuel's legs, and the diver died before a partner could get him to shore.

Many of the sixty commercial abalone divers in the area quit the business after the attack; others began toying with ideas for a protective gadget. That soon led to the mobile cage. It is not clear how many divers use the cages today. Tidswell claims that all but a few depend on them, but others told us that most divers now descend without them, realizing the enormous odds against a white shark attack.

Rodney Fox related his own experience. While making a living as an abalone diver for eighteen years, Rodney logged more than 6,000 hours in the water. During that time he saw only two great whites, neither of which approached him. Rodney's conclusion was that whites are interested in neither abalone nor divers.

For two days, we remained in the Port Lincoln area, while the camera team made filming excursions into Port Lincoln channel. Our goal was to capture underwater footage of Australian sea lions without the hindrance of antishark cages, and we came upon a tiny island where sea lions and their pups bask. Since Fisheries personnel had never noted the presence of whites here, we made conventional dives, and, in fact, saw no sharks at all.

But the sea lions were a rare treat. Most sea lions we have encountered throughout the world are a curious, frolicking lot, but these creatures seemed extraordinarily playful. They cavorted alongside our Zodiac, then gyrated about the divers underwater. When Prezelin, Stern, and Rosset returned to the surface, they described the rendezvous as a "wild party."

On another dive, we came across a lovely creature that, despite weighing only about three ounces, may be as lethal as the great white shark. The blue-ringed octopus injects venom during its bite that has resulted in death to human victims within minutes. The creature's toxin is more potent than that of any land animal, yet the bite is almost painless and can go unnoticed until a victim succumbs, usually within an hour. Toxin researchers believe that many incidents of human death from blue-ringed octopus bites may go undetected, even by coroners, since the autopsy features are nonspecific and the bite fades after death.

As a precaution, we outfitted Thierry Stern with a thick glove impenetrable to such a bite, and he gathered a blue-ringed octopus in his hand as Prezelin filmed. Despite his careful maneuvers around the creature, Stern endured a moment of agony. Something about his face plate aroused the octopus's curiosity, and the creature jetted to the oval glass, where it settled for several minutes. Apparently disappointed, the octopus swam off without bothering the hapless Stern.

Van Alphen and American still-photographer and cameraman Chuck Davis, who would join *Alcyone* several times on our great-white-shark missions, followed Prezelin and Stern into the water. Armed with macrophotography gear, Davis was shooting closeup stills of the octopus when the creature suddenly disappeared in a green flash. Startled, Davis looked about the reef and spotted a green parrot fish yards away with blue-ringed tentacles dangling from its mouth. Davis surfaced to tell Prezelin, who was reloading the cine camera, that he needn't bother with new film. His subject had been eaten.

With only a few days left in which to film sharks, we sailed to English Island, not far from Port Lincoln, and optimistically set to chumming again. Three weeks had passed since our last encounter with a white. Our goal now was to meet up with at least one more so that we could lower our see-through plastic cage and test the shark's reactions to an apparently unprotected diver in the water.

On the afternoon of May 20, we got our wish. The arrival was a female, about eleven feet long, and she appeared eager to be a star, circling close to the stern, taking our bait and coming back for more. While the film team raced to suit up and descend, I joined Martin and Dourassoff, who were pulling in the bait lines just in advance of the shark's strikes. Excited by the opportunity after such a long wait, we were soon shouting and laughing.

Again, I found myself surprised by the shark's manner. Not ferocious, not wildly and mindlessly violent as stories have led us all to expect. Nothing like that, really. Describing my feelings to Dourassoff, I was tempted to use the word gentle, but that was not accurate either. I settled on wary, which seemed to best capture the slow, deliberate, smooth approach of the creature. There was no mistaking its potential for destruction, of course. When its huge maw opened to consume a fish, the rippling muscles in its throat bunched up like white inner tubes. The snout seemed to rise, while the jaws jutted forward to bite— a mechanism science calls jaw articulation. The mouth that maintained a strange, grinlike image when swimming suddenly turned into a protruding pincer, outfitted with upper and lower teeth that fit together in the bite like shears.

It was frightening in the moment of the bite, but before and after, this feared creature seemed no more terrible than any other. I recalled a line written by film writer Bud Weiser years before in describing another animal. "It is just another creature," Weiser wrote, "neither good nor evil, just trying to survive."

When the steel cages were in the water, the plastic cage was lowered. We had constructed the cylinder for maximum strength: it was made from a single sheet of 3/16-inch LEXAN plastic, curled into a four-foot-diameter tube and bolted together, with LEXAN tubes supporting both ends. Two metal pontoons in a metal frame at the top made the cylinder buoyant. In the event the cylinder should be severed from its line, the diver within could blow air into the pontoons using his Scuba, so that it would rise. We had considered several designs, arriving at what seemed the most practical and durable. Yet we had no idea what to expect. The plastic could stop a .38-calibre bullet, but could it stop a two-ton great white shark?

Among those who helped in the design was chief diver Arrington. When the cylinder arrived aboard *Alcyone* at Port Adelaide, I had asked him if he felt the novel cage was safe enough. He believed it was, unless a shark managed to drive it against the hull of the ship and crush it.

"But yes," he said. "I believe it's safe enough."

"Good," I said, "because you're the one going in it."

Now, as he prepared to enter the cylinder, I caught Arrington's eye. He smiled, shaking his head as if to say, "What a way to make a living."

Bruno Gicquel had climbed to the top of a Turbosail, from which vantage point he could keep track of the shark and give Arrington a signal to enter the water. When the shark turned away from the ship, Gicquel shouted and Arrington leaped into the water. We watched him swim quickly to the top of the plastic cage, open its double hatch doors, and squeeze in.

The shark paid little notice to Arrington in the cage at first. On her next approach, she headed for one of the metal cages and made what seemed another test bite. Then, abruptly, she veered toward the bottom of the plastic cylinder and struck a glancing blow off the bottom tube supports.

Within the cylinder, Arrington found himself engaged in a different kind of experiment—a psychological one.

"Underwater," he would tell us later, "the single sheet of plastic between you and the shark disappears to your eye. It's like looking through a face plate. Your rational mind is aware that there is a protective wall, but you don't sense it visually, and your subconscious mind is not at all convinced. When the shark first nudged the bottom, I could see the plastic tubes bend somewhat and her snout enter the cage. Instinctively, I jerked my feet up. She was unable to break through and gobble me up but every motor response in my body seemed to believe otherwise."

On the stern above, we continued to work the bait lines, tossing and retrieving them to keep the white intrigued. While we were concerned about the safety of the men below, an incident occurred on the rear deck that briefly called into question our casual assumption that the only danger was below.

Captain Dourassoff jerked a bait line back to the starboard swim-step, which he shared with Martin, who was manning the crane. Neither was aware that the shark was chasing the bait fish at the moment, and when the fish landed on the deck, a huge shark head rocketed from the water in pursuit, mouth agape. The shark's teeth crunched into the swimstep only inches from Martin's feet, leaving quarter-inch scrapes in the metal deck as the creature slid backward into the water.

Paul Martin is a veteran seaman, calm of temperament. He rarely moves with the speed of a leaping gazelle. This time he did.

The shark remained along *Alcyone*'s flanks for three hours, during which the divers stayed below, chilled to the bone in the cold southern waters. Through the entire time, the shark displayed little interest in Arrington and his invisible cage. Eventually, Arrington tried to attract her attention by waving his arms and pounding on the cylinder walls. She remained far more interested in the dangling bait fish and the metal floats on the conventional cages.

When at last she swam off, and the cages were hauled aboard, the mood was celebratory. Prezelin was uncharacteristically effusive in describing the footage he had captured. Davis was thrilled by his opportunities to take dramatic still photos. And Arrington, while slightly disappointed that the shark found him less interesting than fish heads, was noticeably happy to be all in one piece.

Over a dinner that evolved rapidly into a festive party, we toasted our final shark, naming her after the person who for so long kept Cousteau crews dedicated and involved, my late mother, Simone.

While in many ways the expedition had been frustrating, it had fueled our curiosity and concern for great white sharks. We had seen only four individuals in more than a month: Did this imply they are a disappearing population? We decided over champagne that we must come back to these waters equipped for an unprecedented examination of the white shark's behavior, its numbers, and its plight. We would continue to film, but we would greatly expand our research effort to acquire scientifically reliable data on these creatures.

That night, sitting alone at the chart table on the bridge as we raced toward Port Lincoln to elude an arriving storm, I reflected on our first encounters with the most feared animal on earth. I recalled Rodney's remark, that he "felt sorry for them." Such a sentiment seemed odd as we were embarking on the mission, before we had seen the white shark for ourselves, before we had watched the creature's tentative behavior in approaching *Alcyone*, before we had marvelled at its living elegance as it swam only inches from our cameras. Now, we felt somehow involved with it. It was no longer the abstract monster of legend, but a hungry animal somewhat confused and ambivalent in our presence, searching its realm for the means to survive. The possibility that it might be vanishing from the sea worried us enormously. We had come to see *Carcharodon carcharias* as just another animal, as worthy as any of our understanding, respect, and protection. We were not surprised so much by its size or its might as by its seeming caution in the midst of human beings, and by the unanticipated empathy aroused in us.

from The Coast of Coral
by Arthur C. Clarke

His studies of astronautics led Arthur C. Clarke (born 1917) to an interest in oceanic exploration. He began diving in the early 1950s. The Coast of Coral *describes an eighteen-month expedition he and partner Mike Wilson took to the Great Barrier Reef beginning in 1954.*

It was on a partly overcast day, with the sun breaking through at intervals, that Mike and I made our first dive off Heron Island. We piled our equipment into the Research Station's dinghy, and rowed out across the reef flat until we had got clear of the dead, sandy bottom and were over live coral in about fifteen feet of water. The spot we had chosen was on the lee side of the island, well sheltered from the prevailing wind, and as far as we could judge through our waterscopes—glass-bottomed cans which gave a clear though narrow view through the surface—visibility was quite good.

We put on our face masks and flippers, adjusted our weight belts, blew the sand out of our snorkles, and dropped quietly over the side. Below us was a bewildering profusion of weird shapes; it almost seemed as if we were hanging above a forest of fantastic trees or giant fungi. By comparison, the corals we had seen while fossicking along the exposed reef were no more than withered, stunted shrubs.

The commonest variety was the branching staghorns, whose spikes formed an impenetrable thicket within which countless tiny fish would retreat for safety if we came too close. The larger staghorns resembled the giant cacti of the Arizona and New Mexico deserts, and it was hard to realize that they were animals, not plants. Or, to be accurate, the skeletons of animals, for a piece of coral is almost all dead limestone, covered with a thin and still-growing film of living polyps.

Less common, but equally unmistakable, were the convoluted domes of brain coral, forming massive boulders sometimes a yard or more across the base. The labyrinth of ridges and furrows covering them forms such an uncanny resemblance to the human brain that no other name is possible. Often, as I was swimming among them, I was irresistibly reminded of the "giant brains" imagined by Wells, Stapledon, and other science-fiction writers.

At rarer intervals there were wide, flat plates of coral, often growing one upon the other, and providing shelter for large fish which we could see lurking in their shade. Some of these corals were quite delicate, veined with intricate traceries like those which spring from the tops of the columns supporting the roof of an ancient cathedral. There were, however, none of the frail vertical fans common in the Caribbean and off the Florida coast. Probably the movement of the water was too violent here for such fragile structures to survive.

As a garden on land has its butterflies, so these coral groves had their legions of gorgeously colored fish. They were cautious, but not shy. We could get so close to them that it sometimes seemed easy to reach out and catch a handful. If we tried this, however, they would effortlessly elude our grasp.

The larger the fish, the more nervous they were—and with good reason. Neither Mike nor I approved of the indiscriminate piscicide which has wiped out the underwater populations in some areas of the world, but, when we were in Brisbane, Lyle Davis had given us the most powerful spear gun he manufactured and we were very anxious to try it out. Apart from indulging in what is one of the few sports where hunter and hunted meet on equal terms, we had good moral justification for what we were doing. Our unannounced arrival on the island had caused a slight food crisis in the Hasting household, and a few fish for dinner would be very welcome.

With his first three shots, Mike speared three fish totaling just over fifty pounds. We decided that was quite enough for one day, and heaved fish and gun into the dinghy while we started on the serious business of photography.

For the next few days, when tide and weather conditions allowed, we returned to the same spot so that we could test our cameras in familiar territory. We met no very large fish—above all, no sharks—but we did not expect to do so, for we were inside the boundary of the reef and in comparatively shallow water. When we were quite sure that we had a reasonably good chance of photographing anything that came along, we prepared to make our first dive over the edge of the reef. Mike had made one preliminary reconnaissance, under bad conditions, some days before. The water was still dirty after a recent storm; he had dived off the dinghy, just to have a look around, and had climbed hastily back into the boat with a very thoughtful expression.

"It's weird down there," he admitted, "and there's some big stuff moving around. It won't be safe until the water's clearer—you can't see what's coming at you now."

I was content to take his word for it; there was no point in running unnecessary risks by diving in water which was too dirty for photography—and photographs were, after all, the main object of our expedition.

It was about an hour after noon, and on a falling tide, that we rowed out to the reef and tried our luck for the second time. I slipped quietly overboard, with the Leica strapped round my neck, and found myself drifting twenty feet above a dense thicket of staghorn coral. The anchor of our boat lay supported in the topmost branches of the petrified forest, with a few small fish playing around its stock.

Visibility was excellent; when, a few seconds later, Mike followed me into the water we could see each other clearly when we were sixty feet apart. The sun, though it had passed its noonday peak, was still powerful enough to throw patches of dappled light on the coral beneath us.

There were some very large fish moving sedately over the sea bottom, but never venturing far from the shelter of some cave or cranny into which they could retreat if danger threatened. Keeping one eye on Mike, who was prowling around with his spear gun at the ready, I made several dives to the bottom to take close-ups of interesting coral formations. After a while I decided that there was a better way of reaching my goal than swimming, which used up a lot of energy and air. The anchor line provided a convenient stairway into the depths, so I flushed out my lungs, then filled them to bursting, and pulled myself hand over hand down to the sea bed.

When I arrived at the bottom most of my reserve of air was still intact; I twined my legs around the anchor and relaxed in the water to survey the situation in comfort. I hoped that if I remained motionless for long enough, some of the larger fish would let their curiosity overcome their natural caution.

Nothing whatsoever happened for almost a minute, and I was just about to head back to the surface when the utterly unmistakable shape I had been hoping to see slipped into my field of vision. Thirty feet away a small shark, with a startlingly white tip on his forward dorsal fin, was sailing smoothly above the coral undergrowth. It was no more than five feet long—just about the right size for an introduction to the species. As soon as I had refilled my lungs, I began to stalk it with the camera, and had no difficulty in securing a couple of shots as it passed over sandy bottom and was silhouetted against the dazzling white of pulverized coral.

Then I surfaced and yelled to Mike, who was in the water some distance away. I tried to indicate with my arms the direction the shark was taking, and Mike set off towards it as if jet-propelled. When I again ducked my head under the surface, I had lost sight of the beast, and regretted my missed photographic opportunities. Almost at once, however, there was a flurry fifty feet away, and Mike emerged momentarily to yell, "I've got him!"

Ignoring the excellent rule that one should swim quietly on the surface, without making too much of a splash, I stern-wheeled across to

Mike at maximum acceleration. When I arrived on the spot, I found him using his gun to fend off a very angry shark, which was turning and snapping on the spear that had passed right through its body below the rear fins. Though its crescent-shaped mouth was only about six inches wide, I did not at all like the way in which its teeth kept grinding together in rage and frustration.

I took two hasty photos, then moved in close (or as close as I cared) with my own hand spear, to help push the beast away from Mike if it showed signs of coming to grips with him. He had swum slowly backward toward the boat, towing the spear with one hand and using the discharged gun to keep the still violently wriggling shark at bay.

We had an acquaintance in the dinghy, who had come along for the ride and seemed slightly taken aback when we drew alongside and yelled at him to help haul our captive aboard. He reached down and tried to grab the tail, which was about the only thing he could do—though even this is not recommended in the best circles, since sharks can curl round to snap at their own tails with no trouble at all. They also have skins like sandpaper, which further discourages contact with the bare hand.

We had managed to get the shark halfway out of the water when, in a sudden paroxysm of fury, it succeeded in tearing itself loose from the spear. I caught a final brief glimpse of it shooting away across the coral, apparently none the worse for its encounter. When I surfaced again I found that Mike had climbed into the boat and was doing a dance of rage, accompanied by suitable sound effects, which were being greatly admired by another boatload of spear fishers who had now arrived on the scene. He stated, in no uncertain terms, what would happen to this particular shark if he ever met it again, with or without spear gun. He added several footnotes, containing information which would have surprised ichthyologists, about the ancestry and domestic behavior of sharks in general. In fact, he managed to convey the distinct impression that he did not, at the moment, feel very kindly disposed toward sharks.

When we had succeeded in calming him down a little, we went back into the water and did a search for the weight belt he had lost during the battle. After five minutes' hunting, he was lucky enough to find it on a patch of sand, and this did something to restore his good humor. The loss of these weights would have been quite a serious matter, as without them it would have been difficult or even impossible for him to remain in effortless equilibrium at any depth. Though we had brought spares of all our other equipment, we had drawn the line at an extra ten or twenty pounds of lead, which somehow always seems to be even heavier than it actually is.

While engaged in the search for Mike's belt, I had swum a considerable distance against the prevailing current, and had noticed that the water "upstream" was much clearer than in the region where we had been operating. So we pulled up the anchor, and rowed a hundred yards against the current to try our luck further round the edge of the reef.

The character of the bottom had changed greatly, even in this short distance. Huge coral boulders, ten feet high, were spaced at irregular intervals through the blue-lit twilight. The water was also considerably deeper, and much richer in fish life. Horned rhinoceros fish, coral trout, and grouper swarmed beneath us, playing hide-and-seek around the submerged hillocks when we tried to get close to them. I noticed a fine grouper, well over a hundred pounds in weight, moving along a valley below me, and surfaced to draw Mike's attention to it. As I did so, a large turtle, moving with surprising speed for so ungainly a beast, shot past me and disappeared into the depths. I had no opportunity of giving any of this information to Mike, however, for no sooner had I broken surface than he shouted "Shark!" and pointed back into the water.

For a moment I wondered if our earlier victim had been rash enough to return. It took only a second's glance to dispose of *that* theory.

This was a real shark—a good ten feet of ultimately streamlined power, moving lazily through the waters beneath us. His body was a uniform metallic gray, with no trace of markings. He seemed aware of our presence, for he was cruising in a wide arc as if wondering what to do about us. I swam slowly above and behind him, trying to get a picture every time he was in a good position. If I kept moving steadily toward him, I felt quite sure that he would not come at me; indeed, my only concern was that I might make too violent a move and frighten him away. I was far too lost in admiration of this beautiful creature—the first large shark I had ever met in clear water—to feel the slightest sense of alarm.

But then I saw something that made my blood run cold. Mike, apparently thirsting for revenge, had reloaded his spear gun. He was getting into position to attack this monster who was bigger than both of us put together.

I shot up to the surface like a rocket, and as soon as Mike came up for air yelled at him, "For God's sake—don't shoot!" The spear fishers in the boat fifty feet away heard every word; Mike, a yard from me, appeared to be stone-deaf. I followed him all the way down, making all the sign gestures I could think of to try and dissuade him, but it was no use.

Things sometimes happen so quickly underwater than often one can never clearly recall a sequence of events. I cannot remember the actual moment when the gun was fired; I can only remember my vast relief when the spear missed, and the shark veered away from its course. It did not, however, show any signs of fright as the steel arrow whizzed past its nose; indeed, it swept round in a great circle and swam toward Mike, who had now reeled in his spear but—luckily—had not had time to reload the gun. As the shark came slowly up to him, Mike suddenly realized that it was about time he did something, and began to shout into the water in the approved textbook fashion. The shark took no notice at all, but continued its leisurely approach. Mike jabbed his empty gun in its general direction; still it came on. Not until it was about five feet away, and Mike could see its myopic eyes staring straight into his face mask, did it apparently decide that this was just another of those annoying and indigestible human beings, and swing contemptuously aside. I caught a last glimpse of it, a blurred torpedo lit by the slanting sunlight, as it vanished along the reef.

We climbed back into the boat, and recriminations continued as we rowed homeward. Mike swore, not very convincingly, that he thought

I wanted him to shoot the shark. I produced all the witnesses within earshot to prove the contrary, and loudly lamented the masterpieces my camera had lost. "If you *must* shoot a shark," I wailed, "at least wait until I've finished photographing it."

Looking back on these events from the comparative calm of the present, I am inclined to believe that Mike never actually intended to hit the beast, but merely wanted to express his feelings. He is a dead shot at fish anything more than nine inches long, and it makes no sense at all for him to have missed something that occupied most of his angle of vision when he fired at it. At the crucial moment, his subconscious mind must have decided that this nonsense had gone far enough, and made him deflect his aim.

That evening, as soon as we could borrow the necessary ice from the tourist center, we set to work to develop the color film I had shot during the day. After two hours' work, pouring liquids from one bottle to another and running round with lumps of ice to maintain all the solutions at the right temperature, we knew that our photographic efforts had not been in vain. There was our gunmetal friend cruising over the coral, the undisputed master of the reef.

Undisputed? Well, one day Mike may decide to put that to the test again. I hope he does it when I'm not around.

from The Lady and the Sharks
by Eugenie Clark

Florida had no marine research facilities in 1954, when the Vanderbilt family invited ichthyologist Eugenie Clark (born 1922) to open one. The opportunity to study whatever she wanted on the Gulf Coast helped Clark become one of the world's leading shark experts. The Lady and the Sharks tells the story of her twelve years developing the Cape Haze Marine Laboratory (later renamed the Mote Marine Laboratory).

There is really no effective shark repellent. The Navy Shark Chaser, developed during World War II, is made up of several ingredients, the most significant being nigrosine dye. This dye (or almost any dark dye released into the water) will cause a shark to avoid the area or swim around it if it happens to be in his path—if there is no inducement to enter the dark area. However, if in the center of this chemical cloud (or in an area with any of the numerous other so-called "shark repellents" we've been asked to test) you place a piece of juicy cut fish, a hungry shark will swim directly into the "protected" area.

But the morale factor is important. After a shipwreck or other sea disaster causes vibrations which may attract sharks, a lone swimmer could panic and drown at the sight of sharks. He can be comforted by the thought that he has a little package on his belt labeled "Shark Chaser." And when he releases the contents of his package into the water and nearby sharks swim away, the improvement of his psychological state could be most important for his survival until help reaches him. The fact that the sharks probably wouldn't bother him anyway, and the statistics of the infrequency of shark attacks (your chances of being bitten by a shark when you're in the water with them are much less than your chances of being in a crash when you drive your car), is not much comfort when you find yourself in the water with them. Somehow being mangled in an automobile doesn't arouse the same sense of horror as being bitten by a shark.

But after a sea disaster sometimes a survivor in the water bleeds, vomits, has "nervous perspiration," or releases other excreta which might attract a shark. Dr. Albert Tester, who does research on olfactory and other chemical senses of sharks at the University of Hawaii's Marine Laboratory, visited the Lab and told us about his work. He found that almost all food substances he tried attracted sharks and produced the typical hunting response—surfacing, circling, rapid swimming, and, occasionally, jaw gaping. Oily fish such as tuna can excite a shark more than a "dry" snapper. Dr. Tester found that if he starved blacktip sharks, they responded to much smaller quantities of fish extract. His blacktip sharks showed an awareness of the presence of human urine in the water but were not attracted or repelled by it. Several species of sharks he tested showed an aversion to human sweat.

The plastic bag recently designed by Scott Johnson and tested during a six-month study by Dr. Johnson at the Lab is probably the best protection against sharks for a man stranded at sea. This green bag which can be quickly unfolded and filled with water has an orange inflatable ring. It can be seen easily by rescue workers from a plane or boat, yet it screens the man inside from the shark that gets no olfactory cues. He sees only a large, inconspicuous bag, rather than dangling arms and legs.

Those of us who study sharks (or any animal, for that matter) know that the responses can be different depending on the species, the age of the shark, its state of health, its psychological state, its environment (water temperature and salinity), and its past experience. And, like people, sharks possess individual differences.

All careful investigators working with sharks are cautious to restrict their conclusions to the exact species and individual characteristics of sharks they work with and the exact conditions of the experiment. Sometimes scientific publications can be boring reading for a layman, as they seem filled with uninteresting details, but these details are very important when you are trying to fit together an accurate picture of a situation from which you want to draw true and meaningful conclusions. The Shark Research Panel of the American Institute of Biological Sciences keeps careful record of the details of all shark attacks on which it can get information, and every year reports and tries to analyze these data.

Something that may work as a repellent for one species of shark may attract another. This is true for some acoustical and electric "repellents." An expert diver I know claims he can repel sharks in the Red Sea by hitting two stones together; but in some little islands in the Pacific the natives attract sharks they want to catch by leaning over the side of their dugout canoe and hitting two stones together underwater. The species of sharks involved, however, are not known.

Some businessmen came to the Lab once to demonstrate an electrical repellent which they wished me to endorse. Engineers had worked it out in an electronics lab, and when they tested it on a shark, it had worked. They were vague about what kind of shark it was and under what conditions and for how long a period it repelled the shark. I put the gadget in our shark pen, and when we turned it on, the lemon sharks from the far side of the pen joined those nearby investigating the box discharging into the water.

Dr. Perry Gilbert's most dangerous incident in the water with a shark was when he was testing an electrical gadget "sure to repel a shark" and almost electrocuted himself.

There are supposed to be some effective electrical shark repellents being developed, but I have yet to hear about one that is safe for a diver to use, can drive away all kinds of dangerous sharks, and can continue to keep the shark away after it has discharged for some minutes and the shark becomes used to the unusual current.

Dr. Gilbert, who is head of the Shark Research Panel, has demonstrated that the "bubble curtain" (air pumped to an underwater pipe perforated with holes), thought to keep sharks away from swimmers, is not effective in deterring tiger sharks in captivity.

We all keep hoping that someone will develop an effective shark repellent, but after cooperating with dozens of people who claim they have one, and losing much time on inconclusive demonstrations, I no longer get excited when someone full of conviction and ready to take out a patent offers me the chance to test his shark repellent.

A species we have learned much about recently is the bull shark, *Carcharhinus leucas*. It is the most common of the sharks along the west coast of Florida, one we catch in quantity every month of the year. It can swim upstream from sea water into rivers and has been caught in the fresh water of Lake Okeechobee. In Central America, the bull shark has been called the Lake Nicaraguan shark. Because it lives in fresh water and has a somewhat stunted growth (reaching maturity at a smaller size than when in the sea), the Lake Nicaraguan shark was thought to be a separate species. It is greatly feared in Central America, where it is known to attack people.

Except for the east coast of Australia, the largest number of authenticated shark attacks in the world are in the Durban, South African area, where shark-watching towers are posted at crowded beaches so that swimmers can be warned out of the water when a shark is sighted and where all the doctors in the area are specially prepared to treat shark bites. The problem is so great and affects so many industries associated with tourism that much money is given to support shark research in South Africa, and the expensive process of "meshing" for sharks is practiced around some public beaches, where the nets have to be cleared of sharks and mended every few days. The culprit mainly to blame is the Zambesi shark, which lives in the sea and goes up the Zambesi River. It is the same species of bull shark that is so common around Florida. Strangely, it is not known to have attacked a swimmer in this state except in the case of a "provoked" attack at the Miami Seaquarium, where the bull shark was in captivity and being handled.

The experienced skin diver will usually leave the water with as little commotion as possible if he sees a small six-foot white shark, tiger, or any so-called "carcharhinid" shark coming too close. But he won't mind a full-grown nurse shark of 10 feet, a basking shark of 40 feet, or a whale shark of 60 feet. I've never met the last two monsters when diving, but if I do, like most divers, I'd get into my boat as fast as possible for my underwater camera. When not photographing these big plankton-feeding sharks, divers like to try to ride them, and many divers have succeeded in hanging on to the tail or dorsal fin of a giant whale shark. As these sharks often bask at the surface, some fishermen—even little boys in the Bahamas—jump on the whale shark's back and run up and down until the shark, perhaps mildly annoyed, heads for deep water. The great size of these sharks could knock a ship on its side or injure a swimmer merely by bumping into him, but I don't know of anyone who has been hurt by a whale or basking shark.

The nurse shark can be a little dangerous if provoked. Its teeth are small but arranged in seven or more rows that can shred your skin. Some skin divers who have tried to ride a nurse shark by holding on to the tail or dorsal fin have a small scar from the experience. I've been slapped in the face by the tail of a nurse shark that looked dead as I bent over to examine it on our dock. I was thrown with a snap against sharp corals the first time I tried to ride a nurse shark by grabbing its tail. And I've had a long and wild ride and had my midriff and legs sandpapered when I once grabbed a nurse shark's pectoral fins and clung to its back while I was wearing a two-piece bathing suit. Several of us at the Lab regularly catch babies of this species by grabbing the tail with one hand and the back of the head with the other. I've never been bitten, but one of my friends has.

Jon Hamlin, the son of Alley Oop's creator, doesn't blame the nurse shark for his scar. Jon is a fine diver who has collected many small sharks by hand for the Lab, by pulling them out from under the ledges of Point of Rocks, Sarasota. Jon once grabbed a protruding tail belonging to a shark that was longer than he expected. He couldn't bear to let go of his prize and they tugged in opposite directions until the shark turned and grabbed Jon's leg like a bulldog. As soon as Jon released the shark's tail, however, it released Jon and swam straight out of sight.

For some reason, the nurse shark is not well known. Although it is common all around Florida and looks so different from other sharks, it is usually called a "sand shark," that catchall term applied to any of a dozen or more species even by fishermen. Or they may not recognize it as a shark at all. A male nurse shark made headlines in Florida newspapers until it was identified. "Mysterious monster, caught in St. Petersburg . . . 8 feet long, with whiskers like a catfish and a pair of legs without feet," read the account.

I wish I had a good story to tell about my most dangerous contact with a shark. Oh, I could probably embellish a few incidents when I was awfully close to some big sharks, but the incidents all had happy endings. I've been down in a one-man shark cage in the middle of the Red Sea with big offshore sharks swimming all around me. Another time, I crouched in a depression in a coral reef as Claude Templier and I unexpectedly set off a feeding frenzy among seven sharks and hoped the air in our aqualungs would last until we found a relatively safe moment to swim for the surface. And once, at 80 feet underwater, I backed my air tanks against a vertical drop-off of over 4,000 feet as I watched Dr. Joseph François, just beside me, poke his shark billy at the head of a sizable shark that suddenly rushed toward us from the deep blue clean water near the Suakin Islands.

Just once my arm dripped blood after the teeth of a twelve foot tiger shark sank into it. I was driving my car down the Tamiami Trail when I stopped short for a red light. I was late on my way to give a lecture at Riverview High School, in Sarasota, and had some books and props on the seat beside me, including the dried and mounted jaws of a tiger shark we'd caught. As I slammed on the brakes, I stretched out my arm to try to hold the pile of material from falling off the seat. The students seemed to like the opening of my lecture that day, when I could demonstrate my fresh, though mild, wounds.

There have been only two bad shark attacks on the central west coast of Florida. One happened in June, 1920, long before the Lab opened. I learned about it one day when I went to get gas for my car at the Texaco station in Englewood. The attendant looked hard at me and asked, "Are you the lady who studies sharks?"

He pulled up his pants leg and showed me a terrible scar: From the size of the single huge curve, I judged it must have been a shark well over ten feet, a tiger or possibly a white shark. The man, Hayword Green, had been swimming off the Englewood Beach a good distance from shore beyond the sandbar, in water over his head, one evening at about 6:30, when he felt something grab his leg. He swam to shore and luckily was helped before he bled to death as many shark victims have.

A worse shark attack occurred off Longboat Key, Sarasota, on July 27, 1958, at about 4:10 p.m. The parents and brother of the boy, Douglas Lawton, who was attacked came to see me at the Lab the next day. "How could such a thing happen in such shallow water?" they asked. "What kind of a shark was it?" Doug was in Sarasota Memorial Hospital, where he had to have his leg amputated. He was eight years old. I went to see him and talked with the five witnesses: his parents; his aunt and uncle, who were on the beach; and his twelve-year-old brother, who was swimming with Doug and dragged him to shore with the shark still holding on to his leg. At the water's edge, Doug's uncle held the boy by the shoulders, his father grabbed the shark's tail and pulled, and Doug pushed the shark's head with his hand. The shark finally released its grip and floundered at the water's edge until it was in water deep enough to swim away. It was a small shark, about five feet long.

I went to the office of Dr. John Bracken, the pathologist, and he gave me Doug's amputated leg to examine. The shark had attacked the leg at least three times. The deepest bite, high on the thigh, made it necessary to amputate the entire leg. I found the clue to the species of shark in some superficial nicks made by the shark's teeth just below the knee.

One toothmark, undoubtedly made by a front tooth, in particular showed that the largest cusp of the serrated edge was off center. Dr. Bracken took photographs.

Back at the Cape Haze Marine Lab I studied the photos, my notes, and measurements. I got some clay and made tooth imprints on it, using preserved jaws of all the different species of sharks we had collected. The distance between the toothmarks and the wide curve of the bite for a shark of five feet reduced the possible species involved down to four: the dusky, sandbar, bull, and tiger sharks. The place and time of year ruled out the first two species. The shape of the toothmark ruled out the bull shark. It must have been a young tiger shark. All the witnesses and Doug himself had stressed that the head of the shark was blunt, not pointed as they remembered pictures of sharks. The tiger shark has an exceptionally blunt head. They had told me the shark's body was streamlined, and Doug's father remembered that the base of the tail where he grabbed and pulled was narrow and felt sharp. The tiger shark has a small caudal peduncle with a keel on each side (the only shark with these keels that comes close to shore in the Sarasota area). The swiftest-swimming sharks, especially deeper-water sharks like the mako, have these keels. Everything pointed to the tiger shark as the attacker except for the fact that none of the witnesses noticed any markings. But on looking over photos of tiger sharks of about five feet, I realized that unless you look at this shark from the side, the stripes are hardly noticeable. The witnesses saw the shark mostly from above. They knew it was a shark, and understandably they were so concerned about Doug that no one paid any attention to how the shark looked.

Why did the shark attack Doug? We took the *Dancer* to the spot where the attack had taken place, about 10 feet from the shore in murky water 3 feet deep. We found a long sandbar about 25 yards from shore running almost the entire length of Longboat Key, a distance of nearly eight miles. Low tide on July 27 was at 5:57 p.m. We figured the depth of water over the sandbar at the time of the attack must have been only a few inches. The channel inside the bar was about 5 feet at its deepest point but led into deeper water (10 feet) in Longboat Pass at the north end of the Key and into New Pass (15 feet deep) on the south end of the Key. The water next to the beach dropped sharply from a few inches to 3 feet.

Possibly the shark had swum over the bar earlier in the day and then found itself trapped in the channel as the tide went out. Or it may have entered the channel from either of the passes at the ends of Longboat Key.

The victim and his brother were the only people in the water at the time, and the shark, swimming within the confines of this channel, might easily have detected the vibrations made by the boys slapping their flippers at the surface of the water, the irregular vibrations of boys playing rather than swimming. The victim's feet and ankles were not as deeply tanned as the rest of his legs, as he usually wore shoes and socks on his feet when playing in the sun. It seems possible that the shark, attracted by the vibrations made with the flippers, saw the pale lower portion of the boy's leg and struck at that point first, causing a large wound on the foot. The victim's left flipper was lost, presumably during the attack. The blood and the struggling victim could then have aroused the shark into a feeding frenzy, causing the repeated attacks.

All of us working with sharks in captivity get such a different attitude toward them that it is an effort for us to remember how dangerous they can be and to keep up necessary precautions. The vicious attack on Douglas Lawton by a young tiger shark seemed as incongruous to us as a dog lover might feel who keeps several boxers at home and hears about a mad dog attacking some innocent person.

Newborn tiger sharks are beautifully marked with black stripes and spots on their silvery white bodies. Hera and her friend Zen helped us deliver a litter of 37 tiger sharks, each one 2 1/2 feet long, from the uterus of a dying mother. (Tiger sharks are known to carry as many as 105 embryos at one time.) These babies were slightly premature but some started feeding and one became remarkably healthy. In three months it grew only two inches in length but doubled its weight. It fed from our hands and allowed itself to be stroked. If you walked to the

side of its small pen the baby shark would swim over to see you immediately. We had hopes of raising a tiger shark in captivity and finding
out how fast this species grows and matures—something never done
before. But this was cut short by a vandal who broke into the Laboratory grounds one night and beat the young tiger shark to death. We
found the stout stick near the pen and marks on the bruised dead body
of the young shark matched the shape of the end of the stick.

In the history of the Cape Haze Marine Lab, we had only one
human mishap in the course of our daily work. In 1956, Beryl brought
a class of school children onto the dock beside the shark pen to show
them his favorite shark, Rosy. This big old nurse shark was at the
bottom of the pen and couldn't be seen. Beryl, who often called her up
in this way to feed her, splashed his hand on the water while kneeling
on the feeding platform. He let his hand dangle over the side some distance above the water and turned for an instant to say something to the
watchful children. Rosy lifted her head out of the water and touched
Beryl's hand. It was such a smooth gentle-looking maneuver that it
could have been mistaken for a kiss. But the end of one of Beryl's fingers has been a quarter of an inch shorter ever since.

Diving Into Shark-Fin Soup
by Jim Thornton

A life-long fascination with sharks left journalist Jim Thornton determined to dive with them. Here he finally gets his chance, helping a shark biologist test a new version of an old idea—shark repellant.

The radio receiver crackles with static: "Bilge pump not working . . . poor . . ." Samuel "Shark Doc" Gruber grabs a walkie-talkie from an overhanging bookshelf in the kitchen of his Shark Lab and barks a reply into the moonless Bahamian night. "Are you saying there's water in the boat? And your pump's not working? Over."

A burst of Gatling-gun unintelligibility fires back to us from the skiff, which bears the apt name *SNAFU*. I try to conceal my giddiness. My first night in the Bahamas, and already it's like the end of *Jaws* when the shark almost eats the *Orca*.

Over a 40-year research career, Gruber, who insists on being called "Doc," has published research that has transformed human understanding about this array of mysterious, cartilaginous species—creatures that are, he says, "as different from ordinary bony fishes as humans are from snakes." In recent years, Gruber's interest in shark population dynamics has led him to study lemon shark "nurseries" at the Marquesas Keys, Brazil's Atol das Rocas, and here at the Bimini

Biological Field Station. He has begun to document how complex—and surprisingly fragile—shark reproduction is. In an era when many shark species are being hunted and "finned" (to sate the appetites of Asia's shark-fin soup connoisseurs) to the brink of extinction, Gruber is more than just a world-renowned shark scientist. He is one of the planet's foremost advocates for animals that have rarely attracted anything but human enmity.

Which, of course, explains why he's here in the metaphorical, and often literal, maws of sharkdom.

More difficult to explain is my own quest for a rendezvous with denticulation. Let me not put too fine a point on this: I want to swim, seminaked and cageless, in the proximity of man-biters, and I've wanted to do so for 30 years. The fact that my time at last is nigh seems to be a kind of miracle.

When my loved ones ask me the reasons for this obsession, the best I can offer is that my motivation dates back to tenth grade, when, for reasons too wrenching to go into without exhausting a box of Puffs, I was exiled to Massachusetts, to a Dickensian outpost known as Phillips Academy Andover. It was a bleak, cold, gray, and bully-laden place, and the single bit of enjoyment I managed to find during the entirety of my serotonin-devoid high school years was in watching the occasional Jacques Cousteau special on TV. This world of exotic reefs in which did swim kindly, thin, heavily accented Frenchmen and whopping sharks, side by side in happy harmony, was so foreign to the colorless, cruel misery of my surroundings that I began to fantasize about becoming an ichthyologist and spending my years in tropical waters as far as humanly possible from Massachusetts.

Over the intervening decades, dreams of a tenured professorship at the U. of Eden slowly fell to the reality of successive minimum-wage positions in the Pittsburgh area, each of which featured the word "boy" in the job title. Still, the shining dream of swimming with sharks continued to tickle the back of my brainpan.

An amateur without portfolio, I knew it would be impossible to line up a "research project" on my own. So, like a human remora, I did the next best thing: I tracked down Dr. Gruber at the University of Miami and sucked up. My proposal: Let me serve as a human guinea pig to test out a shark-repellent gizmo called a SharkPOD (about which, more in a moment). Astonishingly, I talked Gruber into this scheme—provided, that is, I agreed to absolve him of all responsibility.

"Doc, Doc," spits the radio in a burst of what passes for clarity in the Bimini night. "Transom cracked . . ."

Just an hour ago, during the orange-sherbet phase of the Bahamian twilight, the *SNAFU* departed the mangrove dock behind the lab. The crew's mission: Check to see if anything had been caught on the "long lines"—nearly a mile and a half of hooks baited that morning with barracuda and amberjack kabobs. Inspecting those lines is a process that has to be repeated every three to five hours, day and night, in order that any captured shark can be measured, sexed, tagged, and released before it expires from stress or hypoxia.

On one of the shark photos that adorn the prefab walls of the lab, a waggish grad student has affixed a cartoon balloon to the mouth of a lemon shark undergoing this procedure. The wide-eyed beast says: "I've just been Gruberized!"

Before the *SNAFU* started to leak, its crew successfully Gruberized a seven-foot nurse shark, which survived, and a small sharpnose shark, which didn't. The big excitement, however, is their reported hooking of a tiger shark, which is considered to be the most dangerous shark species in the world. "Tiger sharks have such broad feeding ecology," Doc tells me, "that they might consider a human or even a pig as legitimate prey."

This bodes ill for a pig-man like me.

Sharks, it turns out, bear a stigma of viciousness way out of proportion to their actual behavior. True, humans do occasionally get attacked, and a handful are even killed each year. In 1999, investigators with the University of Florida–based International Shark Attack File confirmed 58 unprovoked attacks worldwide, including four fatalities.

This statistic, I'll grant, is hardly cause for celebration by the four casualties and their families. But for the vast majority of humanity, what such numbers mean is that your chance of being killed or even injured by a shark is statistically nil. Residents of the United States are at greater risk of being eaten by golf-course alligators. Of course, most Americans don't go out of their way to put themselves in sharkian proximity.

About the only ungarbled transmission we've heard from the *SNAFU* was the length of the tiger: 184 centimeters. As Doc and his grad students ready their Aquasport powerboat for a rescue mission, I do the math. The shark, I calculate, measures six feet, .4408 inch. In my 20s, I stood six one, but the past two decades have definitely begun to shrink me. The tiger shark, I realize, is almost exactly my height—a rather puny fellow as far as these guys go.

Years ago, Doc often caught tigers measuring 12 feet or longer, but such leviathans are becoming increasingly rare. For this decline, you can credit post-*Jaws* overfishing and a notably sluggish reproductive rate.

Unfortunately, the small size of today's specimen won't necessarily render him safe as a swimming partner. Certain species of sharks begin their carnivorous lifestyle while still in utero, with the biggest ones gobbling up their unborn siblings. Those that survive the 12 months of gestation burst into the turquoise sea with abdomens grotesquely swollen with their well-masticated brothers and sisters. A researcher acquaintance of Doc's once made the mistake of palpating inside a pregnant sand tiger's womb. He pulled out a bloody hand.

Doc fires up the Aquasport's propellers and wends slowly through the mangroves until we hit the open sea. By day, the waters surrounding Bimini are a rhapsody in blues. The deep navy of the Gulf Stream to the west gives way to a neon turquoise band that pulses on the horizon as if powered by electricity. Conversely, the shallow mangrove waters sheltered by the islands are glass-clear and tinted the color of baby lemon sharks. It is here, in the makeshift nursery of the North Sound, that more than a hundred camouflaged newborns have their best chance to avoid being eaten during their first year of life. Pockets of this Grey Poupon color stud the aquamarine for hundreds of miles to the east and south all across the shallows of the vast Bahama Bank.

By night, of course, the waters turn into a vat of black ink. There's no moon tonight, and the pollution from south Florida is only a faint smear on the horizon.

Finally we reach the *SNAFU*, which is indeed taking on water, but, alas, much too slowly to sink. Doc dispatches the *SNAFU* back to the lab, then shines several high-intensity Q-Beams into the drink. Thin shafts of the 80°F water suddenly take on their daytime hues. I'm sitting on the edge of the boat, geared up with fins, mask, and snorkel, awaiting my first-ever glimpse of a live shark outside an aquarium.

A sudden gray shadow darts by the boat, and Doc says, "There's the little bastard! Oh, he's tiny! He's a baby!" My heart sinks. The fish seems as threatening as a giant trout.

Doc quickly initiates Gruberization, dispatching one student to pull in the hook line as another maneuvers the "tailer"—a wire lasso—to ensnare the diminutive fellow's tail fin. Pretty soon, the skinny tiger has been secured parallel to the side of the boat. He thrashes about violently with what little freedom he has. He's not looking quite so trout-like anymore.

"Truth is," says Doc, "these little ones make me nervous. Small tiger sharks are constantly under threat—they can be nasty."

This morning, Doc had me sign a blanket waiver that releases him and his lab from any responsibility for anything that might happen to me under any circumstances. I'm pretty sure that he could shoot me through the head with a speargun, and my heirs still couldn't sue.

"OK to go in now?" I ask.

Doc nods, and I fall back into the choppy water. The tiger shark renews his thrashing, and a slight current tugs me toward the back of the boat. I resist, swimming to within a foot of the shark's pectoral fin, which I gingerly grasp.

For the next ten minutes, I fight the chop, currents, and my anxiety, trying to get my head as close as advisedly possible to the shark's teeth. Meanwhile, doc stabs a shallow hole beneath the shark's dorsal fin, and inserts a barbed Casey tag. When and if this specimen is ever caught again, the tag will help researches learn more about growth rates, migratory patterns, and other aspects of tiger shark biology.

Doc is about to release the shark when I make a final request. "Could you turn off all the lights for a minute?"

With the Q-Beams extinguished, and my rods and cones bleached out by their intensity, the world turns completely black. I feel the current pushing me about, knowing full well there's a tiger shark tied up nearby with a small but measurable degree of jaws-moving freedom. It's an exhilaratingly creepy feeling, one I can only hope will help prepare me for tomorrow's exercise: a swim through a feeding frenzy.

During the 1940s, military researchers, responding to the natural human tendency to fear and loathe sharks, developed a noxious chemical they called "Shark Chaser." They gave this to soldiers, along with a dye they could use to hide from sharks if forced into the water. Unfortunately, the Shark Chaser quickly dispersed—and sharks swam right through the dye. Call these shark-repellent placebos, an illusion of safety to keep skittish men from panicking on shark-infested waters.

In the South African coastal province of Natal, government researchers began in the late seventies to work on a new kind of repellent—an electrical curtain, the shark equivalent of an invisible dog fence. Sharks have an organ in their snouts known as the ampullae of Lorenzini. This contains exquisitely sensitive receptors that sharks use to detect faint electrical fields generated by the firing of nerves and muscles in their prey. Perhaps foraging sharks might be effectively repelled by jacking up the volume of electrical stimuli.

The curtain worked, sort of, at least with some sharks. But a new problem soon arose: Currents and waves made it difficult and sometimes impossible to keep an underwater electrical cable in place. In the late eighties, the Natal Sharks Board began developing a portable electrical unit that they christened the SharkPOD (protective oceanic device). The device creates a powerful electrical field that radiates up to ten meters around the person carrying it, effectively repelling tiger, bull, and great white sharks—at least in some testing situations.

Launched with great hoopla several years ago, variations on SharkPOD technology promised soon to find their way into a host of water sports; special units were expected to be fitted onto surfboards. But this enthusiasm proved short-lived, at least in the United States, where tests yielded mixed results. At least one unit was reportedly swallowed whole by a shark.

Last March, I called around in hopes of finding a unit to try out myself. SharkPOD USA, I discovered, had gone belly up. I finally found a warehouse in Miami with an unmarketable unit still in storage, and they were happy to unload it on me for a fraction of the $595 retail price.

It wasn't until I arrived in Bimini that I finally read the manual. In language that sounds a lot like Doc's waiver form, it warns that the SharkPOD *must* be used only in accordance with the instructions. There's a long list of conditions I don't intend to follow, including wearing it on a scuba tank (I don't have one) and never trying it in "induced feeding, i.e. baiting, chumming, etc." type situations. But how else can I hope to flag down some test sharks?

"What kind of sharks have you tried that thing on?" asks Tim Calver, a Canadian with blond dreadlocks. Calver is the lab's underwater photographer, and he'll be attempting to document the efficacy—or lack thereof—of my decidedly unscientific SharkPOD trial.

"You mean me personally?" I ask. "Actually, none. But it did repel a shrimp this morning."

That image still lingers. Fearing the POD's battery wasn't charged, I decided to try the gizmo out in six inches of water. The moment I turned the switch on, a shrimp torpedoed up from his hidey-hole in the muck and skittered in panic across the water's surface. This seemed like a good omen—until a mangrove snapper leapt up and gobbled the shrimp whole.

It's 4:30 p.m. and the Aquasport now hovers over a coral reef five miles south of Bimini. Doc began feeding sharks in this location ten years ago. At first, he was lucky to attract one or two, but their number has steadily grown. Now they are so accustomed to the sound of the Aquasport's motor that a dozen scamper in at the first faint rumble, like cats conditioned to the sound of a can opener.

Still safe on the boat, I see the first gray shadow streak through the cerulean waters, followed by another, and another. Unlike last night's tiger, which was no more stout than my leg, the biggest of these fellows sport the girth of telephone poles. A staffer estimates that the largest is nearly nine feet long.

"Despite appearances, they're really pretty harmless, aren't they?" I say to Calver, fully expecting to receive a reassuring reply.

"Well, not really," he says. "Whenever somebody's bit in the Bahamas, it's usually by a Caribbean reef shark."

A student opens a cooler, which is stuffed with barracuda heads and assorted hatcheted body parts—oily, smelly stuff that is irresistible to these sharks. A half dozen more ravenous fellows have now arrived for the banquet. Today's special: chum-cum-Jim.

"How many other people have you seen try what I'll be doing?" I ask Doc.

"One," he says, explaining that one of the SharkPOD's developers traveled from South Africa a few years back. "It scared me to death."

Though my predecessor in feeding-frenzy investigation emerged unscathed, the reality of my predicament is finally starting to bubble up through a fortress of denial. I begin preparing for the possibility of having at least a small chunk removed from my person. "If I do get bit," I say, "could you throw some kind of stun grenade into the water and fish me out?"

Evidently, Doc assumes I'm joking. He ignores the remark and continues directing what is called "the shark dive protocol." The first step is for Calver to dive to the bottom and plant the anchor.

"Can I go in with him?" I ask. I believe it's best to get on with things like this.

Seeing that nobody else is ready, Doc reluctantly assents. "Stay near Tim, and if any sharks get too close to him, kick them away. Do *not* turn the POD on till I tell you to."

Using a weight-bolt strap, I've cinched the SharkPOD's main unit, a toaster-size gadget designed to fit on a scuba cylinder, directly to my back. I'm wearing a shortie-style wet suit, and I'm hoping the thin skin of neoprene will insulate me from electrocution. The POD's other electrode is a yellow paddle that attaches to one of my fins. The two units are connected by a waterproof electric cord, which is secured to my body by an assortment of Velcro straps.

The moment I hit the water, the whole jury-rigged extravaganza begins to discombobulate. The thigh strap falls off, the fin unit detaches, and the weight belt loosens. A seven-foot reef shark cruises by me, followed by a four-foot blacknose shark. In the distant aquatic gloaming, I count a dozen more.

Doc throws the first barracuda head into the down-current waters. I see a small puff of blood as this hits the water, followed by the darting in of an opportunistic blacknose shark, which snarfs it out of the jaws of a much larger reef shark. More chum hits the water, and in seconds the sea surface is boiling with dorsal fins.

"Can I try going through now?" I yell up to Doc. "I could do it with the POD turned off first and see what happens."

"No!" he yells. "Swim over and back with the POD turned on!"

Grad students throw more bait into the churning waters. The plan is for them to stop five seconds before I reach the frenzy.

"All right, go," says Doc.

I let myself drift and switch the POD unit on. The full-body shock that follows is reminiscent of misadventure with submerged kitchen appliances. *Bzzzzzztttt!* it goes, followed two seconds later by another *Bzzzzzztttt!*, then another, and another, every two seconds. The amps zap through my entire body.

Addled by electrocution and by some misguided sense of duty (and fear of sharks), I leave the unit on, making a slow jerky approach toward the epicenter of sharkdom. There are now 20 sharks darting about. When I get to within five feet of them, they explode away like shrapnel from a hand grenade.

Bzzzzzztttt! Bzzzzzztttt! Bzzzzzztttt!

Seconds later, though, they've circled back and are on me again. One reef shark nearly bites the fin with the paddle electrode.

Bzzzzzzztttt! Bzzzzzzztttt! Bzzzzzzztttt!

Finally, I can stand it no longer, and I turn the unit off. I've drifted a considerable distance away from where I'm supposed to be.

"Well," I mutter. "The battery works."

Doc is yelling something I can't understand, but his body language suggests that I've bungled the protocol. I launch myself back through the feeding sharks, this time with the unit turned off. At this point shark bites strike me as preferable to repeated shocks.

But the sharks make not the slightest move to molest me. I keep my fish-white hands tight to my body and regard the ballet of sharks whose flexing bodies are inches away.

Over the next 45 minutes, I bisect the feeding frenzy another half dozen times, occasionally with the POD turned on, more often with it turned off. Either way, it doesn't seem to matter. Whatever effects electricity initially had upon the sharks, they've quickly habituated to it.

Perhaps the electroshock has had an anti-depressant effect on me, but it's surprisingly easy to will myself to stay calm. Again and again, I swish through these denticle-dappled waters, happy to the point of bumptiousness.

I am the shark whisperer!

from Sharks Are Caught at Night
by François Poli

French writer François Poli decided to fish for sharks after a friend reported seeing Caribbean sharks the size of buses. Poli spent six months fishing in the Caribbean, and in Haiti encountered an unusual means of catching a shark. This passage from Naomi Walford's 1959 English translation of his book describes that experience.

According to an old Haitian belief, the dead leave their graves at night and walk about the countryside: and here and there in the island one can still find old negroes willing to swear by their heads, by the heads of their grandchildren, and by one's own that they have seen these zombies walking through the bush.

"They're not dangerous," they tell you. "They look at you without seeing you, and pass by; all they want to do is stretch their legs a bit."

When we had left Port au Prince and were driving through picture-postcard scenery of rounded green hills, copses, and ponds, with clematis and blue columbine flowering between, I talked to Father Lartigue about this legend.

He was sitting in the back of the car, busy carving his walking-stick with a penknife. He had been doing this for years; he was like those Chinese who polish balls of ivory for generations by turning and turning them in their hands.

I had hardly finished speaking when he stopped whittling the wood and looked at me.

"Let me tell you a strange story," he said.

"Many years ago—back in the dim, distant past—there were sorcerers in this island who discovered a way of paralysing a man's nerve-centres by making him drink an infusion of certain herbs. This turned him into a sort of robot, capable of obeying any order that required no intellectual effort—he could cut wood and use a pick and so on, but was deprived of all initiative. The advantage of the discovery was that it provided unpaid labourers who were given the minimum amount of food and were unable to protest. The damage done by this poison is permanent, and twenty years ago an English scientist published a paper on the subject. At about the same time it was discovered that a young Port au Prince girl of good family, who had disappeared in suspicious circumstances, had been kidnapped, taken into the mountains, and treated with this poison. She was found some years afterwards, and every method known at the time was tried to bring her back to full consciousness, but without success."

Father Lartigue opened his penknife again and added: "That may be the origin of the old belief. And if I hadn't known what I've just told you, and had bumped into one of these robots one night at a bend in the road, I wonder what *I* should have made of it. . . ."

We dropped Father Lartigue and, about an hour later as we were coming to the top of a hill, we saw the sea. A zig-zag road led to a score of thatched cabins lining a track of beaten earth at right-angles to the shore.

At this point on the coast there was a tiny natural harbour, its mole being formed by a rocky barrier jutting into the water in a semi-circle. A hundred yards further on, the sea penetrated the land by a channel barely a yard wide, and then opened into a shallow lagoon, on the shore of which stood about ten other shacks.

Six boats were anchored in the harbour, and three others were drawn up on the beach. We saw two children running along the shore, wearing nothing but big straw hats; they were the only living creatures to be seen in this three-colour landscape—ochre, green, and blue—which was as motionless as a painting.

Having parked the car at the end of the village, we walked along between the double row of shacks as far as the harbour. Three negroes were lying full-length in the shade of a boat; Johnsfair went up to them and tried to make them understand what we wanted; a cabin to rent for a few days and enough food to live on.

There was no cabin to let, but as we insisted, they promised that a small family should be turned out to make room for us by the harbour, in a "house" built of wood and cement and roofed with an old piece of linoleum thatched with straw. There were two bedsteads on the earth floor and an oil-cooker in one corner. Pinned to the walls were photographs cut from the *Schweizer Illustrierte*, a Swiss weekly, which in some mysterious way had turned up here.

Johnsfair carried in our luggage, which we had reduced to the minimum: a rod suitable for big-game fishing, procured the day before, and two carbines which he always carried with him in the boot of his car.

After that we strolled about the harbour. Night had fallen, and one after another the negroes emerged from their cabins like bats; they came up to us in casual groups and shook hands.

They all knew by now that we meant to stay in their village and fish for shark, and they stared in astonishment. The sea was full of sharks, certainly, but they were seldom fished for; only one man, a mulatto of sixty named Felicien Obin, went out after them every day. He regularly brought back two or three, which he butchered himself. Twice a month he took the skins and oil to sell in Port au Prince. The others lived by ordinary fishing, and sold their catch in the mountain villages.

In one corner of the harbour was a shed furnished with benches and a wooden counter; this was the village café where food and drink were served. An old negress brought us two bottles of rum, and about ten negroes sat down with us to drink and chat.

Then Felicien Obin arrived.

He lived in one of the ten cabins bordering the lagoon. His boat was one of the biggest in the village, he told us, yet it was still not large enough for shark-fishing, and he carried a ballast of pig-iron to prevent the sharks from towing him along too easily. He fished only at night, three or four times a week, and was willing to hire his boat to us, starting next day, on condition he might come too.

Unlike the other fishermen, who spoke a fairly comprehensible French, Obin used a sort of lingua franca of French, English, and Spanish mixed with native patois. He spoke in long, musical phrases which he had to repeat several times before we could make any sense of them.

We had just left harbour next day and I was trailing the lure about twenty yards from the boat—more with the idea of showing Johnsfair how to handle his new rod than in any hope of a catch—when the first and only bite we were to get that day came with staggering violence. The rod was nearly snatched overboard. I only just managed to keep hold of it, while the line ran out like an express train. I waited a few moments, and at the first slackening I struck. Three seconds later the line ran out again, more slowly this time, but just as irresistibly. Johnsfair was in luck. He dropped the carbine he had brought with him in the hope of shooting some big fish, and gazed open-mouthed at the sight. The coloured man at the helm wagged his head.

"I know," he said. "Great, great *tiburón*. Line going to break. . . ."

I tried to recover the line while he manœuvred the boat in such a way as to offer the greatest resistance to the struggling monster. But what monster? I had never known any to attack so fiercely.

An hour later the fish was still fighting several hundred yards away, and with aching arms I passed the rod to Obin, wondering if we could have hooked a whale.

At eleven o'clock, three and a half hours after the tussle had begun, the situation was unchanged; we handed the rod back and forth to each other, recovering a few yards of line and then watching it run out again. Other craft were now cruising round us; some of them went back to pick up cargoes of women, children, old men, and two dogs. All were yelling, shouting encouragement, and clapping. We might have been at the races.

At noon we managed to bring the exhausted creature alongside, and the boats drew near, their occupants suddenly silent. Then there was a great shout of laughter.

We had caught a tuna. A tuna barely three feet long. The hook, instead of being in its mouth, had pierced the skin of its round, black body and stuck there—hence its combativeness—while the trace and a good three yards of line were wound round its tail.

For a week afterwards the villagers talked of nothing but this tuna (an exceptional catch at that season and at that distance from shore) and of "the whites who catch fish by the tail." Through this ludicrous incident we won a certain renown, which was spread by the fish-sellers right up into the mountains.

For the next few days I went out fishing alone with old Felicien Obin, as Johnsfair wanted to visit other villages along the coast.

In front of his shack Obin had built a long plank platform which jutted a yard over the water; on this he laid all the sharks he brought in, skinned them, washed the skins in sea-water, and dried them. Lastly, he performed the delicate operation of extracting oil from the livers. This he did by cutting the livers up into large pieces and putting them into a copper; he then poured water over them and lit the fire underneath, and stirred the mixture with a stick for hours on end.

The solids fell to the bottom of the vessel while the oil floated to the top. He filtered it and poured it into kegs. A medium-sized shark produces about four gallons. (Shark-liver oil is used in pharmacy, tanning, in tempering steel, and, more generally, in the manufacture of any products requiring a thin type of oil.)

The fins were carefully cut up before being sent to Port au Prince, where he sold them to a small Chinese colony.

Any meat which he did not keep for his own consumption—he ate platefuls of it every day—was pickled in brine like cod, and sent to the mountain villages. The remains he pounded up to make fertiliser and poultry-food.

"Shark all good," said Obin, "except his bite."

One day he brought back an extraordinary catch: a tiger-shark about ten feet long with a fresh scar a few inches from the tail. While cutting it up a few minutes later he exclaimed in surprise. The wound had been caused by a swordfish, and the sword had snapped off, leaving a piece about eight inches long in the shark's body. (The fish cannot long have survived the battle, for swordfish use their weapon to kill their prey, and without it they cannot feed.)

Obin gazed at the fragment of sword for some time, deep in thought; then he uttered a series of long, melodious phrases, from which I gathered that the shark's chief enemy so far as he knew was not the swordfish, but a creature he called the balloon-fish *(Diodon antennatus)*: although little bigger than a man's fist, it kills the shark in a really fiendish manner.

When angry, the diodon has the faculty of blowing itself up to quite a large size by swallowing water and air, meanwhile emitting through the mouth a liquid which has some of the properties of vitriol. If a shark accidentally swallows one of these balloon-fish, the latter swells up and spits out its caustic liquid, inflicting terrible internal burns on the shark. Then it erects the sharp spines on its body and nibbles its way out through the stomach-wall and flank of the shark, which plunges to the bottom like a torpedoed ship.

When he had done his fishing and cut up his catch, old Felicien Obin would settle down in front of his shack by the lagoon and stay there for hours, pulling at long, thin cigars which he made himself from tobacco he grew behind his cabin.

Sometimes at nightfall Johnsfair and I would join him; then the old man would offer us rum and coffee, and constrain us to smoke some of his murderous cigars. One evening I taught him how to catch flying-fish, according to the method employed by Señor Hornez, and on our return from this trip we realised that his friendly feelings towards us had greatly increased. But alas, the honeymoon period lasted only three days—that is, until he caught us shooting at sharks from the top of the rocks.

The idea was Johnsfair's. While walking on the jetty the day before, we had seen two sharks gliding along only a yard or two out. This was natural enough, as it was here that the village refuse was thrown. Next day we managed to procure a large piece of meat and put it into an open-slatted packing-case, which we cast into the water attached to the shore by a rope. Then we each took a carbine.

"Now, then," said Johnsfair, who, of course, had but one idea in organising this, "ten dollars to the one who kills the first of these muck-eaters!"

We waited all day without seeing a single shark. Yet the bait was tempting enough, and a thin thread of blood trickled from the crate and mingled with the blue water.

At dusk, four sharks appeared at once. We hit one of them, and it began turning round and round, lashing its tail. As we had both fired simultaneously, no money passed. What followed was so fascinating that even Johnsfair forgot to shoot.

The sharks abandoned the bait, surrounded their mortally wounded companion and remained absolutely motionless. For some seconds we had the extraordinary feeling of being able to read their thoughts, as clearly as if they had been written on a blackboard. The wounded shark was twice as big as the biggest of them, and they were waiting until they could safely attack it. It stopped turning and began to rock, dribbling out a thin grey cloud. (Blood mingling with water beneath the surface looks grey.) This was the last stage of its agony; the rest of the scene was played out in the depths, and all we saw was a great flurry of foam and big red bubbles rising to burst on the surface.

Obin heard the report of our guns and came up just as we were reloading. He saw the packing-case and understood. Raising his arms to heaven, he began muttering imprecations in Spanish; then he fell silent, and his face took on an expression of profound grief. We could not fail to understand: we had been taking the bread from his mouth.

Some mornings after that, I came upon Felicien Obin by the lagoon, in the middle of a group of fishermen. Everybody was talking hard. Among them was a tall negro whom I hadn't seen in the village before.

He was naked to the waist and wore blue jeans, and he seemed to be the central figure in the conversation. He left the group from time to time, went down to the edge of the water as if to gauge its depth, then pointed to a particular part of the lagoon and returned to the rest, as if to convince them of something.

I went up to them. The black athlete was speaking Spanish. Obin, who was interpreting, fell silent at my approach, and everyone looked at me as if expecting me to solve a delicate problem.

The unknown negro took two steps towards me and shook hands; I thought my bones would crack. I must have winced, for he laughed loudly and clapped me on the shoulder with a blow powerful enough to fell an ox.

These preliminaries over, Obin explained in his own jargon what it was all about.

The negro in the jeans, with his half-baked look and loud laugh, had suggested a startling plan, which was to drive a big shark into the lagoon through the narrow channel that separated it from the sea, and leave it there "on ice" for a time, until it was hungry. Then he would tackle it with a knife in front of the assembled village and, having killed it, receive a small reward. His name was Sambo and he came from the Dominican Republic, where he had killed some thirty sharks with his own hands. For the moment he was living in one of the mountain villages, where he was to marry a girl he had known in Port au Prince.

Naturally he had heard of the arrival of two white foreigners, and this had encouraged him to come down from the hills. The whites were to contribute fifty dollars each as the price of admission to the show.

The other men were hesitating because they suspected some trick. Attack a shark with a knife? Such a thing had never been seen, declared Obin sententiously. Sambo would merely waste their time and wring a few *gourdes* out of them on some pretext or other. I was asked for my opinion.

In fact, the idea excited them all very much, and as soon as it was agreed that Sambo should receive no money until after the fight, Obin himself gave in. There were few amusements in the village, apart from cock-fighting every other Sunday, which enthralled the men but aroused only moderate enthusiasm in the women. The latter preferred the travelling film-show which came once a month from Port au Prince, in a van driven by two mulattos. The films were shown in the harbour, the screen being a sheet stretched between two poles, and these performances were made the occasion of a tremendous spree which soaked up all the week's profits; for the movie-men brought not only prehistoric films with them, but a whole cargo of cakes, coloured frocks, combs, and other knick-knacks.

Once the plan had been agreed upon, Sambo explained how he would set about it, though without giving too many details. He would stand in the lagoon at a point where the water was no more than five feet deep, and wait, knife in hand, until the shark attacked him.

He showed us his weapon: a broad, two-edged blade about ten inches long set in a curved haft. He told us that he had already been wounded three times, and showed us a deep semi-circular scar on his left thigh. He added that no shark attacked by him had ever survived the battle. On this occasion, too, he expected to earn his money.

Preparations for the show were put in hand.

To drive a shark through a channel seventeen feet long by three wide into a pool which is nowhere deeper than a couple of fathoms is in itself a feat. Sambo began by throwing in chunks of rotten meat at each end of the channel, and in the channel itself. The first sharks appeared at the end of the afternoon. They dashed at the bait floating in the sea at the mouth of the narrows, and then—either because they were no longer hungry or because instinct warned them of a trap—they turned about and disappeared.

The procedure was repeated next day. Sambo stood beside the inlet, ready to block it with boards as soon as a shark passed along it; but none seemed inclined to try.

By the evening of the third day the villagers were getting restless. They didn't want to wait six months. After work the fishermen came to sit in little groups beside the channel, chatted for a bit, and then moved off with wagging heads and suppressed laughter. Then a shark did come in—a blue shark measuring twelve or thirteen feet—which could not have eaten for a week, judging from the ravenous way it devoured the meat at the entrance to the lagoon. The channel had been swept clean of bait, as if with a broom.

Once in the lagoon, its hunger appeased, the monster seemed surprised at the shallowness of the water, and cruised about disconcertedly; then it dropped slowly to the bottom and lay there motionless.

Having blocked the outlet, Sambo rose and squatted by the edge of the lagoon, just above the apparently lifeless shark. There, with a tense look on his face, he gazed at the great fish for a long time, as if trying to guess at the quickness of its reactions and the thickness of its armour.

Relaxed and smiling, he then rose and uttered a series of howls, to announce to the village that the first stage of the operation was completed, and that in three or four days the show could begin.

This delay was necessary, Sambo explained to me, both to give the shark time to become familiar with the shape of the pool and to get hungry. It would then attack as soon as he entered the water.

"He must attack first," said Sambo. "I can't kill him otherwise."

This time he explained to me in detail how he would set about it. It was a neat and simple method.

"The shark dashes at me, and see-saws a little just before snapping at my thigh. I step back quickly, bring the knife forward and plunge it into his throat. As he moves very quickly then, he rips himself up on it, like a zip-fastener!"

It was best, of course, to kill at the first blow.

"For afterwards, with all the blood, the water gets cloudy and Sambo can't see. Comprende, señor?"

Naturally there were risks, but they were not so great as one might think. The whole art lay in knowing when to step back, and to be quick about it. (The terrible crescent-shaped scar was a souvenir of one of these underwater corridas when Sambo had retreated a split second too late.)

He added that in the Dominican Republic, where he meant to return as soon as he was married, he and one other man practised this sport at festival-time, when many people came down into the coastal villages. The idea had come to them after they heard of an American mulatto who regularly earned small fortunes in the Florida swamps by tackling alligators with his bare hands, for the entertainment of tourists.

The mulatto (of whom a short film had been made) was able to do this by taking advantage of a peculiarity in the jaw mechanism of the alligator. The animal has muscles enabling it to seize its prey with tremendous force, but the muscles for opening the jaws are practically nonexistent. Once he could grasp the jaws and hold them shut, he deprived his adversary of its most formidable weapon. A fascinating wrestling-match ensued in a few feet of water and mud at the edge of the swamp, ending as often as not in the beast being dragged ashore, where it was roped by the man's assistants.

"He called himself 'the first man to kill an alligator with his bare hands,' " said Sambo. "So we decided to be 'the first men to kill sharks with their bare hands.' "

What Sambo didn't know—nor I either at the time—was that this hand-to-hand struggle between man and shark was the revival of an old Polynesian custom.

In the Hawaiian islands, some centuries ago, on occasions of popular rejoicing, the native kings organised duels in which men, armed only with a long shark's tooth fixed to a horn handle, challenged sharks to single combat. Tradition says that the Hawaiians attacked the shark from the rear; they seized it by the tail and hung on, and from this comparatively safe position plunged their weapon into the creature's belly.

On Sunday, four days after the shark's entry, at three o'clock in the afternoon, Sambo walked into the lagoon.

The crowd massed on the bank presented a really astonishing sight. In this barren setting, this end-of-the-world landscape, the locals had dressed up as if for a party at the *Cabane Choucoune* (a night-dive in

Port au Prince). They wore ties, stiff collars, and white jackets, or else dark suits, or ancient dinner jackets which looked as if they had attended every gathering in the Haitian capital for a generation, and which the fishermen had bought either from a secondhand-clothes dealer in Port au Prince or from the movie-men. All these garments were shabby and dirty, but meticulously buttoned up.

The women wore frocks with starched trimmings, and carried parasols or fanned themselves with fans made from cardboard boxes.

During the foregoing week the whole village had passed along the shores of the lagoon gazing at the shark, which paraded slowly in wide, concentric circles, evidently searching for something to eat; they had watched it for hours, thrown stones at it, and generally amused themselves. And now, massed side by side, they waited.

At the other end of the lagoon a fisherman threw stones to attract the shark's attention, so that Sambo might reach the spot he had chosen for the fight. He waded out a few yards from the edge until the water reached his chest.

The shark was nowhere to be seen; then suddenly, in a corner of the lagoon that sparkled like a mirror in the sun, a fin appeared at the surface, moved slowly along in the direction of the negro and then sank, leaving behind it a faint trail of foam.

Sambo bent over the water in a waiting position, his knife between his knees. From the crowd not a sound was heard.

About two yards in front of Sambo's feet the sandy floor of the lagoon shelved abruptly to a depth of a fathom or two; here the shark paused, its nose towards him. A tremor that ran through its body made it look as if it were on the point of attacking; but many long minutes were still to pass before that happened. The great fish turned about, went away, came back. . . . At each turn a murmur went up from the crowd.

Then for the last time the shark hung motionless some yards from the negro. Just when it looked like turning yet again, we saw Sambo testing the sand behind him with his foot; then he moved slowly backwards to provoke the attack.

The rest was lost in a maelstrom of foam.

• • •

A few seconds later Sambo straightened himself and almost immediately dived, his eyes apparently fixed on the shark, which we could not see for the flurry of the water. He stayed below for what seemed a long time, then stood up, raised the hand that held the knife and showed it to the crowd. With the other he pointed to the place in the lagoon where the unseen shark had gone to the bottom.

Then, as in the circus when the acrobat catches the trapeze after the perilous double somersault, one could hear a long sigh moving like a wave through the double row of onlookers. No exclamations, however. The general feeling was that the whole thing had happened too quickly and that they hadn't had their money's worth.

Then the shark was dragged up on to the sand, where, with its belly ripped open along its whole length, it appeared nearly twice as big as we had thought it. From the incision, which was as neat as a surgeon's, issued blood and entrails, and this did prompt some nods of satisfaction. It was a nice bit of work.

The rest of the day was spent in dancing and drinking. The people danced not to tom-toms but quite prosaically to the music of an ancient gramophone (another "present" from the movie-men). By midnight the whole village was asleep. Some of the men had collapsed on the sand, knocked out by alcohol, and were sleeping it off in their double-breasted suits and old dinner jackets. It was an extraordinary sight. One might have thought that some vessel had gone down off the coast and that the passengers, in their evening clothes, had been washed up here.

from Tales of Fishing Virgin Seas
by Zane Grey

Known mostly for novels about the American West, Zane Grey's (1872–1939) first writing assignment was a fishing story. He spent most of his free time fishing and sailing in various parts of the world, and held records in at least fourteen deep-sea fishing categories.

W e had come to regard a certain place as the best Marlin water in the vicinity. Probably it was no better than any other locality thereabouts, but having sighted more Marlin there we naturally went back. Captain Heston told us that the hundred-fathom bank directly off the Cape was the best swordfish ground. We had not had any luck there. In the morning early we trolled for bait off the steep wide beach of golden sand along the east shore of the bay. Mackerel were plentiful at times, and rarely we got a golden grouper. The difficulty was to keep one of the big hundred-pound cobias off the hook. This species of jewfish or bass, was a hard fighter, and it was more work than fun to catch him.

When we had caught some bait we ran down the shore, off the rocky point, where the green swells roared and crashed, out several miles into the Gulf. A red desert headland, bleak and barren, furnished a landmark. Usually we trailed teasers behind the boat and watched closely for Marlin. While the tuna were striking it was not worthwhile to try to troll a bait for swordfish.

We had trolled all morning without sight of any kind of a fish. The market boats had worked to the eastward, close inshore. The sea was dark blue, calm, and hot under the noonday sun. I was trying to keep from falling into a doze when Sid roused me:

"They're yellin' for us. Somthin' doin'."

At the same time he opened both throttles. I got up to face forward, with zest and the old curious thrill. R. C.'s boat was perhaps a quarter of a mile from us. R. C. was standing in the stern and instead of a rod he held his camera. Next instant I espied a high sharp black fin not far behind his boat. He yelled and waved for us to come.

"It's a basking shark, like we saw the other day," shouted Sid.

I thought so, too, but when we got within a hundred feet and I had a close view of that enormous fish I changed my mind. Still, it had the shape of a shark tail.

"What do you know about this?" yelled R. C. "Some fish! He's bigger than the boat. Doesn't seem to mind us."

Sid ran my boat closer. I saw white spots on the huge fin. It was not a fin, but the lobe of an enormous tail. I saw a silvery green mass, long and wide, with projections. The sunlight shining through the water upon this fish produced that peculiar green color. We always saw that green made when a whale was moving along under the surface. Then in another moment the green changed to a dark beautiful blue, dotted and streaked all over by a brilliant silver. The dorsal fin was low and stubby, the pectorals huge, apparently fan-shaped, almost resembling the wings of a colossal bat. The fish had a wide flat head, like that of a catfish, and he was close to sixty feet long. I recognized him as one of the rarest creatures in the sea—the *Rhineodon typus*, or whale shark. I had always wondered if I would ever have the luck to see one. Dr. Gudger of the New York Natural History Museum is the authority on this strange fish, and he had sent me his fascinating booklet, containing all that was scientifically known about it.

In 1829 a Dr. Smith of South Africa harpooned a large shark of unusual appearance, and assisted by a number of men finally captured it. The shark was of unknown species. Dr. Smith named it *Rhineodon typus*.

This first specimen was fifteen feet long and nine in circumference. The skin was sent to the Paris Museum.

In 1850 Dr. Buist described a gigantic shark native to Kurrachee in northwest India, forty to sixty feet in length. This no doubt was the *Rhineodon typus*. In 1865 Dr. Gill described an enormous spotted shark of the Gulf of California, called by the natives "Tiburone ballenas," or "Whale shark." A specimen about twenty feet long was sent to the Smithsonian Institution.

In 1902 an eighteen-foot *Rhineodon* floated ashore at Ormond, Florida. From that year writers made frequent mention of the *Rhineodon*; and it became evident that the great shark had a wide distribution. Around the Seychelles Islands north of Madagascar, this species was common. In the Indian Ocean it is called chagrin.

In 1912, Captain Thompson, a local boatman of Miami, Florida, captured a *Rhineodon* thirty-eight feet long. This fish was exhibited as an unknown sea monster, and was finally identified by Dr. Gudger. In 1924, my boatman, Captain Newton Knowles, with whom I have fished for years around Long Key, Florida, harpooned and killed a *Rhineodon* somewhat smaller than Thompson's.

Knowles told me there were two sharks together, and that the one he harpooned was much the smaller. An interesting statement was that the bridge-tender on the viaduct below Knight's Key informed Knowles he saw a number of these huge sharks every June. They came across the shoals from Florida Bay, and were working out into the Gulf Stream. Knowles said the shallow water made the capture of his fish a comparatively easy matter.

I remembered all this in a flash, while at the same time I was keen to photograph that lazy weaving black tail. I was afraid the fish would take fright and sound, but it paid not the slightest attention to either boat. We moved along very slowly, with the fish between us and a little ahead.

"What the devil is it?" called Bob King, leaning over the gunwale.

"*Rhineodon typus,*" I replied, with the satisfaction of being able to classify what none of us had ever seen.

"By golly!" ejaculated Bob. "He shore ought to have a crazy name like that. He's the darndest-lookin' fish I ever saw. Let's ketch him!"

This instinct of capture might never have roused in me but for Bob. He could not see any kind of a fish, little or big, without wanting to catch it. Nevertheless, even as that boyish desire burned up in me, I knew perfectly well we could not hold such an enormous brute, if we did get fast to it.

We had one enormous gaff, and thought to get that in the shark. So, tying it to a heavy rope, we ran almost up on top of the fish. That afforded clearer view. The size was tremendous. From its dorsal fin to its head the length exceeded that of our boat, and it was wider than our beam. Lazily, with ponderous, slow weave of tail, it moved along, six or eight feet under the surface. Its dark blue color changed to a velvety brown, and the silver spots turned white. There was an exquisite purple along the edge of the broad pectoral fins. Altogether its colossal size, its singular beauty, its indifference to the boats, its suggestion of incredible power, made it the most wonderful fish I had ever seen.

"Good night!" called R. C., facetiously, as Heisler prepared to throw the gaff over the fish. "We'll pick up your remains in a minute."

I was standing on deck, beside Heisler, who wielded the heavy gaff. Up to that instant I had not thought of danger. The fish was harmless. But I realized that one blow from its tail could smash and sink us. What a strange cold prickle of my skin. I was all tight, breathless, staring, and as Heisler threw the gaff I suddenly sat down and held on to the hatch. Still I could see. The gaff sank over the side of the shark. Heisler pulled with all his might. It slipped off. The fish did not appear to be aware of our ambitious and evil intent. Bob was yelling, I know not what. R. C. and Chester had the cameras on us, and I was sure they were gleefully expecting to see us go flying into the air, with the debris of the boat. Heisler threw the gaff again. It would not stick. Twice more he failed to get a hold.

"Leave me have that gaff," yelled Bob. "I got six hundred feet of rope."

We gave it over to him quite with alacrity. Then we ran alongside just a little behind. R. C. took the wheel of his boat, while Chester stood up on deck, at the camera.

"Don't blame me if we lose this Bell and Howell machine," he called, in grim humor.

Bob got out on the bow with the gaff. He had put it on the pole, and evidently did not intend to throw it loose on the rope, as Heisler had done. Bob motioned for R. C. to run the boat to suit him, and then drew up close to that weaving black tail. Bob lunged to gaff that tail. He got hold, but not securely. I stood breathlessly, pointing my camera, expecting to see something most startling. The fish did not change speed or position. His tail stuck six feet above the water. Bob took more time, waiting till the tail was right under him. Then he gaffed it. I saw the iron go through.

Next instant the tail disappeared in a waterspout. Then followed a thunderous crash that stopped my heart. But it was a sound of churning water. The shark had not hit the boat. I had been frightened out of securing a remarkable picture. The turmoil at the bow subsided. Then I saw Bob paying out rope, and huge bulges and swirls ahead of the boat. R. C. put on full speed, and so did Sid. We chased the *Rhineodon typus*. It was not a long chase, yet I felt I had never experienced one in any way similar. I could hardly believe what I saw. And I was convinced it would be over quickly. But that fish came up before long and swam on the surface as before. The gaff hook stuck there in the high black tail. We ran alongside and hailed that crew with excitement equal to their own.

Bob got Chester to hold the rope, while he went below. I divined at once that he meant to rig up some kind of an iron. Bob had a reputation in Florida for catching huge rays, sharks, manatees, alligators; and I knew he was bent on outdoing the feats of Thompson and Knowles. Chester had been left a Herculean task. But he was valiant. And when he lost rope R. C. would run the boat ahead so that he recovered it. Sometimes the black tail would slap against the bow.

Presently Bob appeared with some kind of a spear rigged from a file that had been bound on a gaff pole. He attached a rope to the spear. Then with business-like promptness he plunged the thing into the fish. He shoved down on it with all his might. The shark made a roaring hole in the sea, almost large enough to swamp the boat. Then he sounded. R. C.'s boat ran to the edge of the maelstrom and stopped. Quickly the water smoothed out, hissing and seething. Both ropes went slipping over the gunwale until several hundred feet were gone. Gradually then the shark slowed until he stopped. With that Bob signaled us to come alongside.

"Go back to the ship an' fetch ropes, barrels, harpoons, guns," he called. "We'll ketch this rhinoceros tappus."

I tried to persuade Bob that we had no equipment equal to the job.

"Shore we can ketch him," he replied, with a keen flash of his blue eyes.

"But the water is deep," I protested. "Those few that have been caught were found in shallow water."

"This bird will come up," averred Bob. "We'll get a couple more holds, then when he comes to the surface break his back with bullets. Bring your heavy guns."

"But there's danger—leaving you here alone," I replied, hesitating.

"Give you my word we'll keep away from him," said Bob.

At that assurance I consented and we headed towards the bay at a speed never before equaled by the little boat. The stern sunk down level with the water and the bow stood high. How the engines roared! It was impossible for me not to revel in the whole proceeding, however preposterous it was.

Upon reaching the ship we created a great deal of excitement by our hurry, and what seemed mysterious conduct.

"Get Romer, Johnny, Captain Mitchell," I yelled, and rushed to my cabin for guns and shells, more films, a heavy coat, and a flashlight. Heisler was to get the other things Bob wanted. When I emerged Romer and Johnny met me wild with excitement and curiosity.

"We're hooked on to a *Rhineodon typus* sixty feet long," I said, in answer to their queries.

"What on earth's that?" shouted Romer. "Where? How? When? Is it a sea serpent?"

"Get your coats. Hustle," was all the satisfaction I gave them.

In a few moments we were again aboard the little boat. Captain Mitchell forgot his hat. Everybody left on board cheered from the rail. We shot off to the eastward between two sheets of spray. Then I had time to tell the boys what a *Rhineodon typus* was and how we had come to get tangled up with one. If anything this information only served to make them wilder.

We expected any moment to see R. C.'s boat coming back. But we were mistaken, and when finally I sighted it, a dot on the horizon, it appeared to be stationary. They were still fast to the fish. We were thirty-five minutes getting back to R. C.'s boat. They waved and yelled a welcome. I believed R. C. looked relieved. The shark was on the surface, tail and dorsal out, and it was towing the boat.

We gaily hailed R. C. and his men, and running close put Captain Mitchell aboard his boat. Before I could ask Bob what the next procedure should be R. C. pointed out to sea and said:

"I hate to make you feel bad," he said. "But look there."

I looked hastily, with eager thrill. But before I saw anything except water Romer let out a wild yell. "Look! Look! Big Marlin! Oh, he's a whale. Right there!"

Presently I espied the short stubby black fin and the long blade-like tail of a Marlin. The striking thing was the extreme length between dorsal and tail. Fully ten feet! Then the low dorsal and dark color proclaimed the fish a black Marlin. He lay on the surface some two hundred yards out, evidently sunning himself on the glassy sea.

"Boys, you'll have to dispense with our services for a little while," I said. "Here, Bob, take all this truck we brought."

"Gimme some rope an' a keg," replied Bob. "You go an' ketch that Marlin. We'll wait. Our Rhinoceros is millin' round nowhere in particular."

My rod and baited hook lay in the cockpit, just where I had placed them when we quit trolling. Taking them up, I instructed Sid to run round that Marlin so I could drag my golden bait in front of him. When we were about two hundred feet from him I happened to remember the teasers.

"Throw the teasers out," I shouted. "Slow down a little. There. Now keep away from him."

Scarcely had the port teaser begun to twinkle and flash in the wake of the launch when the Marlin woke up and disappeared in a heavy swirl. But I had seen him head toward us.

"Boys, he's coming. He saw the teaser," I said, excitedly, as I frantically wound my bait in. I had let out perhaps sixty feet of line. In that few seconds, before I could reel my bait close to the teaser, the dark purple flash of that Marlin appeared between my bait and the teaser. With what bullet-speed he had come! His thick black dorsal showed above the surface. To and fro he weaved, with the marvelous quickness peculiar to this fish. A few more turns of my reel brought the golden bait in front of the Marlin. He snapped it in, sheered away, leaving a violent swirl in the water. The moment was singularly thrilling. I thought I was cool, but most likely made a mistake. My legs shook as I sat down to drop the rodbutt in the seat-socket. The line whizzed off the reel. When I was about to strike the line went slack. He had spit out the bait. I had let him have it too long. Romer's disappointment exceeded mine, which was great enough. "You let him run too far!" And Sid's comment was similar in import. "These Marlin don't take a cut bait like they do a flying-fish. You ought to have hit him quick."

"A bird in hand is worth two in the bush," observed Johnny, sagely.

Forthwith I forgot another wonderful opportunity to catch a great Marlin; and we sped back to R. C.'s boat.

"He sure was hungry. It was some strike. Too bad!" said R. C.

"These Marlin are like sailfish," added Bob. "You want to soak them when they turn away with the hook. How big was he?"

"I couldn't be sure, but over five hundred, anyway. . . . What shall we do now?"

"Jab a couple of irons into this Rhinoceros," replied Bob, and he instructed Heisler just where and how to hit the shark.

We ran ahead, alongside our quarry, now with dorsal out of the water. I discarded camera for rifle. With calmer eye I judged the *Rhineodon* to exceed fifty feet in length, at the most conservative estimate.

But if he had shrunk a little in size he still retained his strange beauty. We drew close, with the bow at his head. Heisler lunged down with the pole. It was as if he had struck a rock. The iron came back bent. While Heisler hammered it straight the huge fish swam on unconcernedly. Soon Heisler was ready for another try. We had grown somewhat hardened to the presence of the *Rhineodon* and therefore less fearful. We ran right alongside it, so that I had the most wonderful sight of this marine monster. Heisler repeated his harpooning performance, with all the violence of which he was capable. Crash went the mighty tail. We were deluged with water. Everybody on both boats appeared to be yelling hoarse instructions. I heard the impact of the fish against the boat. "Hold on!" yelled Heisler. I thought he meant for the boys to stay with him at the rope. But when the boat began to rise out of the water I knew differently. Then with the lifting motion came a tremendous scraping on the bottom of the boat. The shark had swerved under us. The boys fell with Heisler, all hanging to the rope. I came within an inch of going overboard, but managed desperately to cling to a ringbolt until the launch righted. Then the threshing, thumping tail appeared above water on our port side. What a narrow escape! The iron pulled out, the rope slackened; and that enabled us to run from in front of Bob, who was swearing lustily. When we got in good position again Bob called for Heisler to come aboard his launch. Still the *Rhineodon* stayed on the surface. Bob was soon ready, and we followed close beside his boat. The shark was moving faster now, though still high in the water. While Heisler, Chester, and Mitchell held the ropes, Bob plunged the iron deep back of the dorsal. Roar of beaten water, flooded bobbing boats, blinded fishermen! Pandemonium prevailed for a few seconds, until the deluge subsided. That was surely the most terrific moment in all my fishing experience. My blood ran cold, my heart seemed to freeze, then burst. I had most thought of Romer. But he, with strong brown hands hung on to that boat with the grim zest of passionate, fearless youth. Above the other noise I heard his piercing yell to Johnny, who was likewise strenuously engaged. I had one knee locked on the engine hatch, and my other leg hung overboard. The rifle had fallen, luckily to catch along the rail. When I extricated myself I was relieved to see that the *Rhineodon* had sounded, and was taking line with remarkable swiftness compared to his former movements. Bob had two ropes and Heisler had one. Chester and Mitchell were very busy getting out other ropes.

At about six hundred feet the shark stopped, and swam on at that depth, towing the boat for miles an hour. Presently, at Bob's word, the four men began to haul in on the ropes. It was a slow, laborsome task. The ropes had to be coiled in tubs as they came in. The afternoon was still and hot. Red-faced, and dripping sweat, the men worked incessantly. It took an hour to pull the *Rhineodon* to the surface. How funny to see the big gaff-hook waving in that black tail! He towed the boat a couple of miles inshore, and then to the westward. Then he sounded. The men had a harder job to haul him up. They were wringing wet, and Bob, who had labored longest, was a sight to behold.

To make a long story short, they fought that fish until nearly sunset, during which it sounded five times, going deeper every time, the last being over twelve hundred feet.

When they got him up again Bob yelled to me, "Come aboard this boat with your big rifle." We ran up to them and I went aboard, together with Romer and Johnny. While I watched for a chance to shoot, the boys pitched in to help. But the *Rhineodon* did not come to the surface enough for me to disable it, even with the big fifty caliber.

Sunset came. Our quarry manifestly thought it was his bedtime, for he suddenly sounded. The ropes sped down. Different lengths of rope, tied together, marked how many feet he descended. Six hundred! Twelve hundred! Fifteen! Two of the tubs went overboard to sink. Heisler made a Herculean effort to save his tub, but it could not be done. As the end of the rope left his hands he kicked the tub overboard. Some one else had the white line to which the tub-rope was attached.

Down, slower and slower, but surely inevitably down, the great shark sounded. The boys, with Chester and Mitchell, strove frantically to save a new rope from following the others. In vain! Foot by foot it slipped through their wet, grimy gloved hands. Bob had his rope under the cleat on the bow. He too was in desperate straits, but not vanquished.

Here I put aside my rifle and entered the fray. The spirit to conquer that brute was contagious. When the last few feet of new rope lay in sight, Chester hurriedly tied the last ball of white line to the end. Bob was panting and swearing. "More rope! . . . We'll lick him yet. Somebody get more rope. I'm losin' heah."

"Just tied on the last piece," replied Chester.

Then followed a short intense struggle to stop the fish, before he had all the rope. Heisler nearly went overboard hanging on to his, but he lost it. That was the last I saw clearly, for my eyes grew red with the effort I was making. We knew indeed we were whipped, at least all of us knew except Bob. For when I gave the order to take a half hitch with the ropes and let the fish pull free of the irons Bob groaned loudly. Then he panted: "Got to—hand it—to old Rhinoceros. I've more—respect for him—than I started with."

Upon comparing notes we found that we had seen four *Rhineodon typus* close to the vicinity where the battle had taken place.

Takahashi visited the Japanese fishermen and returned with some interesting information. Two of the large net boats had been towed by one of these sharks for eighteen hours before it broke away. Another net boat caught a fifty-four-foot *Rhineodon* in their net, and turned it loose.

The market fishermen saw a number of them every season in the Gulf of California, and they were especially numerous on the east shore of Santa Margarita Island.

This news only added to the sum of wonderful fish in those southern waters, and fanned the flame of my desire to visit them again, with better equipment and more time, so that all the marvelous fishing possibilities could be realized.

from Last Horizons
by Peter Hathaway Capstick

Peter Hathaway Capstick (born 1940) left a career on Wall Street to spend his life hunting and fishing, and wrote about his adventures for sportsmen's magazines.

José's mahogany knuckles tightened and showed white as the long anchor line came taut. In a practiced motion, the fishing-safari guide deftly dropped a loop over the bow post and the heavy dugout swung to a halt.

We were anchored in "the pool," as the natives know it, where Nicaragua's San Juan River byways merge to form a dread outpost for the voracious freshwater shark. In the vicinity, at the moment, about thirty big, slate-colored dorsal fins cut the surface.

Upstream from us, beyond a shallow stretch, the water became deep again and was flecked with a patchwork of bright jungle sunshine that filtered through the treetops overhanging the bank. Antenna-tailed parrots and colorful dragonflies darted about overhead like spectators to the coming encounter. The heavy air was oppressive and ominous.

As we watched, every few minutes a big shark or two would splash across the shallow water and slide into the deep-water hunting grounds upstream.

Nicaragua is one of the strangest geological areas on earth. It has two major lakes (both densely populated by killer sharks) and a string of twenty-three volcanoes that run down the western side of the country, many of which are still active. In 1835, one of these, Coseguina, blew its top with a roar heard in Bogota, Colombia, 1,100 miles away. Pieces of the cone landed as far as 150 miles out to sea. The capital city of Managua was itself leveled by an earthquake in 1931, with a terrible loss of life.

But the history of life and death in the area seemed much more remote, at that moment, than the possibility of a personal disaster. Watching José study the menacing fins, one sensed that he knew the ferocity of the beasts beneath the surface of the chocolate-colored water better than an ordinary fisherman. Needless to say, I was pleased to have him along.

At last, turning his attention to the twelve feet of hardwood lying along the gunwale, he asked, *"Listo, Patrón?"* ("Are you ready?") I glanced at the heavy harpoon, the hand-forged point glinting from its fresh honing. The silky, white nylon sash cord was securely wired to the ring welded below the steel barbs. It ran along the shaft to the slip-knot six feet up the green wood, and trailed off to a neat coil in the dugout's bow. The rig was ready. *"Listo,"* I said, wondering if this was quite as good an idea as it had seemed an hour ago. José mumbled something in Spanish about his spiritual future, crossed himself, and swung the bloody sack over the side into the murky water. . . .

My first exposure to Nicaragua's dread freshwater sharks came over a very dry martini. I was lunching with Alfredo Bequillard, Jr., the owner of Tarpon Camp, a famous hot spot on the San Juan River, Lake Nicaragua's only connection with the men at sea. I had been sent to Nicaragua by Winchester Adventures, Inc., a subsidiary of the well-known arms manufacturers, to check out the fantastic tarpon fishing on the San Juan. Winchester represents a string of top-notch outfits like Alfredo's around the world, each personally inspected by their staffers before receiving their seal of approval.

Al told me that only three weeks before, a young boy had taken a dive into the river at San Carlos, a small village located at the mouth of the river where it flows from Lake Nicaragua to the Caribbean, some 130 miles away. The boy surfaced and immediately was dragged shrieking beneath the surface by a large shark. No part of the boy was ever found, Al told me. One day in 1944, three persons were attacked by a single shark near Granada, a good-sized city on the shores of the lake. Two were killed and one badly mauled. My own guide, José, told me that his uncle had been killed by a river shark in 1960, just below the location of the present camp. He had fallen overboard and what was recovered of the shredded torso indicated that more than one man-eater was on the prowl that afternoon. When I arrived on the river, a few days later, I was told of eight other definite shark attacks that had had fatal consequences. I spoke with one old man who had been grabbed by the foot in very shallow water by a four-footer. Two toes were missing and infection had set in. He had pried the shark loose with his hands.

Nicaraguans who live along the river say that at least one person each year is taken by the sharks, sometimes four or five. In the village of Castillo, about halfway between giant Lake Nicaragua and the sea, there was one very big shark that hung out at the base of a set of small rapids. This monster had terrorized fishermen for a three-month period, ramming light dugouts and seizing paddles in his huge jaws. He would attack anything that entered his territory. The river people knew it was always the same shark from his extreme size and the definite yellow cast of his hide. Finally harpooned and shot, he was over twelve feet in length.

No one has ever been able to completely unravel the riddle of the freshwater shark. Probably the most logical theory as to how a saltwater animal came to survive and prosper in fresh water is that Lake Nicaragua was once a large saltwater bay. During one of the cataclysmic upheavals of the earth common to this region, a land bridge was raised, cutting off the bay from the sea, forming the lake. In it were, of course, all the species of fish normally found in the saltwater Central

American zone. As the ages passed, the water became less and less salty through dilution by heavy rainfall, and most of the ocean species died. However, the cub shark, also known as the ground or bull shark, did adapt and exists today as the freshwater variant called the Lake Nicaragua shark *(Carcharhinus nicaraguensis)*. The U.S. Navy "Shark Danger" ratings list the Lake Nicaragua shark on a par with the feared tiger shark, giving a rating of 2+.

There are many other species in the lake and the San Juan River that are common to both fresh and salt water, namely the snook, tarpon and sawfish. These species are, however, anadromous, meaning that, like the shad and salmon, they will run into fresh water as a matter of normal course.

The Lake Nicaragua shark is considered to be the only true freshwater shark, but the habit of other species of shark to enter fresh water is not as rare an occurrence as it might at first seem. There is an Indian variety, the Ganges shark, that kills an average of twenty bathers a year in that holy river. In 1959, during a two-month period, thirty-five persons were mauled or killed in the Devi River by this shark.

Sharks have been reported up rivers in such far-flung places as Thailand, Malaya, New Zealand, South Africa, Mozambique, Peru, Guatemala, Australia, Japan, and Fiji. A British military ambulance driver was one of twenty-seven people both mauled and killed in the Karun River of Iran during an eight-year period in the 1940s. A seven-hundred pounder was even found on the beach of Marlboro, New York, fifty miles up the Hudson River, after what was probably a collision with a steamboat in 1926. Eight years later, New York City police flashed a shark alert along the Hudson as far north as Poughkeepsie. A shark had been sighted off the West 42nd Street pier, six blocks from Times Square.

These cases, however, are clearly of sharks that have come from the sea into fresh water and then returned to the sea. The Lake Nicaragua shark is born, lives, and dies completely in fresh water, quite unlike all other species. Natives of the river claim that there are, in fact, two varieties of killers haunting their waters, the reddish-bellied *tintorero* and the white-bellied *visitante,* which they believe does run in from the sea. I think this theory is false. Many of the sharks I have harpooned over several trips to the San Juan would roll upon feeling the steel, clearly showing their snow-white bellies. But, after a long fight against the line, they had pink or red bellies upon being dispatched. It seems to me that the exertion of the fight would break the small blood vessels under the skin, and the blood could be seen through the white skin. Also, if some did run in from the sea, why did they only run up the San Juan? There are many rivers along Central America's east coast, yet only the San Juan and Lake Nicaragua hold these killers.

Alfredo's camp turned out to be an absolute paradise for tarpon. The run of these silver kings (many well over one hundred pounds) between January and June is simply fantastic. But after three days of even this great fishing, I still couldn't get the sharks off my mind. We had caught two on handlines off the camp's dock, and I was amazed to see them clear the water in high, twisting leaps. We had also witnessed their speed and ferocious power as they attacked hooked tarpon we were fighting. They would slash in, either alone or in packs, surrounding the big tarpon. A sudden charge, and they would rip thirty-pound chunks of flesh from the fear-mad tarpon. We would cut the line, but it was always too late as they would glide away in a cloud of spreading blood. It made me sick to see these great gamesters butchered like that. Then José asked whether I was willing to try the pool. Maybe the heat was getting to me, but I said yes.

José hauled the anchor and we went off to the village of Castillo to barter some .22-caliber cartridges for three of the big harpoon heads. We cut a twelve-foot sapling and shaped the thick end of it to fit the skirtlike base of the steel, much the way a hoe head fits its shaft. On the way back to the pool, we stopped and bought the entrails of a cow that had been slaughtered that morning. José put the reeking mess into a burlap sack and tied a short length of rope around the neck. I broke out the long nylon handline and two hundred feet of sash cord, checked the .357 Magnum at my belt and we were in business. . . .

• • •

A cloud of red blossomed from the bag José had swung over the side, and the blood surged downstream into the pool. Thirty seconds went by. Then we saw it. It started with a small V on the dark surface, rising slowly until a foot and a half of the fin gleamed like wet lead above the long, tapered shape. It cut the water like a tiny sailboat tacking as the huge shark cast its ten-foot length back and forth like a pointer trying to locate a running quail. Other dorsals appeared as the bag of bloody cattle entrails seeped its invitation into the current. I slipped the leather glove over my left hand and raised the harpoon as the shark moved out of the pool and headed directly for us, the long upper lobe of the tail waving above the shallow water.

It glided closer to the dugout, the half-open mouth agleam with snaggled teeth, its cat's eyes reflecting dully as it paused in a patch of sunshine ten feet away. A gentle thrust of the big tail brought it nearer. At five feet, I threw with every ounce of strength I had, hearing the *thug* as the steel tore through gristle and muscle. For a fraction of a second, nothing happened. *Then it charged.* It hit the side of the dugout while I was still off balance from the thrust. The long harpoon shaft, jutting from the top of its head, flashed by my face as I felt myself teetering over the enraged shark.

My stomach flipped as I felt myself start to fall over the side. The shark, harpoon-head jutting from its skull, lay four feet away, watching me, wounded but waiting like a striking bushmaster. José's hand flashed out and grabbed my belt, jerking me backward into the bottom of the dugout. We almost swamped the light craft, but somehow we didn't go over. I felt as if I'd been quite literally snatched from the jaws of fate.

The shark reacted by turning and tearing off downstream, the harpoon line melting from the coil of rope in the bow. I grabbed the nylon with my gloved hand and tried to slow down its escape. I might as well have tried to snub a falling safe. There was simply no holding it. The balsa-wood float tied to the end of the line whipped off the bow, and skittered across the surface like a terrified, giant waterbug. José hoisted the anchor and we followed, catching up with the float a half-mile away in quiet, deep water. I plucked the float from the water and felt the throbbing power at the end of the line again. Slowly, I worked it in, only to have it take off again, the line ripping through my fingers. Finally, after almost an hour, we worked it close enough to put four .357-caliber tranquilizers through the Y-shaped brain. That quieted it down quite a bit.

I slipped the big gaff into the killer's gill slits and we tried to haul it aboard. It was useless. It must have weighed over four hundred pounds. I wasn't so hot to share the accommodations, anyway. It took another hour to haul it upstream against the current to our camp, but we were anxious for a look at what the bulging stomach might contain.

It took most of the staff at Tarpon Camp to drag the big shark up onto the shore where José let out the sawdust with a butcher knife. José was a man who enjoyed his work. We took a look into the four-foot incision and got quite a surprise. There, each wrapped in its own little membrane bag, were six very alive pups, thrashing and snapping. I unzipped one water-filled bag and grabbed junior by the tail. As if he had done it every morning of his life, he whipped around and buried a very efficient set of teeth in the edge of my arm. It hurt like the devil as the blood flowed down my wrist, the teeth digging deeper with each jerk of the thrashing, three-pound body. All present, of course, thought this was uproariously funny and it took a few very select phrases in my back-alley Spanish to get somebody to stop rolling around on the ground and cut the infant's jaw hinges. I headed for the bar with ten yards of permanganate-stained gauze trailing from my martini hand. The therapeutic qualities of alcohol had always been extolled by several of my fishing friends, and I am pleased to report that I was back on the river late the next morning, hardly noticing the pain in my hand for the throbbing in my temples.

We killed six sharks the next day at the cost of only three broken and lost harpoons, assorted bruises and rope burns, and about ten years off my life. On the other hand, I picked up four new words for my Spanish vocabulary. I am sure they will do for almost any sort of emergency.

Strangely, all the sharks we killed were females, and all were pregnant. In most cases, birth would have occurred within hours or, at the most, days. Apparently they were using the deep, quiet waters of the pool as a nursery. The stomach of each shark was empty except for double handfuls of tarpon vertebrae. The locals were pleased with the pups, which they claimed made the very best *seviche,* raw marinated fish soaked in lime juice overnight. I tried some of the steaks cut from the adults and found them delicious. The meat was tender and flaky, the flavor delicate. But, as I ate it, I wondered how the talk might have gone around the dinner table at the bottom of that pool if José hadn't grabbed me.

from The Old Man and the Sea
by Ernest Hemingway

Ernest Hemingway's (1899–1961) 1952 novel is a tale of endurance. After eighty-four days without a catch, the old fisherman Santiago lands the fish of his lifetime. The creature is so big that all Santiago can do is lash it to the bow of his skiff, leaving it to drag in the water.

T he shark was not an accident. He had come up from deep down in the water as the dark cloud of blood had settled and dispersed in the mile deep sea. He had come up so fast and absolutely without caution that he broke the surface of the blue water and was in the sun. Then he fell back into the sea and picked up the scent and started swimming on the course the skiff and the fish had taken.

Sometimes he lost the scent. But he would pick it up again, or have just a trace of it, and he swam fast and hard on the course. He was a very big Mako shark built to swim as fast as the fastest fish in the sea and everything about him was beautiful except his jaws. His back was as blue as a sword fish's and his belly was silver and his hide was smooth and handsome. He was built as a sword fish except for his huge jaws which were tight shut now as he swam fast, just under the surface with his high dorsal fin knifing through the water without wavering. Inside the closed double lip of his jaws all of his eight rows of teeth were slanted inwards. They were not the ordinary pyramid-shaped teeth of most sharks. They were shaped like a man's fingers when they are crisped like claws. They were nearly as long as the fingers of the old man and they had razor-sharp cutting edges on both sides. This was a fish built to feed on all the fishes in the sea, that were so fast and strong and well armed that they had no other enemy. Now he speeded up as he smelled the fresher scent and his blue dorsal fin cut the water.

When the old man saw him coming he knew that this was a shark that had no fear at all and would do exactly what he wished. He prepared the harpoon and made the rope fast while he watched the shark come on. The rope was short as it lacked what he had cut away to lash the fish.

The old man's head was clear and good now and he was full of resolution but he had little hope. It was too good to last, he thought. He took one look at the great fish as he watched the shark close in. It might as well have been a dream, he thought. I cannot keep him from hitting me but maybe I can get him. *Dentuso,* he thought. Bad luck to your mother.

The shark closed fast astern and when he hit the fish the old man saw his mouth open and his strange eyes and the clicking chop of the teeth as he drove forward in the meat just above the tail. The shark's head was out of water and his back was coming out and the old man could hear the noise of skin and flesh ripping on the big fish when he rammed the harpoon down onto the shark's head at a spot where the line between his eyes intersected with the line that ran straight back from his nose. There were no such lines. There was only the heavy sharp blue head and the big eyes and the clicking, thrusting all-swallowing jaws. But that was the location of the brain and the old man hit it. He hit it with his blood mushed hands driving a good harpoon with all his strength. He hit it without hope but with resolution and complete malignancy.

The shark swung over and the old man saw his eye was not alive and then he swung over once again, wrapping himself in two loops of the rope. The old man knew that he was dead but the shark would not accept it. Then, on his back, with his tail lashing and his jaws clicking, the shark plowed over the water as a speedboat does. The water was white where his tail beat it and three-quarters of his body was clear above the water when the rope came taut, shivered, and then snapped. The shark lay quietly for a little while on the surface and the old man watched him. Then he went down very slowly.

"He took about forty pounds," the old man said aloud. He took my harpoon too and all the rope, he thought, and now my fish bleeds again and there will be others.

He did not like to look at the fish anymore since he had been mutilated. When the fish had been hit it was as though he himself were hit.

But I killed the shark that hit my fish, he thought. And he was the biggest *dentuso* that I have ever seen. And God knows that I have seen big ones.

It was too good to last, he thought. I wish it had been a dream now and that I had never hooked the fish and was alone in bed on the newspapers.

"But man is not made for defeat," he said. "A man can be destroyed but not defeated." I am sorry that I killed the fish though, he thought. Now the bad time is coming and I do not even have the harpoon. The *dentuso* is cruel and able and strong and intelligent. But I was more intelligent than he was. Perhaps not, he thought. Perhaps I was only better armed.

"Don't think, old man," he said aloud. "Sail on this course and take it when it comes."

But I must think, he thought. Because it is all I have left. That and baseball. I wonder how the great DiMaggio would have liked the way I hit him in the brain? It was no great thing, he thought. Any man could do it. But do you think my hands were as great a handicap as the bone spurs? I cannot know. I never had anything wrong with my heel except the time the sting ray stung it when I stepped on him when swimming and paralyzed the lower leg and made the unbearable pain.

"Think about something cheerful, old man," he said. "Every minute now you are closer to home. You sail lighter for the loss of forty pounds."

He knew quite well the pattern of what could happen when he reached the inner part of the current. But there was nothing to be done now.

"Yes there is," he said aloud. "I can lash my knife to the butt of one of the oars."

So he did that with the tiller under his arm and the sheet of the sail under his foot.

"Now," he said. "I am still an old man. But I am not unarmed."

The breeze was fresh now and he sailed on well. He watched only the forward part of the fish and some of his hope returned.

It is silly not to hope, he thought. Besides I believe it is a sin. Do not think about sin, he thought. There are enough problems now without sin. Also I have no understanding of it.

I have no understanding of it and I am not sure that I believe in it. Perhaps it was a sin to kill the fish. I suppose it was even though I did it to keep me alive and feed many people. But then everything is a sin. Do not think about sin. It is much too late for that and there are people who are paid to do it. Let them think about it. You were born to be a fisherman as the fish was born to be a fish. San Pedro was a fisherman as was the father of the great DiMaggio.

But he liked to think about all things that he was involved in and since there was nothing to read and he did not have a radio, he thought much and he kept on thinking about sin. You did not kill the fish only to keep alive and to sell for food, he thought. You killed him for pride and because you are a fisherman. You loved him when he was alive and you loved him after. If you love him, it is not a sin to kill him. Or is it more?

"You think too much, old man," he said aloud.

But you enjoyed killing the *dentuso*, he thought. He lives on the live fish as you do. He is not a scavenger nor just a moving appetite as some sharks are. He is beautiful and noble and knows no fear of anything.

"I killed him in self-defense," the old man said aloud. "And I killed him well."

Besides, he thought, everything kills everything else in some way. Fishing kills me exactly as it keeps me alive. The boy keeps me alive, he thought. I must not deceive myself too much.

He leaned over the side and pulled loose a piece of the meat of the fish where the shark had cut him. He chewed it and noted its quality and its good taste. It was firm and juicy, like meat, but it was not red. There was no stringiness in it and he knew that it would bring the highest price in the market. But there was no way to keep its scent out of the water and the old man knew that a very bad time was coming.

The breeze was steady. It had backed a little further into the northeast and he knew that meant that it would not fall off. The old man looked ahead of him but he could see no sails nor could he see the hull nor the smoke of any ship. There were only the flying fish that went up from his bow sailing away to either side and the yellow patches of Gulf weed. He could not even see a bird.

He had sailed for two hours, resting in the stern and sometimes chewing a bit of the meat from the marlin, trying to rest and to be strong, when he saw the first of the two sharks.

"*Ay,*" he said aloud. There is no translation for this word and perhaps it is just a noise such as a man might make, involuntarily, feeling the nail go through his hands and into the wood.

"*Galanos,*" he said aloud. He had seen the second fin now coming up behind the first and had identified them as shovel-nosed sharks by the brown, triangular fin and the sweeping movements of the tail. They had the scent and were excited and in the stupidity of their great hunger they were losing and finding the scent in their excitement. But they were closing all the time.

The old man made the sheet fast and jammed the tiller. Then he took up the oar with the knife lashed to it. He lifted it as lightly as he could because his hands rebelled at the pain. Then he opened and closed them on it lightly to loosen them. He closed them firmly so they would take the pain now and would not flinch and watched the sharks come. He could see their wide, flattened, shovel-pointed heads now and their white-tipped wide pectoral fins. They were hateful sharks, bad smelling, scavengers as well as killers, and when they were hungry they would bite at an oar or the rudder of a boat. It was these sharks that would cut the turtles' legs and flippers off when the turtles were asleep on the surface, and they would hit a man in the water, if they were hungry, even if the man had no smell of fish blood nor of fish slime on him.

"Ay," the old man said. "*Galanos.* Come on *galanos.*"

They came. But they did not come as the Mako had come. One turned and went out of sight under the skiff and the old man could feel the skiff shake as he jerked and pulled on the fish. The other watched the old man with his slitted yellow eyes and then came in fast with his half circle of jaws wide to hit the fish where he had already been bitten. The line showed clearly on the top of his brown head and back where the brain joined the spinal cord and the old man drove the knife on the oar into the juncture, withdrew it, and drove it in again into the shark's yellow cat-like eyes. The shark let go of the fish and slid down, swallowing what he had taken as he died.

The skiff was still shaking with the destruction the other shark was doing to the fish and the old man let go the sheet so that the skiff would swing broadside and bring the shark out from under. When he saw the shark he leaned over the side and punched at him. He hit only meat and the hide was set hard and he barely got the knife in. The blow hurt not only his hands but his shoulder too. But the shark came up fast with his head out and the old man hit him squarely in the center of his flat-topped head as his nose came out of water and lay against the fish. The old man withdrew the blade and punched the shark exactly in the same spot again. He still hung to the fish with his jaws hooked and the old man stabbed him in his left eye. The shark still hung there.

"No?" the old man said and he drove the blade between the vertebrae and the brain. It was an easy shot now and he felt the cartilage sever. The old man reversed the oar and put the blade between the shark's jaws to open them. He twisted the blade and as the shark slid loose he said, "Go on, *galano.* Slide down a mile deep. Go see your friend, or maybe it's your mother."

The old man wiped the blade of his knife and laid down the oar. Then he found the sheet and the sail filled and he brought the skiff onto her course.

"They must have taken a quarter of him and of the best meat," he said aloud. "I wish it were a dream and that I had never hooked him. I'm sorry about it, fish. It makes everything wrong." He stopped and he did not want to look at the fish now. Drained of blood and awash he looked the colour of the silver backing of a mirror and his stripes still showed.

"I shouldn't have gone out so far, fish," he said. "Neither for you nor for me. I'm sorry, fish."

from Desperate Voyage
by John Caldwell

The end of World War II found John Caldwell in Panama and his wife Mary in Australia. John faced a year's wait for the next available berth on a ship to Australia, so he bought a twenty-nine-foot sailing ship and set out on his own—even though he was a novice sailor. Here John has been without food for five days, and his ship has suffered severe damage in a storm.

wondered what land it could be. I sat before my guesswork map in the cockpit and studied the scratched-out pattern of sea and islands, and by process of elimination I checked off one island at a time until there was left only the possibility of its being some northerly point of Fiji.

It was a most difficult assumption to make because, first, I wasn't certain of the exact positions of the island groups in the area, and second, I knew little of the layout of islands in the groups themselves. It was pure speculation of the crudest kind. It was based on guessed figures of my speed and the speed and direction of the current.

I re-estimated my speed under jury rig at everything from twenty to fifty miles per day—in the end, all things taken together, I settled on thirty-five miles. Thus by figuring my speed after the hurricane at thirty-five miles a day I had covered somewhere near 700 miles in the twenty-one days before turning south. Add another 150 miles, again purely a guess, for current and various kinds of westward driftage in the nine days since pointing into the south, and I was well on toward Australia.

It was sensible to me, then, under these particular circumstances, to assume from my disproportioned chart that a line drawn south from a point 850 miles west of the Suvorovs would run through the western Fijis, and that this land on my bow was part of that group. This assumption, as anyone knows, was a mistaken one, but as I say, under the circumstances that I made it, it seemed valid.

Thus, I figured, the isle before me was the last for another 600 miles to the primitive New Hebrides Islands just east and north of New Caledonia. Making this island was a matter of life and death. I doubted seriously whether I could survive another 600 miles with a quart and a half of water left aboard and the growing burden of keeping up the pumping. But the hazard of sailing it with the hurricane season underway was the most compelling thought of all.

I was about four miles offshore; I shaped my course so as to reach up to the western point of the island. I was close enough, from the very beginning, to see tangled vegetation on the lower slopes. I thought of mangoes and pawpaws and cool, refreshing, healthful pineapples. Beautiful hunger feelings tingled through me, tickled me and tortured me, and I had to find something to busy myself with so I wouldn't think of food. I readied the anchor to be pushed off the railless decks.

There were hints of palm trees on the shore, but no sign of a village. I stood on the cabin, holding to the short mast, searching for a suitable anchorage.

Hours dragged by with torturing slowness. The sun climbed along its wonted arch to high noon. I had hoped to be in before then, anchored or beached, and on the quest for food. There was something amiss with my calculated approach. I was not closing in properly. After six hours of sailing I should have been through the reef and safe in the lagoon. Instead I was directly west of the island beating hopelessly into the wind. It was evident that my sail area was too small to make any headway. I was actually falling back from the island, losing ground.

By late afternoon wind and current had driven me well back. I climbed to the masthead searching for a sign of life to appeal to, but saw nothing. The shore line was no longer visible. The vegetation and barren upland spots began to blend as one. I was hoping that someone yet might sight me and set off. I retouched the SOS signs with the foul oil from the dead engine. Up to dark no sails broke the horizon. When night closed in, I could see no lights.

For hours I lay on the useless course blinking my weakening flashlight into the low clouds overhead and in a full circle around the horizon. There was always a chance that my spark of light might be picked up and an answering flash bob up on the horizon.

Finally, when my light grew so weak that I could hardly see it myself, I gave up. The island had completely hidden itself in the enveloping dark. It was lost to me. To tarry was fruitless and dangerous. There was nothing to do but turn back to my search for land farther west.

I dreaded the thought of having to cross the landless sea west of Fiji to the New Hebrides. That expanse seemed endless, as I envisaged it in terms of sips of water, hours of drudgery at the pump, and a wet sack. "It's your own fault," I told myself. "You didn't have to come out here, nobody pushed you out of Panama, so shut up."

I set a new course of west by south, that I felt should get me to the southern New Hebrides with good weather in fifteen or sixteen days. I pumped *Pagan* out and went below, wanting day to come so I could consult my map. Also I cut the ration of water to less than a half pint.

At daylight I was on deck for a look at the crude chart etched in the cockpit floor. The next few hours I spent in conjecture over my chances of making the grade with a quart and a half of water. There was water for eight days, possibly nine. I was fifteen days from the New Hebrides, that is, if I could make it in fifteen days, which meant I would be at least six days without water. Humanly impossible.

For the first time in my life, I had a long-term look at death. I had never before had an opportunity to look it in the face.

But now it was before me; and I had a whole week ahead of me to get chummy with it. To my way of thinking—now—death isn't really a dread beast unless you have time to think about him. To be in the presence of death and to have a long-term contract with it are two different things. You can be torpedoed on a ship and be in the presence of death. You can be bombed and set on fire and be in the presence of death. You can be strafed in a lifeboat or under sub attack in a convoy—a lot of things can happen where you are in the presence of death.

But death in such a presence hasn't a sense of finality, or a sense of this-is-the-end; the extreme activity and excitement of action deprive it of that. One can't conceive of death unless it is actually distant.

Strangely, I never once really believed I was going to die. However I will admit I used often to stare stolidly over the restless floor of blue ocean and ask, "Am I going to perish alone out here on the sea?" If I thought of death seriously it is because I toyed with an idea new to me. It never pressed me. My desire, my strength to go on living, was too strong—I had too much to live for. I had overcome too many obstacles. "I am too young to die," I said . . . and believed it! My new faith in God and prayer—thus my new faith in myself—made life something I wanted badly enough, like wanting to see Mary.

Coming on deck in the morning I saw a seaman's nightmare. *Pagan* was dismasted again. Only the mizzen stood. The main and headsails were down across the decks, the shrouds, stays, and mast trailed in the water like bedraggled hair. The rigging, evidently taxed to extreme in the day of beating vainly into the wind and sea for the island, in its tiredness had collapsed in the night. The hard work of restepping the mast, of refitting the rigging, loaded my mind. Working constantly at the pump had fined me down at an alarming rate. I dreaded the work it all smacked of. But I took a sip of precious water and got started.

I dragged the old mast aboard and sawed it flush where it had snapped at the deck, and shave it flat on one side at the base for restepping; it was now only ten feet long. I shortened the shrouds and stays, and made the little mast ready to be stepped. The effort so depleted me that I was forced to lie down before continuing.

After resting I started the arduous task. I raised the mast as nearly straight up and down as strength would allow and thrust it toward the opening in the deck to step it. It missed by an inch, sliding against the cabin, overbalancing me, and crashing from my shoulder. Again I rested.

The next attempt to stand my mast found me atop the cabin staggering beneath the clumsy spar. I tried to drop it straight down into the opening. The closest I could manage the butt end of the top-heavy stick to the deck hole was six inches. My strength was gone: the exertion left me too weak to stand. I slumped to the deck and lay in a heap, puffing with short breaths.

I thought maybe if I shortened the spar it would be lighter, more manageable. I decided against it, because I needed maximum sail up. The mainsail, even on the twelve-foot mast, was nearly as small as the jigger; which looked like a pillow slip. I went below and fell on my bunk.

When I came out again I felt fresher. But in two tries to step the mast I failed miserably. The last effort missed the hole by a foot. Dejection and fatigue swept over me anew. I went below to rest. I intended to make one more try before shortening the mast.

I awakened sometime in the afternoon still weak from the labors of the morning. I took a sip of water. As it coursed down my throat, I felt a return of strength. Putting the water flask back, I saw the shave lotion. I opened it, sniffed it—it was unbearable. Throwing my head back, I downed a hearty portion of what remained of it. As I capped it, I felt an electric sort of surge through my body.

The next thing I knew I was walking over the deck and before I realized what I had done, I had jerked the mast off the deck, had pointed it up like a broom handle, and it was stepped. Everything I did in the next hour was effortless. I lashed the mast in place at the heel; set the shrouds and stays; hoisted all sail; lashed the helm alee. I felt boundless; I even felt like diving over and giving one of the sharks a bad time!

Under her shortened sail *Pagan* took more time to move. She was sluggish, but as she was driven, and as she gained her cruising speed, she tilted slightly before the southern wind. Soon I was plodding along at something less than a knot.

For the next two days I slept eighteen of each twenty-four-hour period, rising only to pump out, or to sip my drops of water, or read from the Bible. Bad dreams slacked off as general apathy set in; I was a broken robot capable of only a few simple actions.

When I finally did come out of hibernation, it wasn't because I returned to my old self. I never felt the same again after the strenuous day with the mast. Working the pump henceforth became a trial—a far cry from the days when I dried the bilges in fifty long quick strokes. Now I had to pump with one hand for a dozen strokes, then with the other. A hundred movements often failed to clear out the leakage. Halfway through each pumping, I lay sprawled in the cockpit to rest.

Each day I read the Bible more assiduously; found more and more solace in prayer and gave more time to it. I learned the Twenty-third Psalm by heart, and spoke it every rising and sleeping, and often in the night as I heaved at the pump. As well, I learned the Ten Commandments and many other Scriptures. My Bible—a gift of my grandpa when I was a boy—I had never read a chapter of. Aboard *Pagan* I read it cover to cover twice, devouring its words, searching out its comforts. I should have gone insane had I not had the comforting solace of my Baptist teaching. Men who sail small boats know the verity of the Good Captain who piloted my boat.

Atheism with me had been an old story. I picked up a good background for it at college. Later, in the war, my experiences at sea, and in particular the invasion of Algiers in 1942, strengthened my unbelief. I saw strange and bewildering things. I shall never forget the trains of wounded soldiers in Algiers just after its capture. German, French, English, Italian, American, all together, their wounds making them brothers. Air raids, submarine alerts, and miles of white crosses—all in a few days.

Aboard *Pagan* the petty arguments of "college" atheism dissolved in the light of faith and the crucial practicality of Godly love under the touchstone of vital need and vital want. The test proves; the argument only conjectures. The test is a full measure, the argument a half measure. I smile when I meet atheists.

All my experiences of civilian life in depression America, and in the war, proved a pattern—a direct groundwork for my meditations alone in the vast Pacific. I cannot agree with Laplace that there is no need in this world for the hypothesis of a creator.

That afternoon of October 12, while I slept to fortify my thinning bones, I heard a heavy thud on the starboard hull. It felt solid enough to be the lip of a reef. I thought I might have clipped a part of it, in skirting it. I hurried feebly out on deck and looked around.

Near the bow, and on the sea surface, plowed a high sharp fin. A new fin from any I had seen before: a new arrival to the school of sharks that loafed constantly in the wake. He turned back to the stern and slid fearlessly along the hull, a foot off, pushing himself with a single effort.

He glided amidships and swung his ponderous body gruffly against the planking. *Pagan* shivered. He wandered gracefully off abeam, then came again. Seeing me moving on deck, he waddled close in and eyed me almost humanly with small pig's eyes, only a few feet away.

There we were, eying each other, each wondering how to eat the other. He, the picture of tropical violence, and I, gone scrawny and desperate.

A most wonderful feeling crept over me. Here was my chance. None of the smaller sharks had dared venture so close. His careless nearness gave me every advantage of the harpooner. The trouble was I had no harpoon. My little fish spear would only tickle him. But I was full of ideas.

If there were only something aboard to make a heavy spear from. I knew that if I could get something big enough into him in a vital spot, he was mine. There were meat and blood enough in him to see me through to the Hebrides. There was at the very least a quart of fresh blood I could draw out of him—enough to last five days. I relished the strength it would give me. I could dry his half a ton of meat, and with plenty to eat I could make out with a quarter pint of water daily. It would be a tight squeeze: but it could be done.

In the bilge, I found an old steel file; under the forepeak was my hacksaw—rusted over, but usable; beneath my bunk lay an eight-inch strip of cold rolled steel, one inch wide, a quarter inch thick. From the workable piece of soft iron, I envisaged a wicked killing spear. How long would the making take, and how long would the shark be around? The work, as I cut it out in my mind, could be done the next afternoon if my endurance could hold. As for the shark, if he were like the others in the wake he would be hovering close astern for days.

The material I was working with was comparatively soft; however, I realized that hacksawing and filing it into shape would wear down my last reserves. The whole venture was a vast gamble—a gamble I was fortunate to have.

I marked the rough outline of a heavily barbed spearhead on the section of steel. I commenced the long task of driving the saw, stroke by stroke, along each mark. I watched the ceiling as I worked so I couldn't see the slow progress of the cutting. Each time I looked down I tried to be surprised at the few hair widths I had bitten away. My thoughts turned to the kill I would soon be making and the heavy feast to follow. Hunger juices flowed and the dryness of my throat eased. The devils of appetite returned to *Pagan*.

It was late afternoon before I finished cutting out the rough outline of the spearhead. I took a recuperative sleep. Before I could work in the afternoon I had to overstep my ration of water: I drank a half pint. But I felt it a worthy risk, since a heavy feast of meat and blood was in the offing.

By nightfall I had notched in four small niches on the upper part of the spearhead so it could be screwed and bound to its handle. I was too worn and weak to begin the filing of the spear point; that would start the next morning. I went to bed early, to sleep hard so that I could hasten my labors on the dawn.

But it wasn't easy to sleep hard. Exquisite hunger played tricks with my dreams and horrible nightmares set me to rolling in discomfort on my bunk. My stomach knotted up and wouldn't leave me in peace. It needed food, and if not that at least something that could be swallowed. Every last edible was gone. I thought of pages from my books—but I had tried that before and it had created unbearable problems of the bowels. Then I remembered the oil in the engine.

I groped out into the night, down into the stern compartment, and loosed the plug to the engine crankshaft. I drained off what seemed a half pint of gurgling liquid and returned to the cabin. With my finger I stirred the thick gritty liquid that had seen many trips through *Pagan's* engine, and made ready to drink it down.

There are people who wonder and doubt how far a man will go when he is hungry . . . they are those, I claim, who have never been hungry. By hungry, I don't refer to the foodlessness of a day or even a week. Desperate hunger doesn't come until one has starved for at least two weeks—and this is best achieved after about a month of semistarvation.

I turned the pan up and drank deeply and quickly. My throat was outraged. My stomach revolted. I blustered and nearly vomited. My head spun in a light swim and I grew faint and drowsy. I remember settling back; and I remember the knots tightening in my stomach and the faraway ringing in my ears that seemed to come close and go away again. And I dreamed I was in the cockpit peering over my roughly hewed map. I was estimating my position anew; and when I shifted the nail and pounded it in, I found myself in Sydney Harbor. There were the harbor bridge, the skyline of King's Cross, and the Manly Ferry steaming into Circular Quay. Then I wakened; the same darkness, the same slapping of water in the bilges, the same soughing of wind in the rigging, the same feeling of a weak stomach.

Before daylight, though I felt slightly queasy, I pumped the bilges at the regular interval, then I stayed out on deck to work. In the waning dark I scraped at the spear point with my small file. Hour on hour I wore away at the weapon, sprinkling mites of steel on my swollen feet. By midmorning it showed a cruel, knife-edged point and two jagged flanges. Before noon it was a formidable weapon, heavy, unbreakable, sinister. I looked past it to the shark whose fin lazed carelessly above the water and who periodically glided up to the bilges and thwacked them sharply.

I had nothing at hand for a shaft to use as a helve for the spear-head. The last of the oars had gone into the mizzenmast. Shark spearing at the moment had priority over sailing; so down came the little mizzen.

With four heavy screws, I tightened the spearhead to the long oar handle. In addition I bound it with a wrapping of shroud wire. In the opposite end of the shaft I drilled a hole with my knife. Through the hole I passed and secured fifty feet of line, bending it to the heavy cleat at the cockpit coaming.

I was ready to spear my shark, but first I went below and slept a few hours.

The shark was off the beam basking on the surface. I stirred the water a bit. He spread the top of the sea with his heavy fin, thrusting it high, and sped straight in for me. Seeing me, he pulled up short, and gave me the once-over. We sized each other up and squared off.

With a thrust of his powerful body he moved up within a few feet of the planking. He stopped in utter defiance, nosing at the hull, loitering purposely. He turned lazily and moved a foot or two toward the bow. Exposed to me was his whole side. A greater favor the harpooner couldn't ask.

I swung the spear high up, ready to drive it down. I braced myself for the shock that would come. I saw a likely point midway between the dorsal and ventral fins. Bone, flesh, vital organs lay there—everything to bed a spear in.

I glued my eyes to his open flank, and drove the spear hard down. The blade hit what felt like rock, but it penetrated. The shark lurched in a spasm. I was shoved upward, off my feet. I held to the spear and thrust it back. The great fish threshed and writhed. I felt the spear push deep into his flesh. My hold weakened and I lost it. I crumpled into the cockpit.

I saw the rope paying out into a frothy wake that broke beamward for sea room. He lunged at the end of the line, tautening it with a slam. He spun around—plunged, and I couldn't see him for the boiling he made, but I could feel his might as the decks jerked.

He flailed the surface white. Tail up he fought his way downward, curving back toward the boat. As slack showed in the line I took it in and twisted it around the cleat. The shark shot under the keel, coming up on the opposite bow.

When he flailed in that quarter he plunged again. I sat down watching his useless battlings against death. I knew the spear had a killing hold in his vitals. When his blood gave out—he would come to terms. I waited and watched for weakness.

In a moment I saw its sure signs. He lay on the surface wallowing gracelessly. I led the slack line between two cleats, wrapping it round and round and taking in slack whenever I found it. The shark was stirring only feebly as I dragged him in. Suddenly with explosive fury he shot to the end of the line. I held the line I had taken in so it couldn't pay out. In a moment he grew limp; I was pulling him in again. He felt like dead weight.

Then again he came to life, or so it seemed, and in an explosive movement bolted away, and then again quite suddenly relaxed. I watched him closely as I towed him in. Another shark was entangled in the line; the other shark was towing him. The other shark couldn't untangle himself.

I tried to pull in more line, to get another bite on the cleat. Then a second shark fouled himself with the line. Once more the line yanked tight. At that moment I saw everything. The sharks weren't entangled in the line. They were tearing the carcass of my shark—eating it!

A third and fourth shark darted in to the death feast. I heaved frantically, and whenever the line showed slack, I wrapped it with mad haste around the cleat. I grew so weak I had to sit down, but I still worked at the line. Every pound of flesh the gluttonous pack was tearing off the carcass was vital to my chance of life. I was fighting for my life. I worked the great shark to within twenty feet of the rail.

One of the greedy pack bit into the tail of my shark, spinning him around in a half circle and racing with him to the bow till the line flew tight. There I could hear a terrifying snapping of jaws as the four set on him, ripping at him, and hastening to rip again. Great holes showed in my shark as he was thrust and pushed and torn.

I worked the mutilated mass of sagged flesh as close in as possible. The thing now was to hook him at the gills and somehow get him on board. I went below for the grappling hook, and hurried back.

The four sharks were jaw deep into the carcass—each thrusting back and tearing from side to side, pulling in opposite directions. The big shark was bent S-shaped. Rusty, blood-filled water nearly hid the heads of his attackers. Like hungry hogs, they were eye deep into the killed victim.

I jabbed my little barbed fish spear hilt deep into the head of the shark nearest me. He was oblivious to the sharp, cold steel. I tried to fit the grappling hook into the gills of the dismembered victim, but weakness felled my arms to my sides.

The grisly feast dropped down to keel depth; and then it dropped beneath the keel to *Pagan's* other side. The line was short, the oar caught against the keel and planking. The extreme pressure was bending it. Through the soles of my feet on the deck boards, I could feel the vibrations of the strained oar. I peered over to see what was happening.

From out of the water came a muffled snap. My oar bobbed to the surface. It had snapped off just above the spearhead.

I moved to the other beam in consternation and below me, gradually sinking into the hiding waters, was the gory feast. I watched it glimmer, and when it no longer glimmered I fell back on the deck boards and lost myself in remorse. I have never been at a lower moment in life.

from In the Slick of the Cricket
by Russell Drumm

Many people believe that shark fisherman Frank Mundus was the model for Peter Benchley's salty Captain Quint in the book Jaws. *Here writer Russell Drumm, on board Mundus's vessel* Crickett II, *listens to the captain's tales of early "monster-fishing" trips. The trips helped start a craze for shark fishing off Montauk, Long Island.*

Now Frank's telling Howard the shark-fishing craze started as a "joke." I've heard him say this before. But his use of the word is not meant to make light of, or simplify, shark fever. For Mundus, "jokes," I find, are firmly rooted in irony, the perception of which, like a shark's nose for chum or helpless wiggling on the surface, is Frank's strongest suit.

"It was a September full moon, and we was chummin' up bluefish outside the Gas Buoy. We hooked a mako, and it was chaos. I remember the charter blowing the leader off with a 12-gauge shotgun. We finally got one and realized what fun it was. It started as a joke at night, but I couldn't build a business at night time, so even when we had a bottom trip for porgies or sea bass, the chum buckets was out, and people didn't know it. We'd put out a line and chum and catch a mako, and people found out how good they was to eat. It took two or three years for people to start charterin' for shahks, and it happened by the twist of a *woyd*."

Frank stands, feet apart, in the center of Cricket's deck, remembering and still, while the endless procession of waves from the southwest rock Cricket, gunwale to gunwale.

"Had the day off, lookin' for a party at the dock. You couldn't say shark fishin'—we needed a fancy name. Three idiots come walkin' down the dock, and I tell 'em we're goin' MONSTER fishin'.' They said okay, like that. They was shark fishin' and didn't know it. It worked. The only thing we caught was sharks. The next time, they said, 'Let's go shark fishin'.' We'd get back and cut up the steaks, because back then, these guys came out to Montauk for meat. I was chummin' people with the twist of a *woyd*, from sportfishin' to monster fishin'.'"

Chumming bluefish, a practice he brought from Brielle, was not common in Montauk at the time. Frank discovered the chumming raised more than fish off Montauk. Howard's listening intently to the history.

How, beginning in the '30s and continuing after the war, Montauk's sportfishing fleet was composed of well-heeled private boaters, including the likes of Zane Grey, Ernest Hemingway, Kip Farrington, and their disciples. These sports pioneered rod-and-reel fishing for swordfish, marlin, and bluefin tuna. For them, fighting a shark would have been an unthinkable condescension.

A separate fleet of charter and party boats catered to the blue-collared hordes fishing food-fish: blackfish, cod, seabass, from the bottom, and in the case of the plentiful bluefish and striped bass, from the middle and top of what marine scientists call the water column. Frank saw rivers of working men meeting rivers of striped bass as the fish moved down their spawning estuaries in spring—the Susquehanna, the Hudson—to meet the warm, food-filled influence of the Gulf Stream, the greatest river of all.

If Frank knew as many words as he knows fish he might think it significant that the word "column" is used to describe classic supports, as in Doric, as well as the body of text in a newspaper, as well as ocean water. Perhaps I see significance only because I know more words than fish. Could be there's nothing to read from the shared meanings of words. Frank's looking at me funny. He goes on.

"The chamber of commerce was upset. If they coulda tarred and feathered me, they woulda," says Frank, explaining how the Montauk Chamber of Commerce thought shark fishing would chase away the tourists. The opposite happened, beginning slowly around the docks, like at Bob Gosman's.

"If he sold a case a beer, he would consider himself good, maybe three candy bars. Halliday used to hang there, and Chester. Those was the town drunks. 'Frank,' Bob says, 'every time you bring in one of them sharks, I always go and ice another case a beer.' They couldn't see we was bringin' more people to Montauk than we was chasin' away."

Frank uses what sounds like the royal "we," but I'm sure he means himself and Cricket and their shared past. Forty years is a long time.

"If we didn't put a million dollars in Montauk, this ain't coffee," Mundus shouts.

Actually, it's instant with that greasy Cremora in it, but I take his point. He tells Howard about the jealousy of the other charter captains as he began getting into the sports columns in the New York daily papers and magazines. *Life* did a two-page spread, and so did an Italian girly mag. The other captains accused him of stealing their charters. He's denying it:

"The silly bastards was givin' me their parties," he says. "They would tell the party, point-blank, quote unquote, 'If you want to catch that shit, then Mundus, he'll take you out. I ain't goin' shark fishin'.' Frank says the other captains saw the shark as a lowly creature, "like goin' snake huntin'. It was a garbage fish to them.'

"The people would come over and tell me what they said. When they climbed on the boat, and they found out they not only catch sharks, but we can catch the same stuff as what the others was doin', they wouldn't bother goin' back, and now I'm the one who stole their party."

Frank says the frenzy grew through word of mouth, and then got into the magazines. "The Italian girly book—I couldn't read it, but I got a lotta mail from Italy," he says with a grin, the kind that rises from the starboard side of his mouth. *Life* had a two-page spread with the archers in it. Sharks fulla aaaaaarows like a pin cushion. Got finger-waved from all the old biddies for that," says the captain gleefully, waving a middle finger to the horizon.

Frank started chumming with the twist of a *woyd*, and appetites changed. The guys who once could only scrape a few dollars together for a head boat began to migrate from Queens and the Bronx onto the Island, to Levittown, and better-paying jobs. More and more could afford the relative luxury of a charter boat. Slowly, at first, sharks became the working man's fish, and a monster—the cerebral niceties about honor between species in mortal combat having mutated to accommodate a street-fighter's requirement for vengence.

But vengence for what? Frank tells of blue sharks nailed high on telephone poles like crucifixions along the route back to New York City or stuffed into phone booths, dumped into the swimming pools of suburbia. Frank has Howard in stitches.

"The archers came out of the woodwork. One of the archers got the bright idea of shootin' a shark with an arrow. 'Ya think we can do it Frank, like they hunt fish? Tie a string on an arrow?' I said sure.

"We drilled a hole in the arrowhead, and then took the leader wire through the hole, twisted it, then gave them 15 foot of leader wire. And you would tease the shark up to the boat with a teaser—a teaser's nothin but a string with a fish on it, no hook.

"So the shark was right underneath their feet. They would shoot and drive the arrow into the blue shark, and then, when the blue shark would take off, we'd have the leader wire attached to the rod-and-reel, so that his buddy could catch him on rod-and-reel. Now, when he got in close, if he stayed up onto the surface, everybody could shoot loose arrows at him.

"One time we'd lost a blue shark—he'd rolled up in the line, rolled up in the 15-foot leader wire, bit it off, and swam away. Now, about a half an hour later, here comes an arrow up the slick, because he's still got this arrow in his back, and it looked funny 'cause it was kinda wobblin' from the water pressure vibratin' it. But it was three-quarters of the way out of the water. The fish was right on the surface, and there was the arrow stickin' up, didn't bother him any. He came back for more bait.

"This was a fad for a while, it caught on real quick. Everybody was talkin' about it. All the archers was talkin' about it. It was in the archers' magazines. Guys standin' alongside of this blue shark he shot with his bow, his 40-pound pull, whatever it was.

"It was a hard shot because when they pull that long bow back and the fish is right there underneath their feet, it's hard to shoot, because the bow would hit the side of the boat.

"We got this one blue shark what's 200 pounds. His back is two foot wide. I tease him right up. The archer's got two foot of target to hit, and he's three feet away from him with the tip of his arrow. He's standin' there, his knees are knockin'. He's shakin', and I say, 'Shoot.' He lets the arrow go and misses.

" 'All right—you ready? okay, here we go again,' and I'd tease that big blue shark in, right there. You could step on his back, put a saddle on him and ride him. And his knees is knockin' again; he shoots again and he misses.

"I take a hold of the leader wire and pull the arrow back. I reach down to the water to grab the arrow, and the blue shark makes a fast U-turn, and he's right there. I make believe I'm gonna hit him, like wid an ice pick. I'm gonna jam it right in him, right there.

"He starts hollerin', 'No, no no, gimme another shot.' The other guy says, 'Joe, what the hell's the matter—how could you possibly miss?' His answer was, he says, 'The reason that I missed, 'cause I'm under such terrific pressure.'

"Terrific pressure? I close my eyes and I see a rhino comin' at him, buddabum, buddabum, buddabum. Now, maybe that's pressure— terrific pressure. Eeeeeeeee," Frank screams with joy.

"What happened with the archers was the fact that the photographer and the writer from *Life* magazine wanted to ride along wid us one time and take some pictures. They did. There was one blue shark. He was a natural, he was, a born actor. He just laid on the surface out there when the guy was fightin him with the rod-and-reel. He musta had 50 arrows in 'im. He was still layin' there. He didn't sink, he didn't do nothin'. We had 11 or 12 archers—that was when I could carry over 6 passengers, up to 20—the arrows are flyin' at him.

"Well, they printed that picture in *Life* magazine, with a story about shootin' sharks with bow and arrows. *Life* magazine goes all over and then people drag it all over, and send it all over. I heard from Scotland and Ireland, a couple other places where people wrote letters 'cause their relatives was in Montauk, and they said what a horrible thing it was.

"One day we're out fishin', and there's a knock at the door. The wife [Janet] goes to the door, and here's a guy standin' there with a blue uniform with shiny chrome-plated badges. She says, 'What can I do for you?' He says, 'Is Captain Mundus home?' She says, 'No, I'm his wife, what can I do for you?' He says, 'Maybe you can answer some questions,' he says. 'I'm from the New York district of the A.S.P.C.A., and we've got so many complaint letters—cruelty to sharks—that I was sent out here special to check up on this.'

"She said, 'He doesn't do it, it's the customers.' He says, 'Oh, that don't make no difference, he's still responsible for what goes on on the boat.' There was a few questions about how many archers does he take out, so on and so forth. How many sharks does he slaughter, all this kind a thing. Then he says, the fatal question was, 'How far off does he do this?' and she said, 'Oh, 15 or 20 miles offshore.' And then he smiled, folded up his pad he was writin' on, and says, 'Well,' he says, 'that's out of our jurisdiction, anyway.' He goes away. 'Well, thank you, ma'am, I found out what I wanted to find out.' "

The *Daily News* runs a story about Frank's wife being visited by the A.S.P.C.A. It runs right before the New York Sport, Travel, and Vacation Show that's held each year at the New York Coliseum, where Frank had a booth.

"They make the A.S.P.C.A. look like a paper bag fulla assholes. The letters to the editor start to come and go. 'He's a no-good bastid!' Another letter, 'No he's not,' 'Yes, he is,' 'No, he's not,' 'Yes, he is,' and I just sit back, laughin'. Got about a week's worth of letters, yes-he-is-no-he-ain't, but better to be talked about this way than not talked about at all.

"Durin' those shows, alotta times, they're four-deep in front of the booth. One guy worms his way through all the people what's in front of the booth, and he says, 'Frank Mundus?' I says, 'Yeah.' He says, 'I gotta shake your hand.' So he puts his hand out, and I shake his hand. He says, I gotta shake your hand because I'm from the A.S.P.C.A.,' and he laughs, and he runs through the crowd like I was gonna chase him. Eeeeeeeeee," Frank giggles in the same octave as the growing wind.

As the years went by, the bluefish populations waxed, but also waned in natural cycles of abundance. Foreign fishing fleets working on rich schools off Montauk and all along the coast were harvesting species that had kept the big predators near shore. For a time, the charter boat meat fishery for striped bass, blackfish, cod, and porgies stayed healthy, but the swordfish which had lured the richer "sporties" were becoming scarce close to shore, where the fleet fished at the time. The years of Montauk tuna fishermen trading vodka and cigarettes for barrels of hook-bait butterfish were over. Finally, even striped bass got scarce from the pollution in the Chesapeake.

Chartermen found themselves stuck between the old pride in gladi-atorial tests—artful angler versus the fast and powerful swords and tuna—and their need to make a buck. Mundus appeared like the black knight.

"Soon people were stepping over piles of tuna at the dock—stepping over dem dirty swordfish," Frank says in mock irreverence for the ocean gladiator, "to go pet one brown shark. That's how it started. They'd drive out from New York City just to touch a shark—so we took their money." This was still before Frank discovered the bountiful 40-fathom line farther offshore and the white sharks following behind the pilot whales, and long before Peter Benchley discovered Frank.

In answer to a question Howard put to him an hour ago, Frank says the author of *Jaws* never spoke to him, but never had to.

"He took his scissors and cut out every article ever written about me. The first scene in the book [and movie] came from a 3,000-pound white in just 75 feet of water off the bathing beach in Amagansett. There was something in every scene that happened to us right out there. The 4,500-pound white shark was the ending, when we tried to bait a white and had motor trouble. Everything was there, but there was 10 pounds of fiction in every scene. I hate fiction," he says with a quick, pointed glance at me.

"*Jaws*, it shook the nuts from the trees, and they rolled in my direction. People come down with machetes, slingshots—they just had to kill *shahks*. They went berserk."

Frank had caught several big white sharks between the time he discovered the wonders wrought by whale meat when sprinkled from the altar of the chum box and June 6, 1964, the day he caught his first monster. The first of the species was off Amagansett in 1961. The second one was the same year but a little bigger, near a dead whale off of Block Island.

"Then we had another one that tried to bite a plank outa the boat, just like the movie *Jaws*. If it had been another boat, it woulda bit the plank out and gone right to the bottom, but because the Cricket's got too much plankin', it didn't bother us none. He come up alongside the boat when we was in the process of takin' him, and he didn't like what was goin' on so he just rolled around and grabbed the side where the side meets the bottom. He went RUFF and hung on, twisting his body, and you could hear the teeth breakin' off like rifle shots.

"Then we get a gaff in him and a tailrope on and dragged him home. Then we started diggin' the teeth out. They was in that longleaf yellow pine three-quarters of an inch. Now, that pine is hard stuff. I made a statement to the press that if that was an average, ordinary charter boat—they only have three-quarters of an inch to play with—he woulda tore that plank out. That's a bad plank to lose where the side meets the bottom. I said the boat woulda sunk immediately. It caused a stir."

On June 6, Mundus caught one that made front-page news. He was fishing south of Montauk Point. His mate was a jockey from Florida who'd lost his mount somehow and found himself dribbling chum into the Atlantic in order to make ends meet. Late in the afternoon, his arm, right down to the little fingers holding a ladleful of reddish-brown whale gruel, went stiff. Rigor mortis had instantly set in when he saw what he did rise up from the fishing spot called the Butterfish Hole, a productive depression 10 miles south of Montauk Point.

"If I'm down in the cabin lookin' up to the cockpit, I can tell you a white shark has showed up," Frank says. "Most of the time, if a guy's chummin', his arm gets stuck." Frank recalls the same great white paralysis on another trip, when Robert Boggs, yet another writer, on night-chumming watch in the Dumping Ground suddenly yelled, "FRANK, FRANK."

"I look out, and he's stuck. He's towards the middle of the deck, away from the edge of the boat. If he'd had chum in that ladle and dumped it, it would have gone in the boat. 'He's here, he's here,' says Boggs. Two or three minutes went by, and he's still stuck, and he says, 'Ah, maybe, ah, maybe it's my imagination.' I says, 'Boggsy, old boy, Cecil B. DeMille couldn't a taught you any better.' I said, 'He's there. I'll be there in a minute.'

"I look over, and Dicky the mate is sound asleep. I give him a shot with my foot in the ribs, bango, and I give Gordon Rynders [the photographer from the *Daily News*] a shake with my arm almost the same time, and I holler, 'let's go—we got a white shark in the slick.' I headed for the door. Those two—I look over my shoulder, and they were runnin' into one another. I was out on deck and threw a few ladles-full of chum into the water. Had to take a wreckin' bar and take the ladle out of Boggsy's hand."

"I throw a few more ladles of chum, and then, pretty soon . . ." Frank lowers his voice until it's slow soft-Brooklyn, full of danger and describing a birth of some kind:

". . . there it is, Old Faithful, little spot, little smudge out there, smudge gets bigger, bigger, now starts makin' color, it's an amber-brown smudge, nowwww it's a head, now here it comes, now you can see it full view. I say, 'Boggsy, old boy, here comes your imagination.' "

• • •

Interesting Frank should describe it thus, like a birth. I boned up on whites before coming aboard—"boned up" is not fitting, of course, as whites and their brethren are elasmobranches of cartilaginous construction, which gives them their characteristic sashay. White sharks give birth to their young alive and big. The males fertilize their mates using either one of their two large penile projections called "claspers." It's possible the lucky bastards can switch tools in mid-stream.

Whites are oophagy, which means *Carcharodon carcharias* are among a small number of species whose stronger young do battle with and eat their weaker siblings while still in the womb. In this way, the strongest survive to meet the world full of purpose and with malice aforethought.

Being top dog of the carnivorous apex predators, whites are built to feed on large animals. They prefer warm-blooded types: marine mammals and penguins. They are known to inhabit every ocean in the world, concentrating in areas like northern California, South Africa, South America, and Australia, where seals congregate. Whales and porpoises, too, are on the menu when they are old or infirm. Or dead. In the New York Bight, Frank's theater of operation, dead whales or those sick and slow enough to catch, are a staple.

Like some other sharks, whites have a sixth sense. In addition to sight, they find their prey by sound: they have the ability to feel pressure waves the length of their body, along lines on both flanks called *acoustico laterolis*. They have a keen sense of smell, and they can sense electrical impulses. Above the smile, that spectral smirk that fades to a deathly gape, the prey sensors are concentrated on the shark's blunt snout.

Two nostrils allow water to flow past with the shark's side-to-side gait, past olfactory cells. The numerous dark pores located on the white's nose cone—looking, as the writer Richard Ellis correctly described them—like a five o'clock shadow, are called *"ampullae* of Lorenzini,"* named for their Italian discoverer. They are jelly-filled receivers, able to detect minute electrical charges of the kind generated by the hearts and other muscles of fish, marine mammals, and, on ever-more-frequent occasions, Homo lemmus of the surfing kind.

It is theorized the *ampullae* of whites and other sharks not only sense what's living and how well, but also serve as compasses by which the animals navigate through the earth's magnetic fields. It's clear something similar guides Frank's idiots to him. The jockey and others froze at the approach of a white shark like the birth of their own worst fears—a birth they are drawn to as surely as if they had ampules of Lorenzini for fillings.

Frank says they saw no pilot whales the day the first real big one found the Cricket in June of '64. The jaws of the 4,500-pound monster continue to amaze the patrons at Salivar's bar in Montauk.

"We had two porbeagles hangin' and a third porbeagle on. We had him on light tackle. He was takin' out too much line, and I had to start the motor to chase him down just to put the line back on the reel again. I was fairly sure I wouldn't have to go that far, just one run, enough to fill up the reel and that was goin' to be it.

"Now, when you have a wet exhaust goin' out the transom, and when you don't have any water goin' through it, it will talk to you, it'll bark at you. So Cricket barked at me when I started the engine. I hollered down to that dopey mate that I had who was a jockey before I got him—this was the first time he decided to go fishin'—I hollered down to him to take a look to see if there was any water comin' out. He said, 'Yeah, there's water comin' out.'

"I said, 'Nah, there can't be,' so, anyhow, I just went ahead a little bit, told the angler to put line back on the reel. He did, so I stopped, knocked it out of gear, and went down below and looked. There wasn't water coming out the transom—it was just blowin' the sea water. The impeller on the saltwater pump had broke when we was runnin'. I have a spare pump, and I figure I'll change that after we catch the fish.

"So the guy was fightin' the fish, and I told him, 'After we get this one, we'll change the pump.' By that time it will be late enough to start back home. As he was catchin' the fish, I was clearin' all the garbage off the motor box so that I can lift it and start with the pump. I look over and my idiot mate is chummin' again. We was chummin' with black-fish whale. I was gonna tell him, 'Don't chum anymore,' but it looked like he was havin' fun, so I wasn't worried about losing a few ladles-full of chum—leave him alone, I think, I got other things to worry about.

"All of a sudden, the ladle stops, arm stretched out tight like a fiddle string. Then he can't talk. Well, I knew what he seen. I got up and ran over to the side, and when I did, I seen this big white shark come right up, and he was lookin on board. The jockey'd sucked him up with this whale meat, aaaargh?

"Nnnnnow, he starts swimmin' around the boat. Whenever this happens, you have organized panic, six people runnin' around in circles hollerin' and screamin'. There was four runnin' around—one guy had a fish on; he still had that porbeagle on—and the mate.

"Then I hollered the worst possible thing over my shoulder as I ran down to the cabin to get the rod-and-reel.

"I hollered, 'Throw him some mackerel'—WRONG—because then everybody grabs mackerel and throws 'em, so now it's rainin' mackerel. I had about 600 pounds of Boston mackerel. So when I come out of the cabin with the rod-and-reel, he's swimmin' around, suckin' up these mackerel, havin' a good ole time. I thought this was good, he's a real hungry fish; won't have any trouble hookin' him. I got the special wire rig out, put a couple mackerel on, threw it over the side, and when I did, he came along and sucked it up.

"When he sucked it up—aaaaaaaaah, I felt like a little kid who just got caught with his hands in the cookie jar. I knew I'd done wrong. How the hell am I gonna catch this fish on rod-and-reel when I don't have any water goin' through my motor, and it's goin' to overheat in 10 minutes? It's goin' to burn up," Frank says. Cricket would not be able to maneuver to help the angler.

"I holler to the mate, 'Don't set the hook. Let him swim around. Don't let him feel anything. Take the rod and follow him around, give him plenty of free spool, don't give him any drag.

"Okay, so now I dived down into the bilge. By this time, I've got about 15 thumbs on each hand, cerebral palsy like you've never seen before. I pick up a wrench off the hatch that's 150 degrees from the sun. Five guys hollerin' and screamin':

"'HERE HE COMES AGAIN LOOK OUT LOOK AT THE SIZE OF HIM . . . HHHHHOLY SHIT.'

"I'm supposed to concentrate on takin' six or seven bolts out of the motor that held the pump on. I've got about one turn on the first bolt when the mate hollers, 'HE'S SPIT IT OUT.'

"I says, 'Good—wind it in, don't put it in the water, let me get this pump changed.' Soooo—

"I started to take off the bolts, he made three or four more passes, got the bolts off, got the new pump, and tried to put the new pump on. You had to line up the gears, small gears, just had to get 'em right, or the holes for the bolts wouldn't line up. Back at the dock, in flat calm water, it would probably take 15 or 20 minutes. Out here, with all this excitement, you'd be lucky if you got it in three-quarters of an hour. He'll be gone, I think, he ain't gonna stay that long, anyhow.

"But the party's screamin' GET 'IM, GET 'IM. I says, 'I can't on rod-and-reel cause I gotta do this.' 'We don't care how you get him—harpoon him, anyway you can, GET 'IM.' Okay, we'll harpoon him. So I told the jockey to bring the harpoon from the pulpit. He brings it down and gets everything ready.

"The shark comes sssstraight up the cockpit, straight to the middle of the cockpit, and I was standin' there like Ahab with the stick in my hand, and I drew back and was gonna pop him right stright between the eyes. No, wait, I think. He should turn, you'll have a backbone shot right in the middle. He got close to the boat, made his turn, *poyfect*, I took the stick and almost scratched it down from his dorsal, down about halfway, and then I come back on it and hit him with both shoulders, the weight of my body, everything, and drove it right home.

"Woooo, he didn't like that one bit, took off towards the bow, the direction he was goin' in. He made half a breach, came half out the water, then headed for the bottom, took off and there went the barrel."

" 'Okay, now,' I holler to these guys, 'keep your eyes on the barrel [attached to the harpoon dart], let me know when it starts to disappear. I'll work on the pump, get it straightened out, and then we'll go out there.

"I get two turns on a bolt, and they say the barrel's almost out of sight. I mash on the starter button. We could run a short distance. I ran up to the barrel and shut the engine off real quick and had everybody standin' over the top of the engine fannin' on it and blowin' on it and everything else.

"Okay, back down to the bilge. Again, I tell the guy, 'Let me know when its almost out a sight.' In five minutes, it is. I hardly got anything done.

"All right, we run up to it, and on the way up there, I say look, 'We're gonna have to put some more pressure on him; we have to slow him down, or I'm never gonna get that pump changed.' I said, 'There's another harpoon with the barrel and everything, just bring it out, and we'll attach it to that one. We'll have another 400 feet of line, two barrels with 800 feet of line.' We get up to the barrel, and I say, 'Grab the barrel, tie on the other. All right now, here we go' and the one idiot customer takes the box with the line in it and turns the box upside down and makes one giant *boydie's* nest. We've got 25 feet between the two barrels and all the line tangled.

"All right, that was our first booboo. Had to shut off the engine and let the barrels go. Holy Gees, I hardly got another bolt done. Out a sight again. All right, start again and take after him. I say, 'Okay take the rod-and-reel and attach the leader to the last barrel and hang on. Maybe that'll slow him down.' I put two guys up on the bow, one to hold the pole, the other guy to hold him and the pole. I say, 'Let me know when you get low on line.' In three minutes, I get one more bolt. He hollers, 'We're almost out of line.' I mash on the starter and come out on the flyin' bridge. I look at the spool. There's still a half a spool of line. I look up, and the barrels are still right there. I call 'em everything I could think of, including dopey bastids. I figure, as long as I got the motor started, I might as well run up on him. I put it in gear, tell 'em to wind up the slack. I put the barrels under the pulpit, come to a stop, shut it off and tell 'em, 'Don't you dare holler unless you're almost out of line. That thing's gonna overheat, and one time it ain't gonna start.'

"All right, I go down, get one more bolt on. They holler and scream, 'We're outa line.' I mash on the starter button, and I'm mad, go up on the flying bridge and look, and they're completely outa line, and one guy is draggin' the other guy toward the bow. They're both tryin' to hold back on the 130-pound test. Before it breaks, I put it in gear—otherwise, we've lost the whole spool a line. Now I'm mad because they waited too long, aaaaargh? They almost cost me a spool a line.

"All right, we done that one or two more times. I got the pump changed and now start up the motor—can't get water. New pump, changed, still no water, the barrels goin' away, come on, we gotta go. Four more times we primed it; finally, we got water. Now we can concentrate on the barrels.

"We picked up the first barrel from the bow. Now we disconnect the other one, put it in the cockpit all tangled up, and I say, 'Untangle it, 'cause we're gonna need it when we get him up.'

" 'Pull, you bastids.' Yeah, the party's pullin' like this," Frank says, demonstrating the weakest effort imaginable.

" 'C'mon, pull,' I'm screamin'. I almost got the black whip out—bang. The dopey little mate's pullin' the same way, 'Oh, my hands hurt!' Holy shit, so I've got some cussed crew: one guy in the whole batch and he got wore out. 'All right, give me the cussed line. You, ya dumb little bastid, get up on the bridge and run the boat.' 'I never run a boat before,' he says. 'Well, run it now—do it, do what I say, follow the line.'

"Now I pull as hard as I can. I'm gettin' him up as I'm tellin' the jockey how to run the boat and I'm tellin' one of the guys to get the other stick ready 'cause when I get 'im up, I'm gonna have to hesitate a minute, take that other stick and put the second one in him.

"Okay. When I get him up, my arms are comin' out of the sockets. I still gotta throw the stick—bang, I got a good shot. He goes all the way to the bottom. Now there's two lines, two barrels. We have a coffee break, and then we go back. We pick up the barrels—'pull, you bastids'—it took another hour to get him back up. I get the other harpoon ready—hit him with the third one. Down he goes, down with three barrels, three lines.

"I say, 'Grab ahold of the barrels now, and watch what you're doin' 'cause somebody's goin' to get killed.

" 'Look out now!' I put the fourth harpoon in him, and down he goes with everything again. I mean, it's really turning into a shithouse mess. Now there's four rigs out, startin' to get tangled up.

" 'Okay we're gonna get him next time. I don't care what you guys do—hang on to everything. Take a turn on everything, your neighbor's leg, anything you want, take a turn on something because we're not gonna let him go.' I hit him with the fifth one and scream, 'Everybody hang on.' They're all slidin' around. We got him to the point where, after five hours, he was fairly much tired. When they can't run away any more, they roll. Well, he started to roll, which was in our favor because it was like the Jolly Green Giant. He was all wrapped up in his work, and after we get the tail rope on, we started untyin' all the other stuff."

The sun was sinking low on the afternoon of June 6, 1964, its bloody light throwing into silhouette the morbidly curious who swarmed around Frank's first monster. It was too big to tow into the harbor, so it was dropped off near the mouth. A man named Alex Joyce put a half-hitch around one of the cement guardposts marking the edge of the Gosman's restaurant parking lot, down where the Montauk Harbor jetty tapers to a small beach.

Alex had come with a bulldozer, Frank's recalling, "and pulls a post out with his dozer blade, pops it out of the sand, so he could get down to the beach with his machine. He puts the bucket down, puts the short rope on the tail, and then picks the tail up. Now he moves the 'dozer back 'cause he's got a lot of the shark's weight in the air, aaargh?

"So he pulls him up, and while this was going on, the fish was half out of the water, half in. There was a bunch of kids and elderly people standing there lookin' at him, gawkin' at him, and they wandered out in the water, up to their knees, and I'm hollerin', 'LOOK OUT, GET AWAY FROM HIM, DON'T MESS WITH HIM, HE'S STILL ALIVE.'

"We'd towed him home for three hours, but an animal like that, you're not botherin' him, nothing to worry about. So now he's laying there, restin'. He's liable to come back alive. Just about this time it happened.

"WOARRRUNNGHHH," Frank says, mimicking a huge wounded animal coming to life. "Then he made a half a turn, and lucky he turned toward where the younger people were. They were agile and jumped out of the way, but if he'd pinned them down, he would have drownded them in three foot of water.

"That was it. I went down to the boat and grabbed my carbine. I put a full clip in there, 15 shots, and I come marchin' down the street like Matt Dillon. By this time, there's 50 people there. Now I wormed my way through the whole bunch of them with the barrel of the chrome-plated carbine *pernt'n* toward the *boidies*, and I says, 'Scuse me, can I get through, scuse me can I get through, GET OUT OF THE WAY, LET ME COME THROUGH, WILL YA?!' And when I got through the crowd—no sense tellin' them to step back—I put the barrel right down to about eight inches or 10 inches from the back of his head and started pouring the lead to him.

"BANG, BANG, BANG, BANG, BANG, BANG, that carbine was throwin' hot fire out the barrel. It was just startin' to get dark. Uh huh, there was a lot said right there. I didn't have any trouble gettin' any room after that. The whole place just cleared right out."

Frank slows his telling here, as though the effort of transporting himself back to June of '64 has tired him out.

"The people'd come from all over, out of the *woodwoyk*, like cockaroaches, when you bring a decent fish like that. By this time, it's just about dark, and I could see all a them teeth and them souvenir seekers, and I said there was only one thing we could do. We didn't have a camera with a flash. There was one little old lady there that had a Polaroid, and she got one or two of the little jockey mate posing at the front of the fish.

"I went down and got my big knife from the boat. I brought my carbine back to the boat and went after the big knife to cut the jaw out because I knew somebody was goin' to attack that. I cut the jaw out, and then I was satisfied, locked it down in the cabin on the boat. I was goin' to get the tail, have the tail mounted. During the night someone stole the tail, yessss, a NICE, CLEAN, NEAT, CUT—stole it.

"The rest of the fish was there next morning. I mean, it was cut, beat, pinched, scratched, and walked on, all the things the tourists do. It was loaded with tourists, but we grabbed a hold of the carcass and dragged it back to the sea."

Great White Sharks

by Peter Benchley

More than fifteen years after writing the book that still keeps beach lovers out of the water, Peter Benchley (born 1940) wrote this article for National Geographic Magazine.

H aai op die aas." Spoken casually, without a hint of alarm, the words meant nothing to me: a puff of incomprehensible Afrikaans. But the crew suddenly tensed, and their tenseness was contagious. Conversations stopped. Cameramen reached for their gear; the soundman rolled his tape. More than a dozen of us, crowded onto two tiny boats rafted together five miles off the tortuous shore of Gansbaai, South Africa, froze and watched the water.

Andre Hartman pointed aft to a spot a few yards behind the outboard motors. "Haai op die aas," he said again, and this time his meaning was clear. "Shark on the bait."

The glass-calm sea was sliced by a steel gray dorsal fin. Behind it— at least six or seven feet behind—the blade of a crescent tail swept side to side, propelling the torpedo body toward us.

Slowly, smoothly, Andre drew in a rope whose end was knotted around and through the skull and entrails of a small cow shark. The big shark followed. No one asked what kind of shark it was; there was no question. Everything about it, from its size to its color to its shape to the cold ineluctability of its assault, broadcast its identity: Great White Shark.

I could see the body now, gray dappling brown as sunlight flooded the misty bluegreen water, and I recalled words I hadn't thought of since I wrote them more than a quarter of a century ago: "The mouth was open just enough to permit a rush of water over the gills. There was little other motion: an occasional correction of the . . . course by the slight raising or lowering of a pectoral fin—as a bird changes direction by dipping one wing and lifting the other."

Andre lifted the bait aboard and dropped it in a box. Quickly he knelt on the wood square mounted between the two motors. Bracing himself with his left hand, he plunged his right into the water, just as the pointed snout and great conical head reached the first motor.

"For God's sake, Andre," I said, "what. . . ." His hand grabbed the snout, moving it away from the shaft of the motor, guiding the head of the shark up as it rose out of the water.

There, in an instant, was the mouth, the most notorious mouth in nature, the upper jaw dropping into view, extending its rank of serrated triangular daggers, the lower jaw falling open, studded with the needle-sharp grabbing teeth that, more than a century ago, gave the animal its scientific moniker: Carcharodon carcharias, "ragged-toothed" one.

Andre's hand cupped the snout, almost caressing it, and as his arm straightened, the enormous head eased back and rose even farther into the air. And there it stayed, motionless, vertical, suspended—apparently by some mystical connection with Andre.

No one spoke. No one breathed. The only sound was the motor drive on David Doubilet's camera as it captured frame after frame after frame of man mesmerizing monster.

The moment seemed endless. In fact, it lasted—what, two seconds? perhaps five?—until Andre pulled his hand back. For one more heartbeat the shark remained suspended, and then—easily, gracefully—it half-slid, half-fell backward, slipped beneath the surface, and, its massive white belly gleaming up at us, appeared to swoon down into the gloom.

Still nobody spoke. We gawked at each other.

At last Andre grinned and said, "The first time it was an accident. I was just trying to shoo a shark away from the motor. Sharks are drawn to motors by their electrical signals and have a habit of biting them to see if they're edible—that's how they decide what and what not to eat—and sometimes they'll knock out a bunch of their teeth." A former commercial fisherman and champion spear-fisherman, Andre has been living side by side with great white sharks for years. "Anyway, my hand landed on its nose, and it sort of paused, so I kept it there, and when I did let go, the shark snapped and snapped, like it was searching for whatever it was that had hypnotized it."

David and I exchanged a glance. The shark's reaction struck us both as quite similar to the phenomenon scientists call tonic immobility. We had heard that other sharks, smaller sharks, can be made to pause in a kind of suspended animation when turned over on their backs. Had Andre's hand somehow had the same effect, perhaps by interrupting the flow of sensory signals that activate the shark's brain? Or perhaps Andre actually overstimulated the shark's sensory organs. No one knows. Maybe the shark simply grew confused by being unable to reach something with its jaws that it sensed was nearby.

What I do know is that neither David nor I had ever heard of, let alone seen, such behavior between a human being and the most feared of all the creatures in the sea.

By now, however, we were growing used to the unusual, for in nearly every encounter we had had with great whites over the past six months, from the stormy Southern Ocean off Australia to here on the southeastern tip of the African continent, the magnificent animals seemed intent on defying conventional wisdom and confounding the experts.

The more we learned, the more we realized how little is really known about great whites. Despite vast leaps of knowledge since *Jaws* was published in 1974, no one—not scientists, fishermen, or divers—yet knows for certain such basic things as how big they can be (how long, how broad, how heavy), how many years they can live, how many of them exist, when and where they mate, how many young they can carry, where they spend their time, and what, specifically, impels one great white shark to attack, kill, and consume a human being and another to bite and spit out the same hapless sort of victim.

I became convinced, too, that considering the knowledge accumulated about great whites in the past 25 years, I couldn't possibly write *Jaws* today . . . not in good conscience anyway.

Back then, it was generally accepted that great whites were anthropophagous (they ate people) by choice. Now we know that almost every attack on a human is an accident: The shark mistakes the human for its normal prey.

Back then, we thought that once a great white scented blood, it launched a feeding frenzy that inevitably led to death. Now we know that nearly three-quarters of all bite victims survive, perhaps because the shark recognizes that it has made a mistake and doesn't return for a second bite.

Back then, we believed that great whites attacked boats. Now we know that their sensory systems detect movement, sound, and electrical fields (such as those caused by metal and motors) in water, and when they approach a boat, they're merely coming to investigate. (Granted, investigation by a 3,000-pound animal can wreak havoc.)

Finally, back then, it was OK to demonize an animal, especially a shark, because man had done so since the beginning of time, and, besides, sharks appeared to be infinite in number.

No longer. Today we know that these most wonderful of natural-born killers, these exquisite creatures of evolution, are not only not villains, they are victims in danger of—if not extinction quite yet—serious, perhaps even catastrophic, decline. Much of the evidence is anecdotal: Fishermen and naturalists are seeing fewer great whites, and in most places those they are seeing are younger and smaller.

Scientists estimate that, worldwide, populations of some species of sharks have dropped by 80 percent. Though precise numbers of white sharks aren't known, there is a growing consensus that they are not reproducing at a rate sufficient to maintain the population. What is known now is that great white sharks—scarce by nature and growing scarcer thanks to contact with man—are, for all their grace and power and manifest menace, remarkably fragile.

Exactly how fragile I discovered one day in the small South Australian resort town of Glenelg, home to the world's uniquely qualified white shark expert, Rodney Fox. In 1963 Rodney was attacked while spearfishing. He was snorkeling, with a dead fish dangling from a float nearby. The shark struck, retreated, then struck again. "I looked down," Rodney said when he told me the story years ago, "and saw that great big jaw rising at me through a cloud of my own blood, and I knew I was in trouble." Trouble, indeed. Only a series of amazingly lucky breaks—including the fact that the strands of his neoprene wet suit held his guts in—saved his life. He spent weeks in the hospital and months in recovery, sewn together, like a quilt, with 462 stitches.

Rodney went on to win the South Australian team spearfishing championships one more time, and ever since he has devoted his life to the study and protection of great white sharks. (As David Doubilet puts it, "The shark bit Rodney and then inhabited him.") He has never held a grudge against the shark that chewed him up ("He was only doing what sharks do"), and he offers advice to any diver who finds himself in the water with a great white: "Make sure he knows you've seen him. Great whites are ambushers, and once one knows he can't surprise you, he's probably not going to expend a lot of energy to get you. Move slowly to other divers or the boat."

Rodney was David's and my cicerone in our search for great whites, and he had heard that the South Australian Research and Development Institute (SARDI) had acquired a huge dead female. Before she underwent scientific dissection, her body was to be shown to the public as part of South Australia's ongoing effort to protect the sharks. (Though not officially designated as endangered worldwide, great white sharks are protected off South Africa and Namibia, Australia, the Maldives, and parts of the U.S.)

The day of the display dawned foul: wind, mist, and a pelting rain. Nevertheless 12,000 people stood in line—some for more than an hour—for the privilege of walking by and seeing and smelling and touching the sad and sorry corpse of this single animal.

To be sure, she was impressive: about 18 feet long, 3,000 pounds, a robust, mature female with teeth two inches long and dark, impenetrable eyes. Child after child, adult after adult touched the shark not only with their fingertips but with their entire hands, as if to commune with the great creature. They were not afraid; they were awed, almost reverent.

For years after the movie version of *Jaws* exploded into the public consciousness, I was asked why I thought it had had such an impact. I had no answer beyond the obvious: People have always been terrified of sharks, of deep water, and of the unknown, and this story touched all those nerves.

Then, a few years ago, I came across some words by Harvard sociobiologist E. O. Wilson. "We're not just afraid of predators," he wrote, "we're transfixed by them, prone to weave stories and fables and chatter endlessly about them, because fascination creates preparedness, and preparedness, survival. In a deeply tribal sense, we love our monsters."

True enough. I, transfixed, had woven stories and fables. And here were these men, women, and children—soaking, cold, and tired— gathered in what was definitely a kind of love for this monster.

They all wanted to know what had killed her. What could kill her? Children especially wanted to know why, why would anyone kill such an animal?

The answer to what had killed the shark was depressingly banal. "A longline," said John Keesing, then SARDI's chief scientist. "A fisherman had set out a longline to catch snapper, and she happened upon it. She got hooked, and in trying to get away, she wrapped herself up in the rope. When it came taut, she couldn't move. She drowned." Like many sharks, she had to keep moving to flush oxygen-rich water over her gills.

Longlines are among the most insidious killers in the sea, for they kill indiscriminately, old or young, pregnant or not, endangered or not. In the open ocean some longlines stretch for 80 miles and contain thousands of hooks.

Unlike some fishermen, the man who caught this shark obeyed the law, notified the proper authorities, and even brought the body to shore. He had requested that he be given the jaw. The government turned him down.

"We couldn't give it to him," John explained. "A jaw this size might bring $10,000 on the open market. If we let him keep it, suddenly we'd find a whole lot of white sharks being killed 'by accident.' "

And so, jaw and all, the shark was hauled off to the Bolivar maceration facility, next door to a sewage-treatment plant on the plains north of Adelaide, where a ton and a half of great white shark could be studied out of the public eye.

This was a rare boon for the scientists. One reason so little is known about great whites is that they are enormous, bulky, and hard to handle. And that's when they're dead. Studying a live great white shark up close and in detail is, for obvious reasons, practically impossible.

Barry Bruce, one of Australia's preeminent shark experts, had flown over from his base in Tasmania to oversee the dissection and study of the shark. He and his assistants got into blue jumpsuits, rubber boots, and gloves, and as Barry delicately—with a knife suitable for quartering an ox—sliced open the belly of the beast, I stood beside him and watched.

"We know a few things for certain," he said. "For example, we know that they're warm-bodied, like all the lamnid sharks. (Others in the Lamnidae family include shortfin and longfin mako sharks.) Their body temperature is sometimes ten to fifteen degrees [Celsius] warmer than the surrounding water, which makes them efficient predators in cool water. We know they're primarily coastal, so they have contact with humans, and sometimes they lose. Then again, they do venture into deep water. They've been found off Hawaii, in the Coral Sea, the Caribbean, and the Atlantic. But we don't know much about their travel and migration patterns."

In my experience the best way to find a great white shark is to go where they're not supposed to be. A ten-footer and I had a chance meeting underwater years ago in the Bahamas, where, at the time, great whites were unheard of. The shark was as shocked to see me as I was to see it. It stopped dead in the water, braking with its two pectoral fins, voided its bowels, and fled. (My reaction? Well . . . none of your business.)

I asked Barry if anyone had a reliable estimate of the number of great whites in the world, and he said flatly, "No. We don't even know how many there are around Australia. Not very many, though."

"A hundred?" I asked. "More? Less?"

He wouldn't bite. "Nobody knows."

Rodney chimed in. "I've heard people claim that 40 or 45 great whites are killed every year here in South Australia, by longlines, nets, and illegal fishing. No question, some people still do target them for the jaw or for what they call 'sport.' But to sustain a loss like that—45 individuals a year—I would think the population would have to be a couple of thousand. I find it hard to believe that there are that many great white sharks in South Australian waters."

Until recently sharks have had no constituency: That is, there has been no public outcry to Save the Sharks, as there has been for whales and dolphins. One problem, of course, is that unlike whales and dolphins, sharks aren't cute, they don't nurse their young, they don't appear to "talk" to one another, and consequently they're hard to anthropomorphize. More practically, unlike whales and dolphins, which are mammals, sharks don't breathe air, so they don't surface at regular intervals and thus are not easy to track and count.

Also, great white sharks do have a documented record of killing human beings. (Rarely though: only 74 times in the past hundred years, according to the International Shark Attack File.)

Nowadays more people are coming to respect and appreciate sharks for what they are: beautiful, graceful, efficient, and, above all, integral members of the ocean food chain. In large measure the change is due to television and the abundance of films documenting not only the glories of sharks but also the dangers to them from long-lines, nets, and the odious practice of finning—slicing the fins off sharks to sell in Asian markets, then tossing the living animals overboard to die. Gradually governments and individuals are learning that while a dead shark may bring ten or twenty or even fifty dollars to a single fisherman, a live shark can be worth thousands of dollars more in tourist revenue to a community. Divers will fly halfway around the world to see white sharks.

Immodestly I claim some credit for the change in attitude, for while the *Jaws* phenomenon was blamed for distorting the public's view of sharks and causing sporadic outbreaks of macho mayhem, it also generated a fascination with and, over time, an affection for sharks that had not existed before. These days I receive more than a thousand letters a year from youngsters who were not alive when *Jaws* appeared, and all of them, without exception, want to know more about sharks in general and great whites in particular.

Great white sharks are among the true apex predators in the ocean. The largest predatory fish in the world, they have few natural enemies. And so, in balanced nature, there are not very many great whites, and the number grows or shrinks depending on availability of food. They breed late in life and pup relatively few.

Again, nobody knows exactly how many, but seven or eight seems to be a safe average. The youngsters appear alive, four or five feet long, weighing 50 or 60 pounds, fully armed and ready to rumble. Still, many don't survive the first year because other sharks, including great whites, will eat them.

Of all the infuriating unknowns about great white sharks, none is more controversial than size. How big can they grow to be? Fishermen from Nova Scotia to South Australia, from Cape Town to Cape Cod claim to have encountered 25-footers, 30-footers, even 36-footers. (Usually the proof offered is that the beast was "bigger than the boat.") There have been reports of a 23-footer in the waters off Malta and a 21-foot, 7,000-pounder off Cuba, but none has held up under scrutiny. The largest generally accepted catch—made by lasso, of all things—was a shark 19.5 feet long. The largest great white shark ever caught on rod and reel weighed 2,664 pounds.

According to British biologist Ian Fergusson, chairman of the Shark Trust, no great white shark longer than 19.5 feet has ever been validated, and in an e-mail widely circulated last spring, he expressed irritation at "this stubborn reluctance by some elements of the media to accept the facts and even more of a reluctance to accept that a 16-foot, 4,500-pound white shark is BIG, very BIG, and should need no further exaggeration to impress even the most discerning of viewers when seen up close."

I can attest that underwater, cruising toward you out of the gloom with the serene confidence of the invincible, a 12-foot great white looks like a locomotive with malice in mind.

When the belly of the dead shark was open, Barry Bruce beamed. "Look at that liver," he exclaimed. "That's a 500-pound liver." The liver is an immense energy-storage facility, and I liked Rodney's clear and simple description of how it governs the shark's feeding habits. "If a shark has eaten a whole seal or sea lion," he said, "it might not have to eat for a month. But the smell of chum or bait or blood in the water will stimulate the feeding impulse, and it may decide to top off its tank of energy."

Barry removed several vertebrae from the shark's cartilaginous spine (like all sharks, great whites have no true bones). He wiped one clean and held it up. "See the rings? Those are growth rings that we use to age sharks, just like rings in the trunk of a tree. In white sharks we are only just starting to understand which ones to count to give their age in years. We think female white sharks start breeding when they're about 12 to 14 years old."

To reach the heart, Barry had to actually climb inside the body cavity of the shark, and the image proved irresistible to everyone with a camera, myself included.

Pores on the shark's snout were oozing what looked like jelly, and I asked Barry what it was. "Those are the famous ampullae," he said, referring to the ampullae of Lorenzini, named after the Italian scientist who first described them in the 1670s. By detecting bioelectric impulses in the water, these jelly-filled canals are among the most important of the shark's sensory organs.

Much of the shark was reduced to reeking flesh and bloody cartilage, but the head remained intact, staring implacably, a constant reminder of what it once had been.

I needed no reminder, for still fresh in my mind were images I had seen the day before, postmortem photographs of a young man killed by a great white shark the previous June, close to shore, in a little bay on an island in the Neptunes, where he and a pal had been snorkeling for abalone. The shark had bitten him only once, severing arteries in a leg and an arm, and the man had bled to death.

"Obviously the shark didn't want to eat him," the man who had the pictures told me. "It bit down, had a taste, and let him go. It knew this wasn't its normal prey."

This episode seems to reinforce a hypothesis proposed by A. Peter Klimley, a shark expert at the Bodega Marine Laboratory in Bodega Bay, California. He holds that great white sharks have an ability to assess the energy value of prey in the microsecond of a first bite. If the prey is perceived as not containing enough energy value to justify the energy expended in a full-scale attack, the shark releases it; if, however, the prey is perceived as being rich in fat (a seal, say, or a sea lion), the shark will pursue the attack. It will deliver a first, devastating bite and wait for the prey to bleed to death, then partake of a leisurely meal.

"If they ingest something that's not energetically profitable," Klimley says, "they're stuck with that for a few days. Fat has twice the energy value of muscle."

Rodney, for one, believes wholeheartedly in the idea. "The shark spat me out, didn't he?" he says. "I was too bony for him."

Over the past few decades the number of great white shark attacks worldwide has increased steadily, according to the International Shark Attack File. This is at least partly because more people (divers, surfers, swimmers) are using the water.

Fatal attacks, however, have decreased. Forty years ago more than half of all attack victims died; today more than four out of five victims survive. Improvements in communications and emergency medical care have, of course, saved many lives, but Peter Klimley believes that in several cases the sharks have simply changed their minds. "Can you imagine?" he said. "These sharks are seizing people and holding them to make this decision. They strike and hold and release."

At the moment science accepts about 400 species of sharks, but the number changes as new species are discovered. Of all known species, only four attack human beings with any frequency: bull sharks, tiger sharks, oceanic whitetips, and great whites.

The old adage is true: A swimmer has a better chance of being struck by lightning than killed by a shark. And around the world many, many more people die every year from bee stings, snakebites, falling off ladders, or drowning in bathtubs than from shark attack . . . none of which, to be sure, detracts from the ghastly, visceral horror of being eaten by a huge fish, but all of which should give some comfort to the recreational swimmer.

In Australia, between 1876 and 1999, 52 attacks by great whites were recorded, and of them 27 were fatal. In the Mediterranean Sea since 1900 there have been 23 reliably recorded encounters with great whites, including one in 1909 in which the remains of two adults and a child were found inside a single 15-foot-long female shark caught off Augusta, Sicily.

Curiously, there has been relatively little progress over the past 50 years in the development of shark repellents. Dyes have been tried; so have chemicals and bubble curtains. The current state of the art uses electricity. So far, though, nothing has been proved to discourage a hungry great white in full attack.

We went to South Africa in the southern winter because of a phenomenon long known to locals but only recently deemed significant by researchers: In wintertime great whites gather in large numbers in a few bays in a little pocket between the Cape of Good Hope and Danger Point.

"The warm Agulhas Current sweeps down the east coast of Africa, out of the Indian Ocean," Andre Hartman explained, "and meets the cold Benguela Current that flows up the west coast. Where the currents mix, there's a temperate zone in False Bay, Gansbaai, and Kleinbaai, and sharks gather there in the winter. The temperature seems to suit them." So does the abundance of yearling South African fur seals, which swarm over rocky islands in the bays and provide a smorgasbord for the sharks.

We drove from Cape Town to False Bay, so named perhaps because early explorers who rounded the Cape of Good Hope thought that their next landfall would be India—until they bumped into the eastern shore of the bay, 20 miles away. Here Robert Lawrence and Chris Fallows run a modest cage-diving operation. For roughly a hundred dollars the young men will take visitors and scientists a few miles offshore and show them great white sharks from their choice of shelters: a small boat or an even smaller cage. They promised to show us behavior that, till now, we all had believed was the stuff of extreme rarity, if not outright legend.

We crowded into two boats and left the dock as day was breaking. It took us only 30 minutes to approach Seal Island, and we smelled it long before we saw it. Some 84,000 fur seals make their home here, and they covered every inch of the barren rock, barking, lounging, squabbling, and sliding clumsily into the water, where they metamorphosed into creatures of sleek and sinuous beauty.

Behind the boat we trolled a plastic seal with a videotape camera mounted in its belly, pointing downward.

We settled down to wait, confident that it would be hours before we . . .

The water erupted. A gigantic body blasted through the surface— white beneath, gunmetal blue above, glinting in the dawn sunlight— with the seal decoy in its jaws. The shark flipped completely over, hit the water with a tremendous splash, and disappeared.

Before anyone could speak, it happened again: a rush from the dark, an explosion at the surface, a balletic somersault, a splash.

"The violence!" Rodney said. "My lord, the violence! We know they attack from below. We know they eat seals. But the violence!" He paused, then said, "If I'd seen this behavior soon after my attack, I tell you, today I'd be a first-class golfer."

It was the breaching that none of us had ever seen, the sheer power of the attack that heaved the huge body out of the water. I turned to Rob and asked, "Does this happen often?"

"Every day," he said. "Early in the day and late, morning and evening, when the seals leave the island to feed and when they come back. There's . . . "

Another shark soared into the air. This time the seal in its jaws was not one of our decoys.

"As I was saying," Rob resumed with a wan smile, "there's what you could call a ring of peril about a hundred yards wide around the island. The sharks patrol it. The seals know it."

Indeed, as we watched, half a dozen seals slid off the rock and gathered at the surf line. All at once they disappeared. A few moments later they reappeared, but not together, each on its own a couple of hundred yards out in the water . . . outside the ring, I supposed.

No one knew why these great white sharks breached during the hunt, while the sharks Rodney had studied in Australia for 35 years didn't. I could not recall hearing about populations of white sharks that breached so regularly and ferociously, nor could Rocky Strong, a young doctoral candidate who had joined us a few days earlier to work on a National Geographic Society grant to study white shark behavior.

Rocky did, however, find the breaching to be a possible cause for concern. "Each unsuccessful breach consumes a tremendous amount of energy," he said. "If there's a lot of debris on the surface, these guys could conceivably wipe themselves out chasing shadows."

Two hours farther up the coast, in Gansbaai, shark-watching and cage-diving operations contribute mightily to the economy. Like False Bay, Gansbaai has a large seal colony close to shore, on Geyser Island, and in a channel around the island that has come to be known as Shark Alley. Here, apparently because the water is slightly shallower (not as much runway room), the sharks don't usually breach; instead, they seem to swarm.

J. P. Botha, co-owner of Marine Dynamics, the company that took us out, told me that most of the operators are former commercial fishermen or abalone divers.

"We're no different from the rest of the world," he said. "Too many people, too few fish. Catches are down everywhere. Great white shark tourism—ecotourism, if you will—is a better business than fishing."

Ecotourism is also joining the vanguard of research. More and more these days it is the naturalists and field operators, guides and dive masters who are contributing to the accumulation of practical knowledge about great whites. To cite just one example: Until recently scientists thought that the scars that mar nearly every mature shark were acquired either from prey that fought back or from ritual biting by prospective mates. Now there is eyewitness testimony of aggressive social interaction between sharks and also of spectacular threat displays that take the place of major—potentially fatal—encounters with other white sharks.

So we are learning—bit by bit, anecdote by anecdote—more and more about these magnificent predators. We must hope that we're learning enough to save them before, through ignorance and inadvertence, we destroy them.

Great white sharks have survived, virtually unchanged, for millions of years. They are as highly evolved, as perfectly in tune with their environment as any living thing on the planet. For them to be driven to extinction by man, a relative newcomer, would be more than an ecological tragedy; it would be a moral travesty.

from Jaws
by Peter Benchley

This first novel by writer Peter Benchley (born 1940) spawned Steven Spielberg's first hit film (for which Benchley wrote the screenplay) as well as three sequels. Here, in the book's opening pages, Benchley offers a portrait of his book's central character.

The great fish moved silently through the night water, propelled by short sweeps of its crescent tail. The mouth was open just enough to permit a rush of water over the gills. There was little other motion: an occasional correction of the apparently aimless course by the slight raising or lowering of a pectoral fin—as a bird changes direction by dipping one wing and lifting the other. The eyes were sightless in the black, and the other senses transmitted nothing extraordinary to the small, primitive brain. The fish might have been asleep, save for the movement dictated by countless millions of years of instinctive continuity: lacking the flotation bladder common to other fish and the fluttering flaps to push oxygen-bearing water through its gills, it survived only by moving. Once stopped, it would sink to the bottom and die of anoxia.

The land seemed almost as dark as the water, for there was no moon. All that separated sea from shore was a long, straight stretch of beach—

so white that it shone. From a house behind the grass-splotched dunes, lights cast yellow glimmers on the sand.

The front door to the house opened, and a man and a woman stepped out onto the wooden porch. They stood for a moment staring at the sea, embraced quickly, and scampered down the few steps onto the sand. The man was drunk, and he stumbled on the bottom step. The woman laughed and took his hand, and together they ran to the beach.

"First a swim," said the woman, "to clear your head."

"Forget my head," said the man. Giggling, he fell backward onto the sand, pulling the woman down with him. They fumbled with each other's clothing, twined limbs around limbs, and thrashed with urgent ardor on the cold sand.

Afterward, the man lay back and closed his eyes. The woman looked at him and smiled. "Now, how about that swim?" she said.

"You go ahead. I'll wait for you here."

The woman rose and walked to where the gentle surf washed over her ankles. The water was colder than the night air, for it was only mid-June. The woman called back, "You're sure you don't want to come?" But there was no answer from the sleeping man.

She backed up a few steps, then ran at the water. At first her strides were long and graceful, but then a small wave crashed into her knees. She faltered, regained her footing, and flung herself over the next waist-high wave. The water was only up to her hips, so she stood, pushed the hair out of her eyes, and continued walking until the water covered her shoulders. There she began to swim—with the jerky, head-above-water stroke of the untutored.

A hundred yards offshore, the fish sensed a change in the sea's rhythm. It did not see the woman, nor yet did it smell her. Running within the length of its body were a series of thin canals, filled with mucus and dotted with nerve endings, and these nerves detected vibrations and signaled the brain. The fish turned toward shore.

The woman continued to swim away from the beach, stopping now and then to check her position by the lights shining from the house.

The tide was slack, so she had not moved up or down the beach. But she was tiring, so she rested for a moment, treading water, and then started for shore.

The vibrations were stronger now, and the fish recognized prey. The sweeps of its tail quickened, thrusting the giant body forward with a speed that agitated the tiny phosphorescent animals in the water and caused them to glow, casting a mantle of sparks over the fish.

The fish closed on the woman and hurtled past, a dozen feet to the side and six feet below the surface. The woman felt only a wave of pressure that seemed to lift her up in the water and ease her down again. She stopped swimming and held her breath. Feeling nothing further, she resumed her lurching stroke.

The fish smelled her now, and the vibrations—erratic and sharp—signaled distress. The fish began to circle close to the surface. Its dorsal fin broke water, and its tail, thrashing back and forth, cut the glassy surface with a hiss. A series of tremors shook its body.

For the first time, the woman felt fear, though she did not know why. Adrenaline shot through her trunk and her limbs, generating a tingling heat and urging her to swim faster. She guessed that she was fifty yards from shore. She could see the line of white foam where the waves broke on the beach. She saw the lights in the house, and for a comforting moment she thought she saw someone pass by one of the windows.

The fish was about forty feet from the woman, off to the side, when it turned suddenly to the left, dropped entirely below the surface, and, with two quick thrusts of its tail, was upon her.

At first, the woman thought she had snagged her leg on a rock or a piece of floating wood. There was no initial pain, only one violent tug on her right leg. She reached down to touch her foot, treading water with her left leg to keep her head up, feeling in the blackness with her left hand. She could not find her foot. She reached higher on her leg, and then she was overcome by a rush of nausea and dizziness. Her groping fingers had found a nub of bone and tattered flesh. She knew that the warm, pulsing flow over her fingers in the chill water was her own blood.

Pain and panic struck together. The woman threw her head back and screamed a guttural cry of terror.

The fish had moved away. It swallowed the woman's limb without chewing. Bones and meat passed down the massive gullet in a single spasm. Now the fish turned again, homing on the stream of blood flushing from the woman's femoral artery, a beacon as clear and true as a lighthouse on a cloudless night. This time the fish attacked from below. It hurtled up under the woman, jaws agape. The great conical head struck her like a locomotive, knocking her up out of the water. The jaws snapped shut around her torso, crushing bones and flesh and organs into a jelly. The fish, with the woman's body in its mouth, smashed down on the water with a thunderous splash, spewing foam and blood and phosphorescence in a gaudy shower.

Below the surface, the fish shook its head from side to side, its serrated triangular teeth sawing through what little sinew still resisted. The corpse fell apart. The fish swallowed, then turned to continue feeding. Its brain still registered the signals of nearby prey. The water was laced with blood and shreds of flesh, and the fish could not sort signal from substance. It cut back and forth through the dissipating cloud of blood, opening and closing its mouth, seining for a random morsel. But by now, most of the pieces of the corpse had dispersed. A few sank slowly, coming to rest on the sandy bottom, where they moved lazily in the current. A few drifted away just below the surface, floating in the surge that ended in the surf.

a c k n o w l e d g m e n t s

Many people made this anthology.

At Thunder's Mouth Press and Avalon Publishing Group:
Thanks to Will Balliett, Neil Ortenberg, Susan Reich, Dan O'Connor, Ghadah Alrawi, Maria Fernandez, Mike Walters, Paul Paddock, Simon Sullivan, Linda Kosarin and David Riedy for their support, dedication and hard work.

At Shawneric.com:
Thanks to Shawneric Hachey for his masterful guidance.

At The Writing Company:
Thanks to Nate Hardcastle, Taylor Smith, Mark Klimek, March Truedsson and Neil Reynolds. Special thanks to Clint Willis for his direction and wisdom.

At the Portland Public Library in Portland, Maine:
Thanks to the librarians for their assistance in finding and borrowing books and publications from around the country.

Finally, I am grateful to the writers whose work appears in this book.

b i b l i o g r a p h y

The selections used in this anthology were taken from the editions listed below. In some cases, other editions may be easier to find. Hard-to-find or out-of-print titles often are available through inter-library loan services or through Internet booksellers.

Benchley, Peter. "Great White Sharks". From *National Geographic*, April, 2000.

Benchley, Peter. *Jaws*. New York: Ballantine, 1991

Cahill, Tim. *Jaguars Ripped My Flesh*. New York: Bantam, 1987

Caldwell, John. *Desperate Voyage*. Boston: Little, Brown and Company, 1950

Capstick, Peter Hathaway. *Last Horizons*. New York: St. Martin's Press, 1988

Capuzzo, Michael. *Close to Shore*. New York: Broadway Books, 2001

Clark, Eugenie. *The Lady and the Sharks*. New York: Harper and Row, 1969

Clarke, Arthur C. *The Coast of Coral*. New York: Harper and Brothers, 1956

Cousteau, Jean-Michel. *Cousteau's Great White Shark*. New York: Harry N. Abrams, Inc., 1992

Dickey, James. *James Dickey: The Selected Poems*. Hanover, NH: University Press of New England, 1998

Drumm, Russell. *In the Slick of the Cricket*. New York: W.W. Norton, 1998

Fraxedas, J. Joaquín. *The Lonely Crossing of Juan Cabrera*. New York: St. Martin's Press, 1993

Grey, Zane. *Tales of Fishing Virgin Seas*. New York: Harper & Brothers, 1925

Hemingway, Ernest. *The Old Man and the Sea*. New York: Charles Scribner's Sons, 1952

London, Jack. *The Night-Born*. New York: Grosset & Dunlap, 1913

Marriott, Edward. *Savage Shore*. New York: Henry Holt and Company, 2000

Matthiessen, Peter. *Blue Meridian*. New York: Penguin, 1997

Poli, François. *Sharks are Caught at Night*. Chicago: Henry Regnery Company, 1959

Thornton, Jim. "Diving Into Shark-Fin Soup". From *National Geographic Adventure*, July/August, 2000.

Williams, Terry Tempest. "A Shark in the Mind of One Contemplating Wilderness". From *The Nation*, November 29, 1999.

Exciting titles from Adrenaline Books

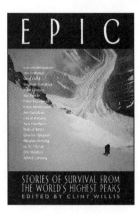

EPIC: Stories of Survival from the World's Highest Peaks

Edited by Clint Willis
A collection of 15 gripping accounts of legend-making expeditions to the world's most challenging mountains, including selections by Greg Child, David Roberts and Maurice Herzog.
$17 ($29.95 Canada), 352 pages

HIGH: Stories of Survival from Everest and K2

Edited by Clint Willis
The first anthology ever to focus exclusively on the two highest, most formidable mountains in the world. Includes accounts by Chris Bonington, Robert Bates, Charles Houston and Matt Dickinson.
$16.95 ($27.95 Canada), 336 pages

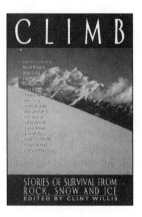

CLIMB: Stories of Survival from Rock, Snow and Ice

Edited by Clint Willis
This collection focuses on the most exciting descriptions of the hardest climbing in the world. From the cliffs of Yosemite to the windswept towers of Patagonia to the high peaks of Alaska and the Himalaya, *Climb* offers more than a dozen classic accounts.
$16.95 ($27.95 Canada), 272 pages

adrenaline ®

Exciting titles from Adrenaline Books

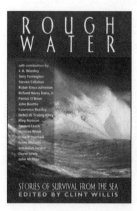

ROUGH WATER: Stories of Survival from the Sea

Edited by Clint Willis

A unique collection of 16 pieces of great writing about storms, shipwrecks and human resourcefulness. Includes work by Patrick O'Brian, John McPhee and Herman Wouk, as well as a Sebastian Junger story previously unpublished in book form. $17.95 ($29.95 Canada), 368 pages

WILD: Stories of Survival from the World's Most Dangerous Places

Edited by Clint Willis

The wilderness—forest, desert, glacier, jungle—has inspired some of the past century's best writers, from Edward Abbey and Jack London to Norman Maclean and Barry Lopez. *Wild* contains 13 selections for people who love the wilderness and readers who love great writing. $17.95 ($29.95 Canada), 336 pages

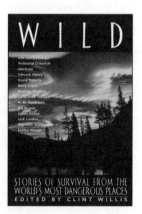

RESCUE: Stories of Survival from Land and Sea

Edited by Dorcas S. Miller
Series Editor, Clint Willis

Some of the world's best adventure writing tells stories of people in trouble and the people who come to their aid. *Rescue* gathers those stories from mountain ledges, sea-going vessels, desert wastes, ice flows and the real Wild West. It includes work by some of the world's best writers, from Antoine de St. Exupéry to Spike Walker and Pete Sinclair. $16.95 ($27.95 Canada), 384 pages

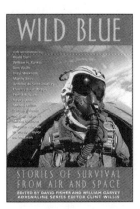

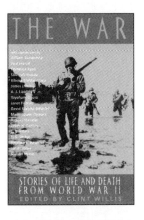

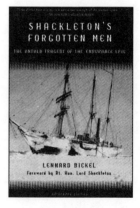

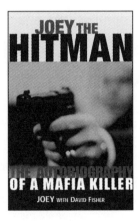